THE WIRELESS
WEB USABILITY
HANDBOOK

THE WIRELESS WEB USABILITY HANDBOOK

Mark Pearrow

CHARLES RIVER MEDIA, INC.
Hingham, Massachusetts

Publisher: Jenifer Niles
Production: Paw Print Media
Cover Design: The Printed Image

CHARLES RIVER MEDIA, INC.
20 Downer Avenue, Suite 3
Hingham, Massachusetts 02043
781-740-0400
781-740-8816 (FAX)
info@charlesriver.com
www.charlesriver.com

This book is printed on acid-free paper.

Mark Pearrow. *The Wireless Web Usability Handbook.*
ISBN: 1-58450-056-5

Library of Congress Cataloging-in-Publication Data

Pearrow, Mark.
 The wireless Web usability handbook / Mark Pearrow.
    p. cm.
Includes bibliographical references.
 ISBN 1-58450-056-5
 1. Web sites--Design. 2. Wireless communication systems. 3. Computer
network protocols. 4. Wireless Application Protocol (Computer network
protocol) 5. Wireless Internet. I. Title.
 TK5105.888 .P422 2001
 005.7'2--dc21
                          2001005709

Printed in the United States of America
02 7 6 5 4 3 2 First Edition

Contents

Preface

The dot-com craze has become the dot-bomb phenomenon. Investors who once would pour millions of dollars into any company with a fancy logo, a trendy "dot-commy" name, and yet, often no tangible service or goods, are now cutting their losses and doling out venture capital to only a tiny fraction of the companies that once were able to get cash just by asking for it. Layoffs prevail around the globe, and the days of extravagant spending are over. Companies have had to re-engineer, rethink, and reorganize or, in some cases, disband altogether. The end of the "Wild Ride" has left lots and lots of Web site developers without jobs, as many companies that once had cutting-edge Web sites have gone the way of the pterodactyl— essentially because the companies themselves had nothing to offer. A company simply cannot survive today if its only useful feature is a Web site. So then, you may be asking, how valid can usability be? Is there room left in the post-dot-com-crazed world for a discipline like Web site usability, when it is symbiotically attached to the entire Web site phenomenon?

Opinions may vary, but mine is that usability has become more important than ever, thereby opening up a path for you, the Web usability aspirant, to attain your goals of specialization. Today a Web site is only as valuable as it is productive. Although aesthetes will constantly find ways to cram more and more features into the aged HTML vessel, the discriminating users (and investors) of today's marketplace will not let mediocrity pass for acceptability. A site must be usable, or it will soon cease to exist. Never before have the bottom line and the survival of the business world been so heavily correlated to the usability of its external face—the Web.

Since I wrote my last book, the *Web Site Usability Handbook*, the need for designing usable information content has also been magnified by the advent of the wireless Web device. This new category of devices, each of which carries its own set of idiosyncrasies and design constraints, will require companies more than ever to create a systematic way of ensuring that their content is usable. The line between consumer electronic goods and rich, full-featured computing systems is blurring rapidly and will soon dissolve altogether. Consumers are predictably intolerant of clunky, user-unfriendly gadgets, and it is unlikely that the case will be any different with Web-enabled gizmos. The closer a technology gets to the "Grandma factor"—that is to say, the point at which you can envision your grandmother using it—the more that technology will need to be thoroughly tested for usability. So, in short, usability specialists have their work cut out for them!

I'd like to impress upon you that this is a good thing. Sadly, part of the job security of being a usability specialist is that it's really easy to make terrible, unusable systems of all kinds. Despite the fact that some of the major players in the field of Web site usability seem to be having some internal problems, the "little people" in usability are on the rise. I've watched the number of open usability specialist positions in the United States go from absolute zero in 1997 to several hundred while I was writing this book. I receive e-mail all the time from people who have moved into the field since having read the *Web Site Usability Handbook*; it's comforting to know that the decision makers of the world are backing the power of usability. Speaking of e-mail from readers, I should let you know that the e-mail I have gotten from you all has been the most edifying aspect of writing my last book and this one. Thank you for the mail; keep it coming! It makes the not-so-pleasant parts of writing a book bearable.

Something important to note about this book at the outset is that it is not intended to be a stand-alone work, but is rather the second in a series on the topic of usability. The first book in the series, the previously mentioned *Web Site Usability Handbook,* is a handy prerequisite to this one. The *Web Site Usability Handbook* covers in depth the techniques needed to implement a comprehensive usability plan for a Web site—techniques that are fully extensible to both the new genre of wireless Web devices and many other types of information appliances. For your convenience, however, some of the introductory material from the first book has been included. Appendix A: Introduction to Usability, provides an overview of Usability that you should read if you are not familiar with the field, and Appendix B: Usability Testing, provides a guide to Usability testing. This book is like a "plug-in" to the first, adding background on the various types of devices and new techniques to the overall comprehensive approach to usability presented in the first. Although this book does not provide the same sorts of hands-on, step-by-step instructions found in the previous one, it will supply you with the information that I have found personally helpful in extending usability techniques to wireless computing devices.

USABILITY AND ACCESSIBILITY

I have taken an integrated approach to usability of both content and device, as well as to accessibility, in this book. The reason for this approach is that Web content is slowly moving away from the safe, well-known tether of the PC/Web browser combination, and since different devices have different quirks, it is no longer possible to treat content entirely separately from the vehicle that delivers it. A usability approach that fails to integrate the physical (hardware) realm with the logical (software) realm is flawed and effectively useless. Thus, until some sort of ad hoc standards emerge, as they did with HTML and Web browsers, the usability expert must place one foot in each sphere of understanding.

Although I've dedicated a chapter to accessibility, I have also integrated accessibility concepts throughout the entire text, where possible. This reflects my recently adopted philosophical stance that it is difficult or impossible to unravel the principles of accessibility entirely from the principles of usability. From a pragmatic stance, I believe that the majority of people involved in usability work are also the people involved in accessibility work, so it makes sense to address them both here. In pursuing better usability for wireless Web devices, I have come to realize several things. First, the name "wireless Web" is really very limiting and incomplete. The Web as we know it today is changing. Information devices will rely on different facets of the global information network(s), screen-driven interfaces will become less dominant, and fully automated interactions will become more common. Throughout this book I have used the phrase "pervasive computing" as an umbrella term for all the different types of information devices that exist today, as well as those that are theoretical or experimental." So while this book speaks to wireless Web usability, it also covers some aspects of usability for other sorts of nonportable devices, like WebTV. I guess the tenet I want to preach is that all human-computer interface methods are worthy of, and desperately require, usability specialists to court them.

In my opinion, many information appliances fall by the wayside because the initial concept for the device is flawed, usually in that the device is created with too many functions in mind or with a single purpose that does not actually address a real need. For example, the Clamshell PC may have fallen out of popularity primarily because it attempted to fulfill too large a niche. The Clamshell is a diminutive laptop, but it is still much larger—and hence, more cumbersome—than a Palm Pilot–like device, as well as being harder to use, less powerful, and offering fewer features. The main problem with the Clamshell, however, is probably that the device is too general. The aim of an information appliance is to provide a minimal set of features and to make those features effortless—or, at least, very simple—to use. The information appliance should be geared toward the mass market, not techies who love to unravel obscure menus of hidden information.

Other devices fail to survive for long because they lack any feature that is truly useful or meaningful. Take, for example, the Modo (discussed in detail later in the book). In my opinion it was designed to help young urban professionals find interesting things to do in their leisure time. The Modo may have been a bad idea to begin with for a number of reasons, primarily because it failed to address an actual need; after all, its intended audience already had several means by which to get this information. The Modo attempted to be a solution for which there really was no problem.

The goal of this book is threefold. First, to provide you with a new awareness of the ways that pervasive computing will affect humans and the way they interact. Second, to give you an understanding of the problems and risks involved with this new generation of devices. The final and most important goal is to give you the tools to ensure that, above all else, the content that you create for pervasive computing devices is usable. Technology is exciting; electronic toys are fun. And, after all, computer science has certainly gotten its share of invigoration from people eager to play games of increasing complexity. In order to stay afloat and make real progress, however, the information appliance has to do more than just be a toy; it has to fill a need. It has to remove complexity from human life, rather than creating more complexity or an artificial need. Although many "latest and greatest" technologies are modeled on the "keeping up with the Joneses" idea, a truly usable tool must be much, much more than this. It must afford the human user more time to be a human and require less time to use than whatever conventional "offline" methods were used previously. In short, it must have a real purpose. The designers must keep that purpose in mind and have a vision of how to arrive at not only usability, but usefulness as well. Although the topics of usefulness, electronic gadgets, and the human condition are outside the scope of this book, that hasn't stopped me from occasionally climbing atop a soapbox within these chapters. I hope the reader will forgive me. After the *Web Site Usability Handbook* was published—and subsequently translated into languages such as Japanese and Korean—it quickly came to my attention that a huge number of my readers were not from the United States, where I currently reside. Since that time, I've received e-mail from around the world. If the e-mail is indicative of the volume of usability efforts going on in those countries, it looks like Australia, Norway, Finland, Sweden, the Netherlands, and Denmark are all hotbeds for usability. These e-mails made me realize how U.S.-centric my previous work had been, and although I have expanded the scope of this book to include international concepts, it cannot address all of the issues involved on a global level.

I would welcome suggestions on how to better expand my scope from readers outside the U.S.; please send e-mail to *feedback@mind-hive.com.*

COMPUTING GOES UNDERCOVER

Pervasive computing. Information appliances. Wearable computing. Environmental computing. Ubiquitous computing. All of these terms are relatively recent, yet the underlying principle is nothing new: the integration of a human-made tool into more and more daily objects to the point where the original device—in this case, a computer— approaches a vanishing point. Consider the evolution of the electric motor, which Dr. Donald Norman describes in *The Invisible Computer*.[1] The motor was initially a novel thing, even though it really didn't do much on its own; it just spun. It took special attachments to make the electric motor turn into something truly useful, like a cooling fan. The motor itself didn't do anything to improve the human condition; it was merely an engine for something that hadn't yet been realized. People were fascinated with it, however, because it was a new, exciting technology; the fact that they were focusing on an object that was only made powerful by integrating it into a system was not a consideration.

Eventually the electric motor's novelty wore off, and its role became much more subtle, much more useful, and pervasive: it's almost impossible to go

---

[1] If you haven't already read this work, you should. Also see *Norman's Design of Everyday Objects* for an excellent, nontechnical introduction to usable object design.

anywhere in the "modern" world without being a stone's throw from an electric motor of some sort. This gradual dissolution into the fabric of everyday life will probably be the shared fate of computing, and the manifestation of this phenomenon will initially be the genre of computing products called information appliances—also known as mobile computing or pervasive computing devices. If science fiction is as accurate a predictor of upcoming trends in mobile computing as it has traditionally been about other technological innovations, then the age of the Star Trek communicator badge is almost upon us! Actually, depending upon whom you ask, that age has already arrived.

People today are spending huge amounts of time learning how to use technology. Companies around the world spend billions of dollars annually to bring their employees up to speed on the latest PC programs, while magazines work at full-throttle trying to keep up with the dizzying pace of new types of technology. So, even though human beings create technology to make life easier, this is generally far from the reality of matters. In fact, the technology that we create has the capability to tie up our time in new ways as we focus on the underlying mechanisms of computation instead of using the technology in an effortless way. The information world is still in its infancy, and our relationship with the computer is much like it used to be with the electric motor. We know how it works and we know what it can do, but the next evolutionary step is to migrate the technology to the inner depths of specialized devices that actually help humans be … humans. Information is a resource, and the electronics that we use to move and manipulate it are the modern-day equivalents of the stone knife, the hammer, and the pulley. Information appliances represent the next phase for information delivery, and this new class of device has the potential to be as ubiquitous as the PC-based Web browser is today—even more so, since these devices can go where PCs have never gone before (see Figure 1.1).

WHY USABILITY?

Once the novelty of a new, exciting technology has worn off, people generally realize that it's time to make use of it in a utilitarian fashion.

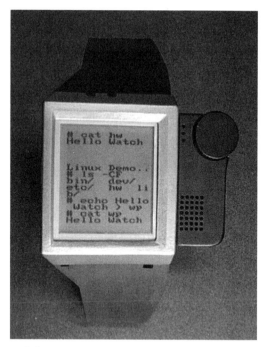

FIGURE 1.1 *An IBM prototype of a Linux-driven wristwatch.*
Courtesy of International Business Machines Corporation.

So many innovations have been integrated into the human way of life—
the telephone, for example, which was initially nothing more than a
curiosity, is today an integral part of life for many people. Devices like
the automobile have had such an impact on society that it is inconceiv-
able to imagine life without it. The common thread between the automobile and the telephone is that human beings have to interface with
the device as a "user" in order to effect change with it. It follows, then,
that any device is only as good as its interface.

One trend of unusable systems is designer-based designs. Many of the
early minicomputers, like the DEC PDP-11, were designed by highly
technical computer scientists, for use by highly technical computer scientists. The same was true of early music synthesizers, like the modular
synthesizer pictured in Figure 1.2. This complex device was not

FIGURE 1.2 *Synthesizer pioneer Mort Garson operates a patch-cord modular synthesizer. Although this early synthesizer was designed for professional musicians who were willing to learn the cumbersome interface, innovations by Moog and other synthesizer manufacturers greatly improved the usability of professional synthesizers over time. © 2001. Reprinted with permission from MoogArchives.com. All rights reserved.*

designed for use by the general population; it was designed to be used by a fairly savvy group of technological musicians. However, over the years, the audience for high-tech music synthesizers grew to include more "ordinary people" who might have been proficient piano or organ players, but not technologically inclined. This shift in audience was a factor in the manufacturers' move to simplify the interface of their instruments, and today the result can be seen in high-quality sounding instruments that are pitched to consumers at department stores.

The interface of the telephone, on the other hand, is well known and has been time tested. Many hundreds of hours of usability tests went into the creation of the common household telephone. As a result, virtually everyone who lives in a part of the world where telephones are common knows how to use one. It is this ease of use, combined with its versatility, that makes the telephone a device that transforms the way humans interact. If the telephone's interface changes or if the manner of usage changes, however, it could go from being an elementary household object to an unusable piece of plastic.

Usability is critical to the life of a system or device, no matter what it is. If humans must use a device, the device must be usable. Companies that rely on electronic information delivery systems like the Internet are starting to realize that the way a Web site looks isn't the only thing that's important; the site must also be usable by the humans who need or want the company's services. Usability affects the bottom line. Since the damage caused by unusable systems is often very difficult to detect and quantify, such damage can erode customer confidence and loyalty, which can short-circuit the longevity of any business. Poor usability means disgruntled—or lost—customers; it's as simple as that. Poor usability can also be damaging in senses other than the fiscal, translating into accidents, lost time, missed opportunities, legal liability, and even worse. Businesses that are not on the track to good (or great) usability will suffer the consequences in today's highly competitive environment. (For more information on cost justifying usability, see Randolph G. Bias and Deborah Mayhew, *Cost Justifying Usability*.)

As information appliances become a common part of everyday life, it will become increasingly important that they be easy to use, reliable, and robust. Imagine this scenario: A medical specialist is on vacation in a remote location. She is away from most sorts of telecommunication but has a two-way messaging device for emergencies. One evening a page comes through. A life hangs in the balance, and the surgeon at the other end of the world needs to know the proper procedure for treating a rare complication. At this point, the design of the two-way messaging device will serve to either save a life or to make it impossible for the two parties to communicate. If the device crashes, does not present adequate feedback to the user, or is unintuitive to use, then there could be a real problem.

Although this example is contrived, it is not far off the mark from the sorts of conditions that users of new mobile computing devices face now and will face with increasing frequency. The process of usability engineering is critical to the ability of information devices to fulfill the needs of the humans who use them; it's important to remember that the end user is ultimately the *raison d'être* for newfangled technology in the first place. As your company moves toward developing content for the emerging mobile and pervasive infrastructures, usability will be the key to their success.

LABELING INFORMATION DEVICES

When humans try to wrap their minds around a new idea, they often use a plethora of new terms to describe it. Rather than throw around a dozen or more terms to describe the innovations we'll be looking at, this book will employ only a handful of terms, including "pervasive computing" and "PCD" (short for "pervasive computing device"). The term "pervasive computing" is commonly used to connote computational power that is used in some component of the human environment other than a standard desktop computer. Some people may argue that pervasive computing is a distinct class of the new genre of Net-savvy devices, but for the sake of simplicity we'll tune out that argument for now.

In the usability and human-computer interface (HCI) fields, a synonym for pervasive computing is "ubiquitous computing," coined in 1988 by former Xerox Palo Alto Research Center Chief Technologist Mark Weiser. The term refers to a world in which people constantly use a myriad complex computing devices without ever being aware of them. For example, any modern automobile relies on a computerized system to function, yet no one has to ask, "What operating system is my car running?"

The Massachusetts Institute of Technology (MIT) Laboratory for Computer Science and the MIT Artificial Intelligence Laboratory are currently engaged in a joint project on pervasive computing called "Oxygen," the name of which speaks to the ubiquity of the subject under study. The goal of Oxygen is to enable people to "do more by doing less," a concept that may bring to mind IBM's "Pollyanna Principle," which states that "Machines should work; humans should think." (This notion is also very similar to the idea put forth by Dr. Michael

Dertouzos in *What Will Be* of "information bulldozers" that would allow humans to throw off a lot of the grunt work of the information age and spend time doing more, well, human things.) Oxygen consists of several key pieces, including specialized networks called N21s, mobile computing devices called H21s, where the "H" is short for "handy," and stationary devices called E21s, which are the components embedded into the work/life environment. According to the Project Oxygen literature, such a pervasive computing environment must meet the following criteria.[2] The environment must be:

1. **Pervasive:** It must be everywhere, with every portal reaching into the same information base.

2. **Embedded:** It must live in our world, sensing and affecting it.

3. **Nomadic:** Its users and computations must be free to move around according to their needs.

4. **Eternal:** It must never shut down or reboot; components may come and go in response to demand, errors, and upgrades, but Oxygen as a whole must be nonstop and forever.

These four attributes are essentially true for any next-generation pervasive computing components—not just Project Oxygen—and will occasionally be referred to throughout the text.

Many of the engineers, programmers, and others responsible for bringing technology to the market are probably hoping that their new electronic gizmo will be the "killer app" that will revolutionize the way humans do things. But the fact of the matter is that no matter how sophisticated, Net-savvy, pervasive, embedded, wireless, dynamic, speech-driven, artificially intelligent, interactive, proactive, nomadic, eternal, or well-marketed any device might be, humans must be able to use it. It follows that if users end up spending more time learning how to use a device or overcoming a bad interface or bad content than they would completing the same task without the device, the device will be a

---

[2] From *http://oxygen.lcs.mit.edu*.

high-priced, elaborate failure. As a usability expert, your sovereign duty is to ensure that the Pollyanna Principle is fulfilled; your tools for making this happen are detailed in this book.

TIME FLIES WHEN YOU'RE MAKING HIGH-TECH GIZMOS

Some of the devices covered in this book will be obsolete by the time you read it (Figure 1.3). In recent months, several of the companies that provide the hardware and software for mobile computing products have gone bankrupt, quit the business, or simply disappeared. Other companies that have not suffered this awful fate have certainly updated their products or have created new families of services. We all know that technology moves at astounding speed, and the area of pervasive computing is certainly no different. It is important, therefore, that as usability spe-

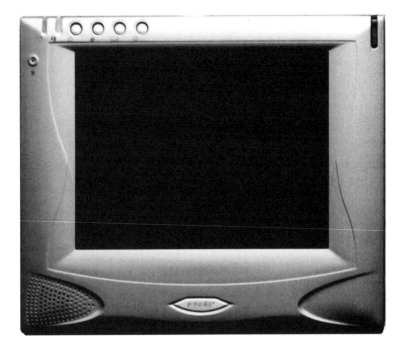

FIGURE 1.3 *The ePods Tablet PC. ePods came into existence and went out of business during the writing of this book.*

cialists we develop methodologies that outlive the short life span of the average information appliance. For this reason, the book will take a wholly generic approach to device and content usability. Specific products have been given only as examples; the methods described should be extensible to any current or future device.

Certain new types of technology, of course, cannot possibly be covered here because they simply can't be predicted. New types of input/output (IO) are likely; there already exists a Mrs. Pac-Man video game that has been wired to accept thought control. Mind control would be the most direct way to express oneself, bypassing the clunky kinesthetic methods that we use now. It's probably not too far off. But covering that in this book would be writing science fiction, not the reality of modern science.

TYPES OF PERVASIVE COMPUTING DEVICES (PCDs)

As mentioned previously, the types of devices discussed in this book have been generally categorized under the umbrella moniker information appliance. Some of these devices and systems exist today as commercially available products , others are still "in the works," either as part of academic research, corporate prototypes, or wishful thinking. Note that each class of device has its own set of limitations and assets, which will be covered in depth later in the book.

Cellular Telephone Devices

Web-browsing services offered as an integrated part of cellular telephony are often referred to as "wireless Web." They usually involve the use of Wireless Markup Language (WML) and Wireless Application Protocol (WAP), both of which were created by Ericsson, Motorola, Nokia, and Unwired PlanetWML and which have been established as open standards. (Note that WAP requires a proprietary server application to serve up content.) Additionally, some phones can handle Compact HTML, another open standard, which is simply a subset of standard HTML that removes graphically intensive features like tables and frames.

Personal Digital Assistants (PDAs)

Since PDAs are essentially handheld PCs (although with less memory, secondary storage, and CPU resources than desktop PCs), they can run applications like Web browsers in a fashion similar to traditional PCs. Their limited graphic resolution (size, colors, etc.) as well as bandwidth limitations put extra constraints on content designed for them.

Some PDAs have flourished, while others have faded from existence. The popularity of the Palm PDA[3] is due in no small part to its simplicity. The Palm OS, which is the core of the Palm approach, does not attempt to make itself a portable PC. It does a few things very well but is also extensible and so adaptable that people have used it for everything from special-purpose dry cleaning tools, like the Symbol® brand information appliance used by Zoots® Drycleaners, to portable medical reference guides.

Television-Based Devices

The first widely implemented device of this nature was arguably Microsoft's WebTV, although experimental interactive television systems have been available since the 1970s in the form of QUBE (an experiment performed in Columbus, Ohio). Information services have been added to many television-based systems throughout the world, ranging from hotel checkout to access closed captioning. The television is an obvious candidate for absorbing more information responsibility since it is already a very familiar part of the ordinary household (in parts of the world where a television set is an affordable commodity) (see Figure 1.4).

The World Wide Web Consortium (W3C, *www/w3.org*), an international organization that focuses on Internet-related standards, has recently gotten involved with the technical dream of integrating the

---

[3] Note that a Palm PDA is no longer called a "Palm Pilot," since Palm voluntarily agreed to remove that part of the name from their product after the Pilot Pen company notified them of potential trademark infringement.

FIGURE 1.4 *The Nokia Media Terminal. © 2001. Reprinted with permission from Nokia. All rights reserved.*

Web with television itself. The consortium has considered a number of proposals for schemes that would allow for hyperlinking inside of broadcast television programs.

Network Computers

Several companies have invested heavily in the idea that simplified, "thin-client" PC replacements will eventually become the successor to desktop PCs. One example of a network computer class device is the i-Opener, which is made by Netpliance (*www.iopener.com*). The i-Opener is a simple device that consists of a ten-inch LCD display that incorporates all the "brains" of the system and a keyboard. The device has limited functionality—basically e-mail and Web browsing—which means that it can be made easy to use. This sort of device is normally targeted at users who are either unwilling or unable to use more complex devices like PCs. Note that while network computers usually don't have the steep learning curve associated with a traditional PC, this does not always equate to more usable systems! Database giant Oracle also has an offering in the network computer, the NIC, which is a lightweight PC that sells at the time of writing for U.S.$199. Although this class of device generally offers a lower price tag than a conventional PC (although not by much; vendors like eMachine have been pushing the cost factor closer to zero with each new permutation of product), this is mainly due to a lack of expandability and power.

Pager-Based Systems

Information services that run over pager systems are typically restricted to two-way messaging. An example of this sort of device is the popular BlackBerry two-way wireless handheld from RIM (Research in Motion). Since these devices often rely on one or both of the common wide-area digital messaging protocols (DataTac and Mobitex), their applications are limited to short text messages. Clearly, delivering menus and other interactive content to this class of device isn't an option—yet.

Modo, a recent concept from Scout Electromedia was apparently designed to provide young urban professionals with information on local happenings, and, although it did show some promise, the device ultimately didn't attain the market penetration it could have since the project was cancelled due to a lack of funding (Figure 1.5). Modo blended style with usability in a fashion that is pretty rare; it even caught the eye of usability guru Jakob Nielsen.[4] Despite its lack of success the Modo device did have one exceptionally useful feature: when the user moved from city to city, the device reconfigured itself to accommodate the new location. As such, it met the nomadic criterion specified by the Oxygen Project, in that the user never had to worry about reconfiguring the device to work in a new environment. Wouldn't it be nice if, for example, devices like laptops and watches had

---

[4] http://*www.useit.com/alertbox/20000917.html*

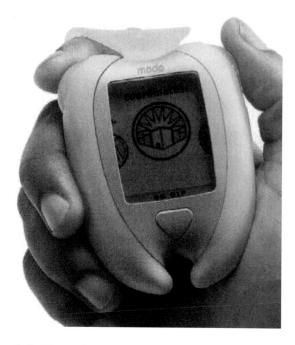

FIGURE 1.5 *The Modo pager-style information device. Image courtesy of Modo. © 2001. Reprinted with permission from IDEO. All rights reserved.*

the option to key on GPS (Global Positioning System) signals and automatically update the time? (Note that this would need to be an option, not a hard-coded feature; to hard-code the feature would be to take control away from the user.)

Automobile-Based Systems

These days, most luxury class automobiles have some sort of information device built right into the dashboard. One example is the system from OnStar, which provides a variety of services while exposing only three buttons to the user. The current feature set of OnStar includes air bag deployment notification, which actually contacts the authorities and lets them know the location of the driver based on their GPS coordinates. Additional features slated for inclusion into the system include voice-actuated cell-phone service and voice-based e-mail; a logical next step will be to provide Web access to traffic conditions, weather forecasts, and so on. As of this writing, the OnStar system is almost completely voice based. The only nonvoice-actuated part of the system is the "three-button" service used to initiate a cell phone call to the OnStar call center. Note that this system still requires human beings at the remote site to produce any useful results. There's no telling if this "person behind the curtain" approach will cease to be necessary in the future.

Wearable Computing

Probably the most prominent example of this form factor is MIThril, the wearable computing system developed at the Massachusetts Institute of Technology's Media Lab (Figure 1.6). The system consists of a "body bus": a Linux PPC core (there's a version for devices that use the ARM microprocessor on the main system board as well, which also runs Linux) and wireless Ethernet. Although this ensemble frequently conjures up space-age images, the fact remains that additional types of wearable computing are in the works. IBM, for example, has begun work on a Linux-based[5] wristwatch computer (example shown in Figure 1.1). Although the notion of wearable computing may initially seem superfluous to many people, this is probably because in some ways the velocity of available technology exceeds our ability to grasp it and make it into something truly useful.

Often the military is the first place that high-tech toys like wearable computing devices first appear. A heads-up, computerized display of a warfare environment, complete with additional data about objectives, surrounding threats, and so on, has been a research interest of the military for some time; the same sort of gadgetry has been featured in lots of futuristic blow-'em-up movies. Some more down-to-earth applications include vision assistance for the visually impaired. In January 2000 the *New York Times* ran an article about a wearable system that is allowing a

---

[5] See *www.research.ibm.com/WearableComputing/factsheet.html.*

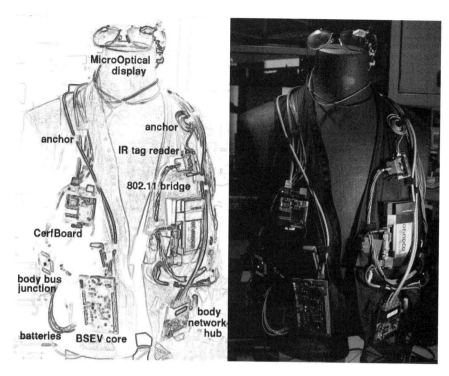

FIGURE 1.6 *The MIThril wearable computing system. Image courtesy of Massachusetts Institute of Technology.© 2001. Reprinted with permission from MIT Media Lab: Alex "Sandy" Pentland, Rich DeVaul, and Steve Schwartz. All rights reserved.*

blind man to have a crude form of low-level vision via tiny cameras mounted on his glasses.[6] The field of medicine could clearly benefit from different sorts of wearable computing as well as from a sort of "embedded" human computing that would accommodate insulin delivery systems and the like.

To a degree, all the current portable computing devices are "wearable,"—at least in the sense that most devices, like interactive pagers, Palm-size PCs, and cell phones, can be worn on the belt. There is, in fact, a phenomenon known as the "Batman syndrome," which results when a person wears too many mobile computing devices on

[6] See *www.abcnews.go.com/sections/science/DailyNews/blindman000116.html.*

the belt and thereby creates the effect of Batman's utility belt! This book assumes that the average person wants to reduce the Batman factor.

Tablet and Pad Devices

These types of devices, which basically take the form of a writing surface with built-in computational capability, were first seen in science fiction standards like *Star Trek.* The tablet offers several advantages over the smaller PDA form factor: namely, a larger, more readable display. There are several major vendors in the e-tablet business, including 3Com with its Audry information appliance. (Early advertising literature for Audry emphasized the fact that the device comes in "colors to match your kitchen.") Some tablet devices attempt to integrate handwriting recognition; others utilize on-screen keyboards or even alternative input mechanisms. Typically these devices use some sort of a stylus for the majority of input.

Embedded Systems

Some may argue that "embedded systems" is truly another name for pervasive computing. These systems take the form of computational capabilities built into just about anything that can physically house an embedded node and benefit from the addition of this logic: desks, entertainment systems, refrigerators, musical instruments, home surveillance systems, microwave ovens—the list goes on. Many households are becoming wired for automation using small devices that work with a simple protocol called X10.[7] The devices allow a central computer system to automate everything from house lighting to alarm systems, temperature regulation, sprinkler systems, and so on. This sort of system is not particularly intelligent, since it must be preprogrammed to perform the automation. A research effort being

---

[7] See *www.x10.org.*

led by Michael Coen at the MIT Artificial Intelligence Lab[8] has demonstrated, however, that a human's work and living environments can be made to autonomously adapt to the human, rather than the other way around. The key to this sort of built-in autonomy is, of course, embedded computing.

Fun Stuff

Arguably, life itself is intolerable without some degree of fun. Games are a diversion, reduce stress, and often sharpen some important, evolutionarily adaptive skill. The computer world itself owes much of its existence to games: gamers are almost always the first group of users to push a new computing system's resources to the outer limit. The UNIX operating system, for example, was born out of the desire to play a game (Space War) on the Digital PDP-7 computer. Moreover, the operating system that helped propel the Internet to its current state was created so hackers could play computer games. The gamers, therefore, will naturally benefit in some way from all this pervasive computing. Here the lines between wearable computing, embedded computing, and whatever else you may call it, begin to blur. Take, for example, the popular LEGO Mindstorms toy inspired by work from the MIT Media Lab.[9] This set of LEGO building blocks contains embedded computing to drive motors and various sorts of sensors and to facilitate communication back to the host PC. Another recent product of the Media Lab: electronic body-actuated music systems for the Flying Brothers Karamazov.

THE FUTURE

While even the general categories of devices presented here will eventually melt into one another, new types of devices that take advantage of

---

[8] See *www.ai.mit.edu/projects/abstracts2000/pdf/z-mhcoen1.pdf.*
[9] See *http://el.www.media.mit.edu/groups/el/projects/programmable-brick/.*

engineering advances that have only been hinted at as of this writing will also emerge. Optical computing, displays that are very small (microdisplays) or that use organic matter as emitters (OLEDs, or organic light-emitting diodes), advances in wireless technology, and even quantum computing will make today's hot computers look as antiquated and underpowered as Univac. The dividing line between wearable computing and PDAs will vanish. The distinction between all of the classes will approach an even horizon, beyond which all that will remain to be seen by the end user will be the resulting functionality. But the principles of usability will persist.

It is important, therefore, that you design a framework for usability that is extensible and relatively insulated from the frenetic pace of technology. After all, human beings aren't evolving nearly as fast as their own creations, and they are still the end users of new technology.

You Can't Please Everyone

If you think trying to ensure that your Web content is usable on two platforms and two browsers is difficult, consider the fact that the sheer number of types of wireless devices is constantly increasing, and the number of potential user agents people could use to view your site is likewise increasing. So, you may be wondering, how is a usability specialist supposed to make sure that content works in all of these potential scenarios?

The truth is, it simply isn't possible to ensure usability on every possible platform. You must pick your battles wisely; you have to make choices. Which platforms make the most sense for you to support? If you are going to produce a Palm OS Web clipping for your site, and your marketing department is going to draw attention primarily to this portal, then you'd probably be wasting time to fret about how your site looks, say, through a wristwatch browser. Choose the slice of wireless life that makes the most sense for your particular goals and audience, and make sure that you have a comprehensive test plan that includes all of these devices.

THE HUMAN FACTOR

One of this book's not-so-hidden agendas is to encourage you, in whatever role you may play in the development of pervasive computing systems, to keep in mind that technology doesn't always solve problems that are inherently human problems. Some devices create more work for humans. Throwing silicon at a solution without understanding what the problem is in the first place will result in uselessness. The human race has created an environment that is now so complex that it takes an incredible amount of adaptation and maintenance to survive in it, and each poorly designed tool, each ill-conceived bit of content, will increase the amount of chaos in everyone's world, either directly or indirectly.

Technology has an overwhelming power to isolate humans while maintaining the ruse of "connecting" them, and as a person who will have some direct impact on the future of technology, it is important that you not overlook this fact.

TRADITIONAL WEB VERSUS PERVASIVE WEB

Although the testing methodology and tools for inspecting and improving the usability of pervasive computing devices are similar to those used for Web sites and traditional desktop PC/browser combinations, some new considerations result from the very device-oriented nature of PCDs. For one thing, human factors knowledge plays a greater role in the usability engineering of these devices and the content they provide. As a usability specialist you may need to refine the content targeted for a mobile-computing device that uses speech as its primary input and text display as the primary output, for example. How do you deal with ambient noise? How do you ensure that your content is navigable with one hand, using the scroll wheel on the device? Will your device cause car accidents when frustrated users stop paying attention to the road to focus on your interface? Knowing a bit more about human factors will empower you to design more usable content and will also allow you to understand how to troubleshoot content that is difficult to use (or even dangerous, in the case of mobile applications).

These sorts of considerations typically don't figure into traditional Web site usability engineering, since the target device is well known (despite the multiple architectures and operating systems and browser differences) and tends to not be used in very many scenarios. Although people use laptops in a variety of locations, the paradigm for usage is still almost identical to that of a stationary desktop PC. The nature of mobile computing, on the other hand, dictates that there be few or no limits on where and how a user can use the device.

Ethical Considerations

Since you're reading this book, chances are that you are living on the edge of technology, and you're anxious to start implementing innovative new systems. You owe it to yourself and your users to understand the implications of this new technology and the potential impact that networked electronic devices can have on everyone. Following are some common areas of concern for you to focus on. Hopefully, you'll take these things into account.

Privacy

Some computer visionaries have predicted that, sooner or later, virtually everything—from office desks to clothing to toilets—will be connected to the vast information network. As more and more of our everyday environment becomes "wired" (or wireless, as the case may be), many new problems may emerge. Perhaps the most ominous side effect of all this connectedness is the reduction of personal privacy. Voice recognition, for example, through which one may pinpoint the location of an individual via their phone conversations, is certainly not a distant technology; it's available off the shelf to any consumer. The technology to track a person's location down to meter resolution is also available to parties that can afford it, via satellite photography systems and other means of triangulating a person's location. A real concern for both developers and users of PCDs, therefore, is that of privacy and anonymity.

Would you use a device that identified you via a unique serial number to anyone on the other end? Some PC chip vendors use these, often without users' knowledge. In Japan, super high-tech toilets are becoming more popular. These toilets contain sophisticated computers, sensors, and readouts that can be networked. Some of them even have optional camera attachments designed to let a family doctor make a diagnosis remotely. The convenience of wireless technology comes at a steep cost in the area of privacy. Wireless devices like cell phones and pagers have reduced the privacy of people all over the world. Adding features to PCDs that disallow the user to remain anonymous while using the device can further complicate this invasion. *It's important that you let users stay in control by giving them the option for anonymity wherever possible.* There are obvious instances where anonymity doesn't make sense, as in the case of a 911-like medical device. If you're having an infarction, you probably want the right people to know exactly where you are and what your vital signs are. Nevertheless, in the majority of cases, users don't want their personal information to be easily obtainable. The fact that many information appliances are wireless means that anyone savvy enough to modify a radio scanner can intercept their information as it passes through the air in clear text, so encryption is even more vital to ensuring the everyday user's privacy.

The issue of privacy brings to light the real importance of strong encryption for the masses, a topic that is currently being hotly debated. Many devices that transmit data over insecure channels—which accounts for just about every way data is transmitted today—are capable of using digital encryption, usually of the public key variety. Public key encryption helps ensure users that their sensitive data—health information, social security numbers, credit card numbers, and so on—is difficult enough to intercept to ward off most prying eyes and ears. It seems as if strong public key encryption is finally available to users in many places around the world, which means that the transmission of data can be reliably secured in just about any pervasive computing device.

Strong public key encryption, however, does not solve any of the security problems that stem from misuse of data once it reaches its destination. Virtually no one stores this information in an encrypted format. When you provide your credit card info over a secure HTTP link, the data usually ends up on the other end in a database that may or may not be safe. A disgruntled employee could easily post all of the numbers in that database on the Web, sell them to other criminals, or use them for their own devious intentions. Transmission encryption is simply one link in the chain of data security; we all know the adage about the weakest link.

Your Information for Sale

In 2001 information gadget manufacturer TiVo came under fire for their virtually covert use of two-way communications on their popular line of television devices.[10] A privacy advocacy group named the Privacy Foundation brought to light the fact that TiVo had, in fact, gathered personal preference data from its 154,000 subscribers. Evidently the TiVo device has built-in logic that allows it to monitor users' viewing habits and to create a table of these preferences, which it periodically uploads to the parent company. The Privacy Foundation has alleged that the privacy statement that ships with the TiVo is much outdated and skirts the fact that end users are being watched. Clearly, there is reason for alarm here. It's relatively simple for nonopen-source software, whether it ships on a chip set in a television or in the form of a precompiled binary Web browser, to contain hidden "hooks" to allow this sort of privacy invasion without the user ever being aware.

As vendors look for ever more aggressive ways to generate revenue, personal information has become an even hotter item for anyone doing direct marketing. The availability of broadband and other high-

---

[10] See *www.cnn.com/2001/TECH/industry/03/26/tv.privacy.ap/index.html.*

bandwidth technologies in the everyday household makes it almost too easy to beam information back to the vendors; consumers, therefore, have reason to worry. This trend will probably only worsen as more and more people find ways of gaining access to personal information.

This heightened need for a sense of security, of course, leads to users feeling disgruntled, unsure, and unsafe, which in turn impacts the bottom line. Take, for example, the situation with the Intel Pentium III processor. Early rumors that the processor contained a unique identifier that could be detected across the Internet, enabling a sort of "permanent cookie," led many people to decide not to buy it. It was only after Intel encouraged system integrators to include a BIOS feature to disable the serial number, as well as making many public statements about the ability to switch this feature off, that the majority of consumers who knew about the feature felt comfortable buying it.[11]

If you are planning on collecting information electronically, make it your business to provide the user with a truthful statement about your intentions. If you truly want to be ethical and provide excellence to your users, you should also provide a means by which users may disable any such information-reporting device if they so desire. Anonymity may be the precious commodity of the twenty-first century.

Frustration

Many studies of human-computer interaction have shown that humans can feel invaded—as well as intimidated, isolated, and frustrated—by technology.[12] You may have seen the little video clip of the man who gets frustrated with his computer and eventually smashes it to the ground and identified with his plight. Just imagine if you also experienced the frustration you feel when things go wrong on your PC with your refrigerator ("Mom! The fridge crashed again and all the stuff in

---

[11] If you own a Pentium III processor, you owe it to yourself to know the facts. Start by looking at the Intel Pentium III serial number FAQ at *http://support.intel.com/support/processors/pentiumiii/psqa.htm#4.*

[12] Ben Shneiderman, *Designing the User Interface* (Addison-Wesley, 1997).

the freezer melted!") or your entertainment system ("The song you selected cannot be played because of an unexpected system error. Please reboot your stereo and choose the 'safe' mode"). Although most computer users are familiar with the reboot as a way of life, users of consumer electronics aren't. Is it acceptable for a cell phone to crash during a conversation? We're not talking about those irritating interruptions of service from signal loss, but about the software that drives the phone acting in an anomalous fashion. How about a VCR? Consumers of these sorts of devices aren't as forgiving as computer users have been regrettably trained to be.

Information devices that look and feel more like consumer electronics than PCs will invite expectations for performance similar to the former, not the latter. This means that messages like, "You are seeing this message because you have disabled JavaScript or need to upgrade your browser," will be unacceptable. PCDs and their content must be robust against all sorts of conditions that designers of traditional PC/Web browser content have never had to think about—or, at least, address in a fail-safe fashion.

Depression and Isolation

Other studies have linked frequent use of electronic communication methods with depression.[13] In spite of the fact that electronic device manufacturers sell their wares as solutions for connecting people with people, there is an undeniable gap that is created or at least reinforced by frequent use of these surrogates for human-to-human interaction. There are certain facets of human existence that are simply not meant to be replaced—or in some cases even augmented—by machines. Frequent use of PC-based means of communication has been shown to result in depression, even if the goal of the communication is to bridge a gap between people who wouldn't otherwise be able to communicate. Again, this goes back to the idea that technology isn't always the panacea.

---

[13] See *www.psu.edu/dept/medialab/research/depressionnetuse.html* and *www.stanford.edu/group/siqss/Press_Release/internetStudy.html*.

Throwing technology at a problem rarely solves the problem; in fact, it can complicate it further.

Content versus Vehicle

Another divergence between traditional Web and pervasive Web is that as a content developer, you will also sometimes play a role in the development of the device itself. If you're not in a situation where you can create your own new device, you'll probably be involved in the decision-making process regarding which platforms to target for your particular content. In either case, you cannot avoid the fact that you need to be familiar with device platforms and their plethora of quirks.

As mentioned previously, this book takes a holistic approach to design that integrates the vehicle with the content, since there is currently little hope of divorcing content entirely from the device, at least from the user's point of view. It is entirely necessary for developers who work solely in content to have at least a working understanding of the mechanics of usability—the physical part—in order to gain insight into usable content methods.

As pervasive computing's popularity grows, the role you play may change. You may find yourself on a team that's putting together a new sort of PCD. You may also find that the new device calls for content presentation that breaks away from any existing modes of delivery. You may end up using established standards like Compact HTML or WML, or you may need to create a new markup language in XML—or even invent a new protocol entirely.

Although these sorts of tasks are outside the scope of this book, here is a single suggestion: avoid contributing to a high-tech Tower of Babel as much as possible. The more incompatible protocols and languages there are in the world, the more costly and painful it becomes to implement and use PCDs. Take advantage of existing standards; 99 percent of solutions can leverage these without requiring that the wheel be reinvented. On the other hand, if you find that your company has created a device that is utterly unlike anything in existence (a PDA that's driven by brain waves, for example), consider making your protocol/solution open source/free software[14] so that others can build upon and improve your solution. XML, the eXtensible Markup Language, in particular is an excellent platform for a great many sorts of content delivery. For example, an industry standard for content delivery called VoiceXML[15] is being used to deliver audio dialogs that feature synthesized speech, digitized audio, recognition of spoken and DTMF (Dual Tone Multiple Frequency, the tone signaling standard used for dial phones] key input, recording of spoken input, telephony, and mixed-initiative conversations. This is an open standard, so many vendors and users can benefit from it and build more compatible systems. WML, or Wireless Markup Language, is another example of XML in action. WML is an application of XML[16] that has gained in popularity for use in cellular telephones.

In Chapter 3 of *Information Appliances and Beyond*, authors Isensee, Kalinoski, and Vochatzer develop an idea called the "prism portal,"[17] a system that reformats legacy data formats for delivery to a variety of target devices, such as set-top boxes (like WebTV), cellular telephones, and PDAs. This approach is probably going to be key to reducing the Tower of Babel factor. A sort of metaserver could listen for incoming requests for content, and, based on the request headers passed from the client to the server via environment variables, could serve generic XML content to an intermediary "plug-in" server. The plug-in server would then custom tailor the content from the generic XML to a language appropriate for the target, including any sort of style information or additional binary data required for delivery. Note that this method eliminates the need for many different sorts of server processes for incompatible protocols (thus eliminating the need for a specialized WAP server,

---

[14] A debate about the differences between free software and open source software is beyond the scope of this book, but for more information, see
www.fsf.org/philosophy/free-sw.html.
[15] See *www.w3.org/TR/voicexml/.*
[16] Here the term "application" means a particular markup language created using the XML metalanguage. It does not mean "binary executable."
[17] Eric Bergman, ed., *Information Appliances and Beyond* (Morgan Kaufmann Press, 2000), 57.

for example). Proprietary protocols that break the current model for information delivery will probably not survive. Evidence of this can be seen by the WAP backlash.[18]

Useful Inventions or Playthings?

A frequently asked question about pervasive computing's relevance for the average person goes something like, "Aren't PDAs and fancy cell phones just playthings for people who have money to burn?" The reality is that many executive-types do use these sorts of devices for little more than show—just to be the first on the block to own the latest gadget. However, this is virtually always the case with cutting-edge technologies: the wealthy technology fanatics are willing to pay for first access to these sorts of tools. This situation usually lasts until the tools become refined enough and affordable enough to take on their true role as utensils for the masses. The Palm PDA is just such an example. Initially, few people had them, but once the price of this device came down its appeal spread. The same was true of televisions, telephones, VCRs, DVD players— well, you get the picture.

So while much of the early acceptance of electronic tools may be the domain of people with disposable income, this population does serve a critical role in the evolution of such devices. Eventually most digital tools that survive their initial release and can manage the vicious sea of competition will find their way into "household item" status. This is by no means a new concept, nor is it likely to change anytime soon.

CHAPTER SUMMARY

Computing power has the potential to be everywhere, embedded in things that benefit from the power of computation without externally exposing the underlying "brains" directly. Usability techniques will be needed for driving usability evaluation of these devices, and many new challenges are on the horizon for usability experts.

---

[18] See *www.useit.com/alertbox/20000709.html.*

HANDS ON

1. Find three devices in your environment at home that could potentially benefit from network interconnectivity. Make a list of the ways in which each device could leverage the power of connection to the Internet, or a smaller autonomous network (like a personal area network that only functions near your person or inside your home)

2. Make a list of three devices that have become more computerized over the last 20 years, but that aren't necessarily "network savvy" yet.

3. Make a list of three portable computing devices, and discuss how each has or has not made an impact on the human race as a whole. What fundamental human problem does each device attempt to solve? How well does it work to this end?

MECHANICS OF USABILITY

2

ERGONOMICS

In many cases, PCDs require human interaction in a fashion that is very unlike customary input with a conventional desktop PC. Users of PCDs, moreover, can be in almost any environment: making hospital rounds, inside the cooling tower of a nuclear reactor, on board a train, and so on. As a designer of PCDs, it is therefore critical that you have an understanding of ergonomics. This chapter will function as an introduction to that topic for those who are unfamiliar with it. It is not intended to be an exhaustive course on the matter; there are many schools that offer graduate degrees in the field, and the amount of literature on the topic is sizable. (Note that if you have a strong background in ergonomics or human factors psychology, you may not find anything new here.) The primary goal of this chapter is to equip you with an understanding of commonly used metrics for evaluating the use of devices of all sorts. These metrics can be generalized to PCDs, as you will see shortly.

Ergonomics is the study of how the human organism interacts with objects in the environment. The word comes from two Greek terms: *ergon*, meaning "work," and *nomos*, meaning "laws." Hence, ergonomics focuses on how humans accomplish work within the framework of the tools that they use. Ergonomics has its roots in the military, developing specifically from the time of the Second World War, when the military was involved in efforts to overcome failures caused by human error in new high-tech weapons systems. The goal of ergonomics is often cited as "fitting the job to the worker, not vice versa." In short, this is the same goal as non-Procrustean design.[1]

Knowledge of ergonomics is critical to the developers of information devices of all sorts; without it, unusable systems result. Most well-known vendors of consumer electronics devices have a full-time ergonomics lab, realizing that if they don't do their homework, their customers may be unable to use their products, or, even worse, that they run the risk of creating a product that is hazardous to the user. Although there is little research focused specifically on the possible negative effects of PCDs, it can certainly be argued that the potential for harm is there.

Much research has gone into the ergonomics of the conventional desktop PC, particularly with regard to the monitor, often called the CRT, which is short for "cathode-ray tube"(note that some monitors, namely LCD displays, do not use CRT technology). Over the years, much important information has been gathered about the way humans interact with, and react to, PCs and their displays. The earliest commonly used CRT displays used a harsh green phosphor for the visual component. The designers believed that this color would be the most effective since it would be the easiest to see, as light in the 530-nanometer range is the most visible color to the average human eye. Over time, however, user testing showed that the color was actually hard on the eyes since it was indeed so bright and powerful. The result of this discovery was the invention of CRTs that used other colors—blue and amber being among the most common.

Eventually, full-color CRTs became economically viable for PC monitors, and research into the refresh rate of the device became a focus (Figure 2.1). Since a CRT "paints" the picture onto the monitor screen one line at a time, there can be a noticeable flicker associated with how quickly the CRT can redraw the screen. Fluorescent lights, which are the

---

[1] See Pearrow, Appendix A, 321–322.

(unfortunate) de facto standard in most office environments, can create an irritating and tiring "beat" effect that can have the optical effect of exaggerating the flicker of a screen with a low refresh rate (around sixty redraws a second, which represents a redraw frequency of 60 Hz).

Besides research into the display itself, much study has been done on the physical effects of using various input devices for PCs, such as the keyboard, the mouse, stylus-based input, trackballs, and chord keyboards. You are probably familiar with the term Repetitive Strain Injury (RSI), a condition that results from the overuse of PCs and similar devices and that represents one of the most common workplace-related maladies. Carpal tunnel syndrome, for example, can occur when the tissue surrounding nerves in the arm become inflamed from the

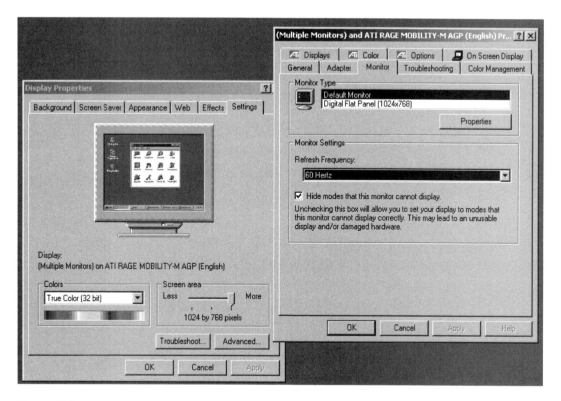

FIGURE 2.1 *Increasing the refresh rate in Windows 2000. Many users are unaware that increasing the refresh rate on their video setting, which is easy to do, would improve the picture on their screen.*

overuse—or improper use—of mice and keyboards. Many companies have sought to create devices that are more ergonomically correct in the hopes of reducing the number of these types of injuries. Kinesis, for example, makes a keyboard with two scooped-out regions that let the hand and fingers rest more naturally, thereby putting less strain on the sensitive nerves (Figure 2.2).

FIGURE 2.2 *The Kinesis ergonomic keyboard. © 2001. Reprinted with permission from Kinesis (www.kinesis-ergo.com). All rights reserved.*

All of this research falls under the umbrella of ergonomics. You can probably surmise why it's important for you to have a working knowledge of ergonomics if you are going to be designing an information appliance or the software that runs on one—or even the content for an existing system. You need to be able to ensure that your design won't endanger the safety and comfort of your users, and it's simply impossible to do so without at least a rudimentary understanding of ergonomics.

HUMAN FACTORS

Another issue to consider along the lines of user-device interaction is human factors. Some people, in fact, use the terms "ergonomics" and "human factors" interchangeably. There is a slight difference between the two, however: while ergonomics focuses on the impact that use has on users, human factors emphasizes designs that reduce the potential for human error, frustration, and wasted time. Human factors studies tend to focus more on goals and objectives and the methods that users employ to achieve them. Human factors (which will be abbreviated as "HF" from now on) typically concerns itself with ways of making actions more efficient, less stressful, and more productive, rather than focusing on the kinesthetic minutiae of a device itself. This small but important difference should be kept in mind as you read the rest of this chapter.

LAYERS OF INTERACTION

When considering the dimensions of human-device interaction, it becomes clear that there are several discrete levels at which this interaction occurs. The outer layer of interaction is the physical layer and is concerned with the user's ability to hold, activate, access, manipulate, and otherwise operate the device. The next layer of interaction is the logical layer, at which the human navigates and utilizes the software, whether visible or invisible, that drives the device and allows input to and output from the device (and any associated "back-end" computing resources). Finally, there is the cognitive layer, at which the human should be able to grasp the meaning of the content itself in a fashion that is as timely and effortless as possible (see Figure 2.3).

If any of these three layers of interaction presents a difficulty to the user, then it follows that the device as a whole is a failure, since it is only when the system is taken as a whole that it is a useful tool. Therefore, our usability methods must necessarily be concerned with all three layers—at least until the day comes when PCDs all share a unified, or at least standard, set of features that have been thoroughly tested and debugged. As Web designers, we take the physical layer for granted. Why? Often, it is because the hard usability work of GUIs (Graphical User Interfaces) and input devices has already been done; we are presented with a time-tested device to deliver our Web content. There's

FIGURE 2.3 *The layers of interaction: physical, logical, and cognitive.*

usually nothing surprising or novel about a mouse or a computer monitor, for example. But what about a pager-sized device that you speak into to get full-color information displayed on a tiny LCD monitor? This sort of device hasn't been around as long as the ancient CRT. We've all read about the Dick Tracy two-way wrist TV, but no usability testing has been done on it!

To a degree, we also take the logical layer for granted, since the operating system–level infrastructure of most Web browsing systems is widely known, well-documented, and standardized. Even the differences between major operating systems like Windows and Mac OS are small when compared to the differences between tiny operating systems found in embedded devices. When the device's design goals require that the software that drives the system fit in a small amount of memory, the navigation features provided may be sparse and possibly incompatible with other similar devices.

Although several OS vendors are releasing compact versions of their systems—for example, WindowsCE[2] and Embedded Linux—there is no guarantee that the method of navigating a device built with one system will even be close to that of the other. General-purpose browsers like Netscape Navigator and Microsoft Internet Explorer are essentially unusable on tiny information devices, especially ones that feature a main input method other than typed input. Therefore, we can no longer assume that the browser and OS vendors are going to make everything nice, clean, and homogenous; before there will be widespread standards there will probably be a cacophony of disparate systems.

The final layer—and possibly the one that you will personally have the most control over—is the cognitive layer. This is the layer at which the user receives your well-thought-out content and uses it to accomplish important tasks. This is analogous to the content you are probably used to creating: menus, navigation elements, images (in some cases), and so on. Many techniques used in Web site usability can be implemented at this layer largely unmodified.

The Physical Layer

The sorts of physical actions a human may take to interact with a device can include, but are not limited, to the following:

- Pressing buttons
- Scrolling with a scroll wheel
- Handwriting input
- Using speech input
- Listening for audio cues
- Listening for speech output
- Operating a pointing device (such as a mouse)
- Reading text output
- Being able to see a screen under varying conditions

---

[2] Appropriately abbreviated "WinCE."

All of these tasks have the quality of being physical in nature; so far, we're not concerned with the higher levels of processing (like making sense out of the text that's been seen, or understanding the meaning of a phrase that's been heard). We're only concerned with the mechanics of interaction at this point (see Figure 2.4).

There are five human sensory domains that could potentially serve as conduits to and from the physical layer:

- Vision
- Hearing
- Olfaction (smelling)
- Haptics (touch)
- Taste

Although olfaction and taste probably served us well throughout the evolution of the species, these two senses just haven't yet been able to

FIGURE 2.4 *A user interfaces with a Palm PDA at the physical layer.*

make it onto the interface scene. This may change one day, but don't hold your breath. Vision and hearing are, by far, the two dominant domains, in that order of general preference. The haptic channel plays a role, too, since devices often need to provide tactile response to the user in case the other two senses are temporarily unavailable. For example, a vibrating cell phone or pager provides a tactile alert to the user when the user is in a noise-polluted environment that would otherwise mask the alert sound of the device.

There are quantitative and qualitative ways of measuring the efficiency of devices along all three of these sensory channels. In addition to this information, there are other physical means of measuring human inter-action, including a handful that are used to gauge what's going on inside the human user—the user's physiological/emotional states. Taken together, these techniques allow us to describe human-device interaction accurately. The rest of this section will detail some of the better-known techniques.

Movement: Fitt's Law

Fitt's Law is an old standby in human factors psychology and ergonom-ics (Figure 2.5). The law, distilled into a sentence, is simply this: The time to acquire a target is a function of the proximity and size of the target. This relationship is expressed by the equation

$$\text{Movement time} = a + bID$$

where *a* and *b* are constraints, and *ID* is the index of difficulty. The index of difficulty is expressed by the equation:

$$ID = \left(\log_2\left(\frac{2A}{W}\right)\right)$$

where *A* is the amplitude (size) of the movement, and *W* is the width of the target. Note that the width of the target and the accuracy needed to hit the target are inversely related: the bigger the object, the easier to hit. This can be a real concern if you are using a device that requires manual pointing and selection (like a PDA/stylus combination) and the screen real estate is tiny to begin with.

FIGURE 2.5 *Fitt's Law in action, illustrating the amount of time it takes the user to move the pointing device to the target and actuate.*

It is unlikely that you'll ever need to plug values into Fitt's Law in order to arrive at a solution for your particular design tasks. Rather, it is more important that you understand the implications of the law and adjust your design accordingly. The formulae have only been included for the sake of reference and completeness.

What are the implications of Fitt's Law as applied to Web navigation? Perhaps one of the best explanations has been given in an article written by Bruce Tognazzini[3], which includes numerous thorough examples of design influenced by application of Fitt's Law. For now, we'll focus on just two of the implications of the law. They can be summarized as follows:

- Bigger is better, especially for menu selection.
- Screen edges and corners should be used.

---

[3] See *www.asktog.com/columns/022DesignedToGiveFitts.html.*

The first tip is basically self-explanatory: make buttons and other navigation items as large as you can afford, since this makes them easier to hit. This also has the side effect of making the content more accessible, which is a bonus. This tip is unfortunately in direct opposition to the design goals of many aesthetes, since using really tiny type and other elements is in vogue in Web design. You may have to provide hard data to support your recommendation to increase the size of navigation items to sway the decision makers at your organization. Note that this design implication may also be potentially problematic in small user interfaces, where the maximum size of an interface widget may be limited by the host operating system, or by the small amount of screen real estate available. Some potential solutions for this dilemma include the following:

- Allowing users to navigate the screen by using nonpointer input methods, like a scroll wheel or voice input

- Providing an appropriate amount of hysteresis to help the device "snap" to the selection area

- Offering a highlighting mechanism, like a rollover, to help indicate which area is about to be made active

The second implication of the law is true because of a powerful principle of design: constraints. A constraint, used in a positive design sense, is a limitation placed on the user in order to assist the user at a task. Putting menu items in the edges and corners of the screen is a type of constraint because it makes it impossible for the user to accidentally move the pointer beyond the edge of the navigation item. Unless your PCD display employs a type of "virtual desktop," the user cannot move past the 1-pixel edge of the screen. This makes it hard to miss items that are positioned there.

You might be wondering what kind of interface wouldn't use screen edges. The answer is that essentially any floating window that has an area that's nonclickable on two or more sides fits this description. Menu items on floating windows require greater precision than menu items that are found at the extreme edge of the display area. Hence, windows found in the Macintosh OS are easier to use than the windows found in any Windows variant (Figure 2.6).

FIGURE 2.6 *An example of Macintosh OS windows. Note the way the menu is located along the extreme edge of the screen, making it easier to "hit" menu items. © 2002 Google.com.*

Another implication that follows is that there is a speed/accuracy trade-off. If a user is confronted with a screen with many selections crammed together, it will be difficult to locate the "correct" choice and successfully activate it in a timely fashion. For interfaces that are used in highly time-sensitive tasks, consider presenting the bare minimum number of options needed at any one time, and make those items as large as possible.

It is worth noting that at least one study[4] has found significant differences in accuracy and speed in navigation between the point-and-click style and the drag-and-drop style. In the study, children were given the task to move icons around on a screen using one of these two styles. Overall, the point-and-click method was the fastest and most reliable.

---

[4] See *www.cs.sfu.ca/~inkpen/Papers/TR20_DD/tr20.html.*

Evidently, some component of drag-and-drop can be more time consuming. This may sometimes be observed when adult novice computer users manipulate on-screen items, but whether this study can be generalized to adults has yet to be shown.

A study done in 1996 has demonstrated that the addition of tactile feedback to an input mechanism can add considerably to the effectiveness of the device, resulting in a reduction of task time and a decrease in errors.[5] This finding can and should be applied to the field of information device design, since tactile feedback can be especially effective in augmenting navigation in situations where vision and hearing are limited. This sort of mechanism has become popular recently with force-feedback devices like game joystick controllers and steering wheels. The same principle can be applied to mobile computing devices.

Finally, bear in mind that there are many ways to reduce the amount of screen clutter while maintaining an adequate amount of information at hand; a little planning and an understanding of human search techniques can assist here. For example, according to Microsoft Usability Training Manager Scott Berkun, many search engines waste space and force users to struggle against Fitt's Law by including multiple links for pages of search engine hits.[6] Although this isn't too much of a problem when the display area is large, like a desktop PC monitor, it is a real problem when the display area is a PDA screen, or when the primary input/output method is nonvisual. Berkun suggests that the solution is simply to provide a link from each search result set to the next (and previous) set, since most search engine users are going to want to look at results in rank order anyway. When was the last time you used a Web search engine and jumped straight to the least pertinent hits? When was the last time you just jumped around from search result page to search result page? These behaviors are not typical of task-oriented

---

[5] Motoyuki Akamatsu and I. Scott MacKenzie, "Movement Characteristics Using a Mouse with Tactile and Force Feedback," *International Journal of Human-Computer Studies* 45, no. 4 (1996): 483-93.

[6] See *msdn.microsoft.com/library/welcome/dsmsdn/hfactor9_3.htm*.

users; therefore, implementing the minimalist design should not detract from the utility of the interface, at least for the vast majority of users.

Miller's Law

In all likelihood you have heard about this famous law, often known as the "magic number" or "seven plus or minus two" law. Although the amount of literature on this subject is vast, Miller's Law essentially states that human short-term memory can accommodate about seven unrelated pieces of information, plus or minus two, at a time. As a result of this famous study performed by George Miller,[7] most telephone numbers in North American telephone exchanges have exactly seven digits. This law has been at the center of many heated debates on Usenet newsgroups and other HCI mailing lists, but may actually be considered to have little bearing on the amount of information that can be displayed on a screen without causing "overload." While the original study demonstrated the short-term memory retention capability of humans, activities such as scanning a page of information does not put such a load on the short-term memory, but rather calls upon it to "weed out" incorrect or useless information.

So then, what are the implications of this study for our purposes? It can be argued that the peripheral discoveries of this study—namely, the phenomena known as "chunking"—may have a far greater impact on PCD design than the "magic number" itself. Certainly, a display that is crowded with information that isn't relevant—noise, in other words—is going to be very difficult to understand and navigate. It is debatable whether adequate research has yet been done in this area to produce concrete theoretical limits for what people can and can't handle, however, limiting the amount of information to just what's needed is a good rule of thumb.[8]

---

[7] Originally published in the *Psychological Review* 63, (1956): 81–97, the entire report can now be found at *www.well.com/user/smalin/miller.html.*

[8] To my knowledge no one has yet developed a complete theory of feng shui for Web pages. However, *www.newmediastudies.com/fengshui.htm* is enlightening, if not totally correct from a usability standpoint.

Human Stress: Galvanic Skin Response

One of the prime goals of usability engineering and user-centered design (UCD) is to create devices and systems that cause the least amount of stress—optimally, none—to the humans who use them. One concrete physiological metric of human stress is skin conductivity. As human stress increases, the electrical resistance of the skin decreases due to an increase in activity of sweat glands when the sympathetic nervous system is active. This change in resistance permits increased electrical flow across the skin's surface. Jean De Tarchanoff first discovered this phenomenon in 1890, although science has only been able to understand what causes it within the last thirty years. Galvanic skin response (GSR), which is used as a reliable metric for measuring human stress in the fields of medicine and psychology, can also be used to measure stress levels in users of mobile computing devices and the like. Many usability labs have a GSR meter, a variety of which range from USD $59.00 to USD $450.00.[9]

Even more useful than a standard GSR meter is the real-time GSR system, a device and software package that connects to a PC and that retails for around USD $500. The combination allows you to monitor a person's stress level over time, which, when combined with video footage of usability tests, will allow you to pinpoint stressful events. In turn, this will help you identify tasks that are too stressful for whatever benchmark you have established.

Human Speech

Speech is becoming more and more popular as a form of computer input/output. Although we're still quite a distance from the likes of Hal from the movie *2001: A Space Odyssey*, we're closing the gap every day. Affordable commercial software that is available today can transform a desktop PC into a speech-driven word processor, although a general speech-driven interface to most popular operating systems is not yet

---

[9] I would be interested in hearing from you if you have a recommendation for one of these meters. Send mail to *equipment@mind-hive.com*.

available.[10] Systems like TellMe[11] have been able to achieve fairly robust speech-driven systems by implementing specific domains of control for speech input. In Chapter 3 we'll take a look at how speech recognition works in greater detail. For now, we'll just focus on the purely physical aspects of speech.

Audible Spectrum versus Speech Spectrum

It is generally believed that an average human can hear sound frequencies in the range from 20 Hertz (Hz) to 20 kilohertz (kHz). In reality, various factors affect human hearing over time. Illness, trauma to the auditory system, and other considerations can cause hearing loss in narrow bands and even above or below a certain threshold entirely. It is not necessary for a human to possess the full range of hearing in order to function normally in this regard, however. Certain types of "important" sounds—namely speech—occupy a relatively narrow slice of the total audible spectrum.

Most of the human voice characteristics that are crucial to speech recognition by a human take place in the 300 Hz–3 kHz range, which is really a small slice of the whole spectrum. This is because most of the fundamental, or dominant, tones created by the human voice are in this range. Anything above 3 kHz is likely to be a harmonic, which is an overtone caused by certain types of resonance in the speech mechanism. These harmonics are not regarded as important for speech understanding. In fact, the telephone system capitalizes on this principle to save bandwidth in telephone transmissions.

Since the range 300 Hz–3 kHz is critical to speech understanding, it's important that any microphone and/or speaker system you implement on your information device be at least capable of this range. Vendors of sound reinforcement components will usually provide you with the fre-

---

[10] Unless you count the Macintosh speech system that has been available for years. Note that this system is still rather limited in terms of what it can recognize.

[11] See *www.tellme.com*.

quency range that their products are capable of; if they don't, you may need to use a different vendor.

Ambient Noise and Channel Distortion

Two factors that can interfere with speech recognition systems and human understanding of speech output are ambient noise and channel distortion. Ambient noise is simply any sound in the environment that is not the target signal, e.g., not the intended speech signal. Other conversations nearby, engine and cabin noise in an automobile, wind, echoic noise inside large structures, and static, for example, can all contribute to the degradation of a speech signal's capacity for recognition. Since this type of noise is generally unavoidable, systems must be crafted to be robust against such interference.

Channel distortion is an effect caused by a shift in the properties of the communication channel itself. Moving the mouth close to a microphone, for example, will result in the bass (low frequency) tones registering very high, often causing signal distortion. Another example of channel distortion is digital artifacts caused by certain types of cellular telephony methods. "Spattering" or other types of electronic noise caused by the communication channel itself can be controlled to an extent, but this type of interference is still nondeterministic and system design must reflect this.

Repetitive Strain Injury (RSI)

No text on the subject of ergonomics would be complete without a discussion on RSI, or Repetitive Strain Injury, which was introduced at the beginning of the chapter. RSI can occur in almost any environment, and a user is at risk any time it becomes necessary to repeat an action over and over. Carpal tunnel syndrome is only one of many possible afflictions that can signal RSI. Eyestrain, bursitis ("tennis elbow"), and other types of nerve damage can result from overuse of almost any device. The research on RSI risks with traditional desktop PCs is well known, and a whole host of accessories and ergonomic input devices have emerged in response. Since the RSI risks posed by mobile computing devices and other PCDs are not well known at the moment, however, you must be aware of the possibility that your device/content may contribute to RSI in your end users. In fact, if you are part of a project that is creating a new type of device, you should seriously consider hiring an RSI specialist.

Although each style of device will require a slightly different mode of physical interaction, there are some simple guidelines that you can follow to reduce the risk of RSI posed by your creation. The following are some basics to consider:

- Increase text font size to help reduce strain on eyes. Use the largest font you can manage.

- Use high-contrast displays to help reduce strain on eyes.

- Reduce glare on displays; consider using an anti-glare coating on displays if feasible.

- Eliminate unnecessary repetition. As simple as this may sound, it is often overlooked. For example, requiring users to type text input via a ten-digit keypad means pressing a button multiple times to register a single character.

- Use speech recognition and speech output. This lightens the load on the human musculoskeletal system and frees up the hands for other activities.

- Consider the user's other activities in the usage environment. If using the device interferes with them or requires the user to contort to use it, redesign the device. A related field study would be informative.

- Don't require a heavy touch to operate the device. If you need to safeguard the device against accidental operation (i.e., while it is switched on and inside a pocket), use a strategy other than making all the buttons hard to push/actuate.

The Logical Layer

Sometimes it is hard to distinguish between content and operating system, especially in smaller systems that use little memory and few other resources, since the two necessarily blend. For this discussion, however, we will assume that the host system has some sort of distinct operating system (OS). Take, for example, the Palm OS, which runs on many popular PDAs from Palm and Handspring. This OS is very simple, since it was designed to run in a small amount of memory, yet it is fairly robust. There is a great amount of support for programmers for the Palm OS, which is able to do many things that the big operating systems can do. A main attraction of the operating system from a usability standpoint is its consistency in and standards for interfaces. All devices that run the Palm OS have several things in common:

- A way to view types (or categories) of applications from a sort of "home screen"; applications can also be launched from this view

- Consistent menu bar options across applications (equivalent to the menu bars in Windows and MacOS)

- Online help (even if it is minimal)

- A way to associate applications with the push buttons on the physical device

Although this list could go on and on, the important thing to grasp is that this OS has made gains in usability by being standardized and well known. (Please note, however, that being standardized and well known does *not* automatically make a system usable.) Of course, the designers of the Palm OS spent many hours testing the user-friendliness of the system before it was publicly released, and it is a usable system.

The Palm OS is very minimal, providing only the visible functions needed to glue together the system. There are no registries to edit (and to become corrupt in obscure, irreparable ways), no extra blinking lights to add to the marketing list of features. It's small and solid; hence its popularity and resilience in a competitive market. When you consider the fact that the logical layer is a necessary evil in most cases—since it is the foundation upon which your content and applications must run— you must also take into account the fact that it is also a barrier for the user in the process of getting to your content. Your job, therefore, is to make sure that it is as transparent as possible. This was the original goal of the Macintosh operating system: for the OS to disappear from view and fade into the background, providing only iconic cues to allow the user to navigate. This was a vast improvement in usability over command-line interfaces.[12]

Depending on the nature of the device you're working with, the operating system may be extremely minimal. Take, for example, pager-type devices. These usually have fairly limited operating systems, although this is starting to change with the increasing popularity and availability of two-way pagers and text messaging.

In short, the logical layer is the element of the system that is visible to the user and with which the user must interface to effect change in the device and subsequently accomplish tasks (Figure 2.7). In trying to make this

FIGURE 2.7 *The Palm OS "home screen." This represents part of the logical layer of this device. Palm VII. © 2002 Palm.com.*

---

[12] Note that a GUI is not inherently more usable—or even more useful—than a command-line interface (CLI). In fact, in many cases a GUI can be difficult to use if it has been poorly designed.

layer as transparent as possible to the user, remember that your users don't buy your product/content to play with the infrastructure; they want results and information that is managed by that infrastructure. Sounds simple, but many designers turn a blind eye to the fact.

The Cognitive Layer

The final layer of the information "onion," the cognitive layer, is comprised of the user's own conceptualization of what's going on inside the device. Sometimes, this is called a "mental model," since humans tend to create and add to schemata in order to understand how something works and, in turn, how to use it properly. The art of design requires that you make it possible for the mental model to be as simple as possible while still allowing the user to accomplish any given goal. For example, a user of a DVD player generally only needs to know that, in order to get a movie to play, they need to:

1. Open the disc tray.
2. Insert a disc.
3. Close the tray.
4. Press play.

Note that users don't necessarily need to develop a complete mental model of how the device works internally; they can develop a simplified model that serves the purpose just fine. In the same way, your users should not need to keep a map of the system in their heads at all times just to use it.

Is Multitasking Safe for Humans?

One of the most important debates in the area of portable electronic devices is the one concerned with the safety of using such devices while doing other things. A recent study conducted by the Harvard University Center for Risk Analysis has suggested that it is not really the physical act of using a cellular phone that can contribute to accidents, but rather the cognitive act of having a conversation that is at fault. Since carrying on a conversation is usually a cognitively expensive task, it is believed that this action may take away from the cognitive processes needed for safe, observant driving. Stressful, emotional conversations have been cited as being particularly high risk for causing accidents.

Cell phone-related accidents are just one of the types of distraction-based accidents that can happen in automobiles and other forms of transportation. The potential for serious accidents is great when the drivers of vehicles also use mobile devices like two-way messagers or palm-sized Web browsers. Using any such device will necessarily consume some of the driver's cognitive resources—quite possibly making it too difficult to dedicate enough attention to driving. So, while the new generations of portable computing devices will offer a plethora of handy features to mobile users—including lifesaving features like those found on some in-car systems—these new technologies could also pose a serious risk to users.

CHAPTER SUMMARY

There are three layers of interaction with any information device: the physical layer, in which the user directly interfaces with the real-world, physical object, like a PDA; the logical layer, in which the user interfaces with the operating system that enables the device; and the cognitive layer, in which the user interacts with and comprehends applications and feedback that enable task accomplishment. Usability specialists should have a thorough understanding of each layer of each system that they are testing.

HANDS ON

1. Pick three devices that you use frequently, and make a list of properties from each of the three layers of interaction for each device. For example, a VCR has a physical layer that includes control buttons (Fast Forward, Rewind, Play, Stop, and Eject), a slot for loading the tapes, a power button, and a remote control that also provides all of these functions. The VCR's logical layer corresponds to the "operating system" of menus for programming that are

accessed through special keystrokes (setting the clock, programming times to record shows, setting playback speed, and so on). The cognitive layer includes functions like the actual playback/viewing of tapes.

2. Do all devices have three distinct layers of interaction? How would it be possible or impossible for two layers to blend? Discuss.

3. What liability should a system manufacturer have in the safety of its users? In other words, should cell phone manufacturers be responsible when a driver has an accident while chatting on a cell phone? Why or why not? How could this concept extend to other forms of portable computing, like PDAs? Discuss.

CONTENT DELIVERY
TECHNOLOGIES

3

The world of pervasive computing is driven by much more than plain old HTML. Long the staple of the Web, HTML is ill suited for the vast majority of content markup needs for information devices. HTML is very display-oriented, with little support for semantic markup (and the HTML tags that are semantic in nature are almost never used, like the "<cite>" tag). Furthermore, HTML is nonextensible, meaning that it cannot readily be adapted for devices other than a traditional PC/browser combination. For all of these reasons, and because HTML is a general-purpose markup language that has already been stretched far beyond the bounds of what its inventor intended, it follows that next-generation information devices cannot rely solely on this mechanism for content delivery.

A natural fit for PCDs is XML, the eXtensible Style Language. XML is a metalanguage that combines the power and robustness of its larger parent, SGML (Standard Generalized Markup Language), but that also delivers the ease of use and Web savvy that has made HTML so popular in spite of its numerous shortcomings. Many PCDs, in fact, are already employing some application of XML.[1] VoiceXML, for example, puts

---

[1] The term "application" is used in the sense of "instance of," not as in "binary executable."

XML in action in the world of computer-driven telephony; other variations on this theme are popping up all over the place. In general, this is good: the software used to parse and manipulate XML documents is freely available, time tested, and well documented. Since a design goal of XML was to divorce content from presentation, XML can act as a neutral base language for expressing documents for dispersal over many divergent systems (Figure 3.1).

Some vendors have chosen to go the proprietary route, however. A variety of factors can influence a company's decision whether to go with an open standard or a proprietary standard, not limited to but

FIGURE 3.1 *An example XML document, as rendered by Microsoft Internet Explorer 5.5. Note: This is how the document appears in lieu of any style sheet information.*

including technological barriers, revenue structures, weaknesses in existing open standards, and the need for something totally unaddressed by existing standards. As mentioned earlier, all of this adds up to a lot of different technologies for the PCD designer and PCD content creator to keep up with.

The purpose of this chapter is to provide an overview of technologies that are currently in use, as well as of some that have not yet been widely adopted. By understanding some of the common threads of these technologies, you will gain insight both into their strengths and their limitations. The information that follows is not meant to be an exhaustive listing of all known content delivery technologies, but rather an introduction to new content delivery mechanisms by way of several real-world examples.

WIRELESS MARKUP LANGUAGE (WML)

It is unlikely that you will ever see a reference to Wireless Markup Language (WML) without also seeing a reference to Wireless Application Protocol (WAP), and vice versa. This is because WML and WAP were designed to go hand in hand. Although they will be discussed separately here, it should be kept in mind that the two are designed to interoperate.

A consortium consisting of Unwired Planet, Motorola, Ericsson, and Nokia was responsible for creating WML and WAP. This group, known as the WAP Forum, now leads most of the development of standards in the area of WAP and WML.[2] WML was designed specifically with the constraints of small narrowband devices, like cell phones and pagers, in mind: their small display and limited user input facilities, their limited memory and computational resources, and their narrowband network connection (Figure 3.2).[3] The functionality of WML includes four primary features:

---

[2] See *www.wapforum.com.*
[3] Summarized from *www1.wapforum.org/tech/documents/WAP-191-WML-20000219-a.pdf.*

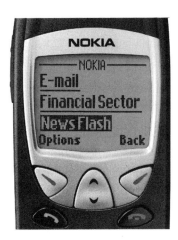

FIGURE 3.2 *A WAP-enabled telephone. © 2001. Reprinted with permission from Nokia. All rights reserved.*

- **Text presentation and layout:** WML includes support for text and a limited form of image support, as well as lightweight layout capabilities.

- **Deck/card organizational metaphor:** Instead of using Web "pages," all information in WML is organized into a collection of cards and decks.

- **Inter-card navigation and linking:** WML includes support for explicitly managing the navigation between cards and decks.

- **String parameterization and state management:** All WML decks can be parameterized, using a state model.

WML is a departure from HTML in several ways. It offers a different paradigm for document organization, which takes some getting used to—particularly if you're used to the old page-of-info paradigm. Since WML documents have all the constraints of well-formed and valid XML documents, they are probably not well suited to creation by hand, but rather via automated processes and/or XML-capable editors.

Designers who are used to being able to specify layout down to the pixel will discover that WML has no such provisions for control. Layout control is not a primary goal of WML, so crafting cards that look a certain way will be next to impossible. However, since WML is an application of XML, it is likely that at some point in the future it could offer support for styles via Cascading Style Sheets (CSS)or XSL, the Extensible Style Language.

Since WML was designed to be delivered using WAP rather than HTTP, you'll need a special server to deliver WML content. WML content must be compiled into a byte stream at the server side before being pushed to the client; as a result, most common Web servers cannot serve WAP/WML content as is.[4]

Despite these major differences, WML shares much with HTML. There is still some enmeshment of content structure and presentation; for example, WML supports tags like "<input>," "
," and "<table>," each of which is tied at least somewhat to appearance. WML, in other words, shares many of HTML's limitations.

Here's an example of a typical WML document:

```
<?xml version="1.0"?>
<!DOCTYPE wml PUBLIC "-//WAPFORUM//DTD WML 1.1//EN"
"http://www.wapforum.org/DTD/wml_1.1.xml">
<wml>
<card id="card1" title="First card in deck">
<p>
Hello World!
</p>
</card>
<card id="card2" title="Second card in deck">
<p>
Hello Galaxy!
</p>
```

---

[4] Note, however, that some people have figured a way around this. See *www.isoc.org/inet2000/cdproceedings/3b/3b_1.htm.*

```
</card>
<card id="card3" title="The last card in the deck">
<p>
Hello, Universe!
</p>
</card>
</wml>
```

There are several things worth noting about the structure of the preceding. For one thing, it is both a well-formed and a valid XML document, meaning that it complies with two levels of strictness imposed upon XML documents. The document is well-formed in that it has no syntactic problems: all attribute values are in quotes, all tags are properly nested, and so on. It is valid in the sense that it can be validated against an existing XML document type definition, such as the one referenced in line three of the sample code.

The document is made up of one parent object called the "deck," which is basically everything between the "<wml>" and the "</wml>" tags. Inside the deck are three cards. The card is the basic unit of display in WML and roughly corresponds to one full screen of information.

WIRELESS APPLICATION PROTOCOL (WAP)

As mentioned earlier, WAP and WML are closely tied, since WAP is the transport mechanism for documents encoded in WML. According to the WAP architecture specification, wireless solutions implemented with WAP must be:[5]

- **Interoperable:** Terminals from different manufacturers should be able to communicate with services in the mobile network.

- **Scalable:** Mobile network operators should be able to scale services to customer needs.

---

[5] From *www1.wapforum.org/tech/terms.asp?doc=SPEC-WAPArch-19980430.pdf.*

- **Efficient:** Quality of service should be suited to the behavior and characteristics of the mobile network.

- **Reliable:** A consistent and predictable platform should be provided for deploying service.

- **Secure:** Services to be extended over potentially unprotected mobile networks should still be able to preserve the integrity of user data; devices and services should be protected from security problems such as denial of service.

The key components to a WAP system are a WAP protocol gateway, which manages the transformation from the WAP stack to the HTTP stack, and content encoders and decoders, which are used to convert WAP content into a proprietary binary format before transmitting in order to reduce bandwidth needs. Although, technically speaking, WAP/WML content is delivered from a standard HTTP server, a WAP proxy server is also needed to convert the WAP content into binary form.

The next bit about WAP might be of interest to people who possess some understanding of network protocols or to anyone who likes to know a little about what's going on behind the scenes. If you don't fit either category, you might want to skip ahead to the next section.

WAP can be described as a protocol stack similar to the OSI network protocol stack. Think of the stack as a sort of onion: each layer encapsulates the layer beneath it, and each layer is only responsible for communicating with the layers immediately above and below itself. The six layers in the WAP stack are described below. They are ordered from the closest to the human-interface level to the closest to the hardware level.

The Application Layer (WAE)

This layer is the closest to the user; it is the layer in which the micro-browser is located (usually built into the telephone or other device).

Other objects that appear in this layer include WMLScript (described in detail shortly), wireless telephony application, and WML itself.

The Session Layer (WSP)

This layer provides the WAE with an interface to two critical services: a connectionless[6] service called Wireless Datagram Protocol (WDP), which is analogous to UDP protocol in the TCP/IP stack, and a connection-oriented service called WTP (a description of which follows), which rides on top of WDP. This layer is also designed with the low bandwidth and high latency of cellular telephony in mind.

The Transaction Layer (WTP)

This layer is analogous to TCP. Its main function is to provide three classes of service:

- Unreliable one-way requests

- Reliable one-way requests

- Reliable two-way requests

The Security Layer (WTLS)

This layer differentiates the WAP stack from the TCP/IP stack. WAP has built-in support for employing digital encryption of data via Secure Sockets Layer (SSL), a well-known standard for data security and integrity. This layer provides several features that are critical due to the nature of cellular transmissions, which can be intercepted by anyone

---

[6] "Connectionless" means that the bits of information that travel using this mode don't do anything to confirm delivery or content integrity. Using a connectionless service can be compared to using the U.S. Postal Service in that users don't receive confirmation that letters they sent were ever delivered. A connection-oriented session, on the other hand, has delivery confirmation built right in, allowing the system to automatically redeliver any parts of a message that may have been damaged or lost the first time around.

with a modicum of electronics know-how and a modified radio scanner.[7] These features include the following:

- **Data integrity via digital signatures:** This ensures that content has not been corrupted or manipulated by a "man-in-the-middle" attack.

- **Privacy:** Sessions are encrypted, making it difficult for eavesdroppers to succeed.

- **Authentication:** Cryptographic identification of client/server is provided.

- **Denial of service protection:** Protection is supplied against several well-known types of denial of device.

The Transport Layer (WDP)

This bottommost layer (next to the actual telephony protocols used to transport the upper layers) provides the connectionless service described above. This is essentially the backbone of the WAP protocol stack.

The Bearer Layer

This layer is analogous to the physical layer in the OSI model. It consists of the actual services over which the WAP stack can run. It currently includes GSM-900, GSM-1800, GSM-1900, CDMA IS-95, TDMA IS-136, and 3G systems IMT-2000, UMTS, W-CDMA, and Wideband IS-95. The list of compatible bearer services will grow over time to keep up with emerging technology.

WMLScript (WMLS)

WMLScript (WMLS) rounds out the WAP/WML suite by adding a scripting language for added programmatic functionality. WMLScript is

---

[7] It should by now be common knowledge that you should never say anything over a cell phone—unless the entire session is encrypted—that you wouldn't want repeated to the entire world.

similar to JavaScript, but with several major differences. First, WMLScript relies exclusively on collections of functions and objects, called libraries. Although the use of libraries is possible in JavaScript, it has not become a widely adopted practice. Some commonly used WMLScript libraries include Dialog, which is a collection of dialog functions and features that facilitate interaction with the user; Float, which is a floating-point math library; and WMLBrowser, which is used to access components of the actual microbrowser itself.

Another big difference between WMLScript and JavaScript is that WMLScript delivers scripts to the client in a precompiled format. This improves performance of the application and decreases the amount of bandwidth needed. Also, WMLScript functions are called in a curious way, since there is no embedded WMLScript support. A call to a WMLScript function looks like this:

```
<?xml version="1.0"?>
<!DOCTYPE wml PUBLIC "-//WAPFORUM//DTD WML 1.1//EN"
"http://www.wapforum.org/DTD/wml_1.1.xml">

<wml>

<card id="credit_card" title="Credit Card Validation">
          <do type="accept" label="Results">
<go href="cardValidate.wmls#validateCC($(CC))"/>
          </do>
          <p>
Enter Credit Card number: <input type="text" name="SSN"/>
          </p>
     </card>
     <card id="Results" title="Results:">
     <p>
     You entered:<br/>
 Credit Card Number: $(CC)<br/>
     </p>
     </card>
</wml>
```

In the example just given, the line we're especially interested in is the one that begins with "<go." This line specifies the function to be called, "validateCC." Note that it is referenced using a method that is similar to a named link inside an HTML document. The WMLScript code that contains the function is named "cardValidate.wmls."

If you've had some experience using JavaScript and HTML, then you know that JavaScript can be used to make an interface much more user-friendly (even though it can also be used to create user-hostile features, even ones that crash the browser). WMLScript is no different. Some of these features include the following:

- Client side input validation: This is especially important, since WAP/WML applications may have high latency and expensive transaction overhead.

- Automatic manipulation of client-side input based on previous user input: Default values, for example, can be filled in for a given option depending on what the user selects for a top-level option.

- Determination of information about the client device in order to redirect to more appropriate content.

The WMLScript standard states that if a browser does not implement a particular function that is part of the standard WMLS libraries, that function must at the least return the special value "invalid." If you read between the lines here, it appears that there's room for inconsistencies between versions of WMLS. So be warned! By the time this book is printed, there may be a "special" version of WMLS produced by Microsoft.

VoiceXML

VoiceXML is designed for creating audio dialogues with human beings. The language allows for a combination of synthesized speech and digitized audio (output from the server side), recognition of spoken and DTMF key input, and recording of spoken input (user response/input methods). The major goal of VoiceXML is to bring the advantages of

Web-based development and content delivery to interactive voice response applications. Since VoiceXML is an application of XML, it possesses the same structure, restrictions, and benefits[8]

The VoiceXML 1.0 specification emerged from years of research and development at AT&T, IBM, Lucent Technologies, and Motorola. Formally, the growth, development, and management of VoiceXML is governed by the VoiceXML Forum, which consists of many member companies. The forum's Web site can be found at *www.voicexml.org.*

VoiceXML possesses the following capabilities and attributes:

- It minimizes client/server interactions by specifying multiple interactions per document.

- It shields application authors from low-level and platform-specific details.

- It separates user interaction code (in VoiceXML) from service logic (CGI scripts).

- It promotes service portability across implementation platforms; VoiceXML is a common language for content providers, tool providers, and platform providers.

- It is easy to use for simple interactions and yet provides language features to support complex dialogs.

Here's an example of a VXML document that represents a dialog with a user.

```
<?xml version="1.0"?>
<vxml version="1.0">
<form>
<field name="department">
<prompt>
Greetings! Which department would you like to speak to?
</prompt>
```

---

[8] From *www.w3.org/TR/voicexml.*

```
<grammar src="dept.gram"
type="application/x-jsgf"/>
</field>

<block>
<submit next=
"http://www.mumblebunnies.org/dept.pl"/>
</block>
</form>
</vxml>
</xml>
```

The resulting conversation between computer and user might go like this:

Computer: Greetings! Which department would you like to speak to?

User: I like oatmeal.

Computer: I'm sorry, I didn't understand your response. Which department would you like to speak to?

User: Marketing.

Computer: Please hold for the marketing department.

In the preceding example, the system is prompting the user for speech input. The "<field>" element represents an input field, similar to an "<input>" element in HTML. The difference is that instead of typing, the user speaks. Note that there is a tag called "<grammar>" that represents the limited vocabulary that will be considered acceptable input for this selection. In speech recognition, a "grammar" is a small set of words that fit a specific target application. The benefit of using grammars is that it makes the job of speech recognition vastly easier. By constraining the types of words that could occur in a given input, the amount of processing needed decreases and the accuracy rate increases. Clearly, this approach means that you can't build a superintelligent system that can understand every combination of possible speech, but it's a start.

If you'd like to hear an example of VoiceXML in action, just call (inside the United States) 1-800-555-TELL. This number will connect you to a system based entirely on VoiceXML. Once connected, you can choose from topic areas like Ski Reports, Stock Quotes, Sports, News, Traffic, and Weather, simply by saying the name of the category you want to choose. You can also check out developer info on the TellMe Web site, *www.tellme.com*.

Applications built on VoiceXML will bridge the gap between traditional, type-text driven Web applications and more natural (human-like) interactions with information systems.

Speech Recognition versus Natural Language Processing

It is worth noting that speech recognition is not the same thing as natural language processing, which is a much more advanced, powerful, and complicated technology. Speech recognition is only concerned with transforming human audio speech into a temporary digital form, comparing the digital blueprint of the words with a database of known words, and checking for a match. The matched words can then be used to trigger an event, like switching the user to a new menu or playing a recording. For example, in a simple speech recognition driven system, the computer may prompt the user for a response. The user may say the word "three," which matches one of the words in the known grammar. The word "three" is matched with a specific action, namely to go to menu number three.

Natural language processing, on the other hand, can use speech recognition—or not—in order to derive meaning from strings of words and sentences. A natural language processing system, for example, would be able to accept a spoken query from the user ("How much is the cheapest plane fare from Boston to Taiwan?"), derive meaning from the query, and find and deliver an answer to the user (usually via text or speech synthesis). Although the amount of processing needed to accomplish this task is significantly greater than that needed to do simple speech recognition, it can all be done on commodity hardware. The Spoken

Language Systems Group at the MIT Laboratory for Computer Science[9] has been able to implement just such a system on hardware no more expensive than an ordinary laptop PC.

COMPACT HTML (cHTML)

Although Compact HTML (also called cHTML) and i-mode are usually discussed together, they are in fact two different constructs, so they'll be covered separately here. Compact HTML is a subset of HTML 2.0, 3.2, and 4.0. The goal of the language is quite similar to that of WML: to enable document markup and presentation for small handheld devices, mainly telephones and the like. The Compact HTML standard really only exists as a W3C note,[10] meaning that it hasn't garnered the W3C's official blessing as a recognized and stable standard. Compact HTML, in fact, hasn't been able to gather much steam, since WAP/WML has a lead in the area. It shouldn't be discounted entirely, however, since it does offer the benefit of using normal HTTP for data transfer, thus making it a lot easier to serve up content for handheld devices that support it.

Compact HTML essentially strips the HTML you are probably familiar with down to the bare bones. The major features of "regular" HTML that are missing from Compact HTML include the following:

- JPEG image format
- Tables
- Image maps
- Multiple character fonts and styles
- Background color and images
- Frames
- Style sheets

---

[9] See *www.sls.lcs.mit.edu.*
[10] See *www.w3.org/TR/1998/NOTE-compactHTML-19980209/.*

Design Requirements of Compact HTML

With Compact HTML, the emphasis is clearly on a reductionist model. Its design requirements are as follows:

- Compact HTML is completely based on the current HTML W3C recommendations.

- Since it is defined as a subset of HTML 2.0, HTML 3.2, and HTML 4.0 specifications, Compact HTML inherits the flexibility and portability of the standard HTML.

- Since Compact HTML has to be implemented with small memory and low-power CPU (central processing unit), frames and tables that require large memory are excluded.

- Compact HTML can be viewed on a small black-and-white display. It does not assume a fixed display space, however, but can adjust to the display screen size. It also assumes a single character font.

- Compact HTML can be easily operated by the user. It is defined so that all the basic operations can be done by a combination of four buttons: "cursor forward," "cursor backward," "select," and "back/stop" ("return to the previous page"). Functions that require two-dimensional focus pointing, like "image map" and "table," are excluded from Compact HTML.

i-MODE

In Japan, electronic devices play a major role in everyday life, and the Japanese are frequently far ahead of the rest of the world with regard to implementing innovative new technologies. While the rest of the world has finally caught onto the power of Internet access via cell phones, for example, the Japanese have been drawing on its potential for a while now. Rather than waiting for a worldwide standard to emerge, in 1999 NTT DoCoMo, Japan's leading cellular phone operator, introduced a service called i-mode (short for "information mode") that would allow mobile phone users to surf the Web using a special new sort of

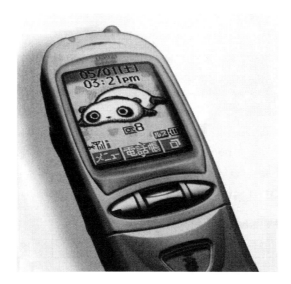

FIGURE 3.3 *An i-mode telephone. Image courtesy of DoCoMo.*
© 2001 NTT DoCoMo, Inc. All rights reserved.

telephone (see Figure 3.3). i-mode directly competes with WAP/WML; they both fulfill the same niche in the information world. NTT chose to implement i-mode and Compact HTML as a standard simply because it was unwilling to wait for WAP to mature. This is understandable, given the technologically superior state of Japan's cellular telephone network and ability to make the move to wireless Web access long before most of the rest of the world.

The Makeup of i-mode

i-mode is really a combination of several distinct components:

- An i-mode-capable phone
- An i-mode gateway
- Content providers that have sites composed entirely of Compact HTML

Note that a gateway is required for the i-mode phone to connect to. The sites themselves, however, are simply required to be written in Compact

HTML, which means that the content providers have little extra work to do. Regular HTTP Web server software can be used to deliver the content.

Since, at the time of this writing, i-mode is almost exclusively used in Japan, it is very difficult to get information about the platform in any language other than Japanese. One excellent resource in English for learning more about i-mode is *www.AnyWhereYouGo.com.* You can also check out NTT's Web site, *www.nttdocomo.com,* for developer information.

HDML/HDTP

Before there was WAP/WML in the United States there was HDML, or Handheld Device Markup Language. HDML and HDTP, the accompanying transport protocol, were created by Unwired Planet in 1997. Unwired Planet also created a browser called "UP.browser" that would run on cell phones[11] (primarily those officially licensed by Phone.com) and similar devices. Together, this trio introduced the U.S. to the notion of wireless Web browsing.

WML came along after HDML had blazed the trail, so to speak, and smoothed out some of the rougher facets of HDML. The popularity of HDML has been waning; in fact, it is deprecated in favor of WML. A sort of "bridge" between the two has been created in the form of WML with Phone.com extensions. A listing of the additional tags in the extension set is given below.

- <spawn>
- <exit>
- <throw>
- <catch>
- <send>

---

[11] A full listing of HDML-compatible phones can be found at *http://updev.phone.com/ dev/ts/up/phones.html.* Note the caveat about choosing a markup language.

- <receive>
- <reset>
- access key attribute

Many of the concepts of WML, such as the notions of "decks" and "cards," come from HDML. HDML has been covered in this chapter mainly for historical reference. You should not strongly consider using this suite to deploy any new rollouts, but instead focus on WML, which is now the de facto standard.

WEBTV

Although the concept of interactive television is not new, WebTV may be the first offering to actually bring it to the table in an economically viable and solvent fashion. WebTV Networks, which is based in Santa Clara, California, has been wholly owned by Microsoft since 1997. At the time of writing, they offer four categories of service:

- **WebTV Classic:** The basic service that uses a special WebTV receiver to connect an ordinary TV set to the Internet. The service allows the subscriber to browse the Web (with certain constraints that are covered in depth later in this book) and exchange e-mail.

- **WebTV Plus:** This service, along with a WebTV receiver, gives the subscriber the above benefits plus interactive television (ITV). ITV allows subscribers to play along with a game show, participate in a poll on a television show, and so on.

- **UltimateTV:** UltimateTV works only with DirecTV subscribers; it adds lots of TV-oriented features like automatic recording of shows.

- **WebTV Personal TV Service:** This service works only with DISH Network DISHPlayer users and mainly offers TV-oriented features.

The primarily TV oriented features are outisde the scope of this book. We're going to mainly be concerned with the function of WebTV as a device for accessing the Internet.

SIMPLE MESSAGE SERVICE (SMS)

SMS, which is short for Simple Message Service, has been around since 1991 but isn't nearly as well known in the United States as it is in Europe and other parts of the world. SMS, simply put, is a technology that allows devices to transmit and receive short text-only content over wireless networks. In the United States, SMS is generally provided over networks based on code division multiple access (CDMA) and time division multiple access (TDMA) standards. In Europe, SMS is carried over GSM (Global System for Mobile Communications), which has included the capability for short messaging from the start.

The beauty of this service is that many types of very useful communication can be provided via short text messages. Often, elaborate tables and images are not helpful when all you want to convey is market closing information, weather advisories, or a message to your spouse about unexpected visitors coming over for dinner. SMS is a reliable service, as the delivery of messages is guaranteed by the system (Figure 3.4). If you

FIGURE 3.4 *A user sends a message via SMS.*

transmit a message via SMS and there is a glitch that prevents the recipient from getting it, the system can compensate by storing the message until delivery can be completed.

SMS fulfills the directive for PCDs to be nomadic; many features that allow for tracking of a user have been built into the system to ensure that message routing is performed successfully. This capability does not extend to mapping the location of a user with pinpoint accuracy, but it provides enough detail for the system to work. Note that SMS's tracking abilities could certainly be seen as a privacy issue, especially if such a device were also paired with a GPS device.

Many types of devices are capable of taking advantage of SMS: PDAs, wireless phones, pagers, and even other types of embedded devices. In theory, SMS could be used by completely autonomous devices for reporting information to human users or to one another. For example, an SMS system tied into a home automation system could send a text message to a user's pager or cell phone if the house temperature went above or below a threshold or if there were a security breach in the home (Figure 3.5).

FIGURE 3.5 *Home automation allows you to remotely control appliances in your house while you are away. © 2001. Reprinted with permission from Home Director. All rights reserved.*

GLOBAL POSITIONING SYSTEM (GPS)

Once reserved only for military use, the GPS, which provides round-the-clock worldwide positioning and navigation information, is now a resource that is available to anyone. The Global Positioning System is composed of a collection of satellites owned by the U.S. government. Development of the $12 billion GPS satellite navigation system was begun in the 1970s by the U.S. Department of Defense. Until recently, only the military could get the full potential of GPS data; civilians were restricted to Selected Availability (SA), a built-in crippling of the GPS designed to protect the whereabouts of top-secret military bases. The U.S. government discontinued SA in 2000.

A constellation of twenty-four NAVSTAR satellites makes up the GPS. The satellites orbit 12,000 miles above the earth and are constantly transmitting the precise time and their position in space. GPS clients are generally handheld receivers used on the earth's surface that receive information transmitted from three to twelve satellites. From this data, the client can determine its precise location, as well as how fast and in what direction it is moving. The time information given by GPS satellites are based on atomic clocks that are accurate to within one second every 70,000 years.

Naturally, positioning data such as that provided by GPS is critical for the functioning of many types of mobile computing devices. Take, for example, a smart PDA that uses GPS data and a database backend to automatically provide the following information to the user, based on their current locale:

- The current time and date
- The currency type(s) and a currency exchange calculator
- A phrase handbook for the dominant language(s) of the area
- Travel information
- Local weather information

None of these features is far-fetched; each can be implemented using only current technology. Clearly, however, GPS is at the core of such a system. A cursory search on the Web will turn up several vendors who sell GPS development kits that you can use for integration into your own systems. One of the world's most popular such vendors is Magellan.

SUN JAVASOLUTIONS

Since Sun originally designed Java as a programming language to be used in embedded devices, it is a natural fit for the job. Recently there has been an explosion of additions to Java in the way of platforms and application programming interfaces (APIs) that focus especially on small embedded computing devices. There are so many that we'll cover them only briefly here; by the time this book is in print there will undoubtedly be others.

J2ME

In recognition of the fact that different applications require different tools—and different sizes—Sun has broken Java into three distinct classes:

- **J2ME:** Java 2, Micro Edition
- **J2SE:** Java 2, Standard Edition
- **J2EE:** Java 2, Enterprise Edition

J2ME is the variant of Java that has been optimized to run in small amounts of memory, such as that found on handheld computing devices. It has support for multiple device profiles, such as set-top box, personal digital assistant, car, and screenphone.

JavaPhone

JavaPhone is essentially an API that provides standard libraries of functions for developers of mobile (primarily cell-phone-based) computing devices (Figure 3.6). The objective of this API is to shorten development time and provide a standard for developers. If you're a Java hacker already, this may be something to pursue. Some fairly big players are on

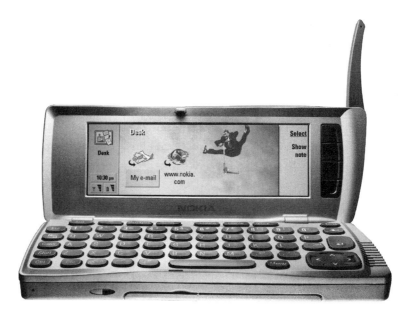

FIGURE 3.6 *JavaPhone technology. © 2001. Reprinted with permission from Nokia. All rights reserved.*

board the JavaPhone wagon, including Ericsson, Nokia, and Motorola. It remains to be seen how big a role JavaPhone will play in the market.

Some of the functionality that JavaPhone provides includes the following:

- Direct telephony control
- Datagram messaging
- Address book and calendar information
- User profile access
- Power monitoring
- Application installation

Jini

Is the genie out of the bottle? If you ask Sun, the answer would probably be yes, at least as far as their Jini technology is concerned. Jini is an

API built on Java that lets programs use services in a network without knowing anything about the wire protocol that the service uses. Jini allows for the dynamic addition and updating of devices in a small area network, as well as communicating the types of services that each device can provide to the others. This means, for example, that a user with a Jini-capable PDA could walk into a room that features Jini-capable printers and print to those printers without ever needing to actively download driver software or remove traces of the printer from the system.

In essence, Jini is the essence of nomadism in computing, since it is completely geared to this sort of ephemeral connectivity. Such an environment would allow for complete adaptation of devices in a network under constantly varying conditions. Jini works by causing a Jini-capable device to begin advertising itself to the network in the form of a Java object, which contains references to all the resources any other Jini device would need to communicate with it. This means that as soon as another device "senses" it, it can begin downloading the needed software. This is transparent to the user.

Java TV

The Java TV API is another extension to the core Java language that enables developers to produce interactive Java-based television content. Essentially, programs written with the Java TV API are able to access and control compatible set-top boxes and television receivers. The API makes it possible for developers to transparently access a variety of information, regardless of the service protocol that is currently in use. For example, a common feature of television service is an electronic program guide; Java TV allows for the access of information in the EPG, regardless of the way it is being delivered. A Java application written with the Java TV API, for example, could build an automated list of all times and dates that a particular show will be televised. Java TV represents a major step towards truly interactive television, since it will help effect a blur between traditional TV-only services and Internet-only services.

Kilobyte Virtual Machine (KVM)

The goal of the Kilobyte Virtual Machine, or KVM, is to bring Java technology to even very, very small embedded devices. It has been designed to run in tiny amounts of memory. Such a virtual machine would be especially useful in devices that might have design requirements of extremely low cost or very tight space (both virtual and real).

Symbian OS

Symbian Ltd. was formed by, and is owned by, wireless giants Nokia, Motorola, Matushita (Panasonic), Ericsson, and Psion. This entity has a mission of setting mobile wireless operating standards in order to enable a mass market for wireless/mobile information devices.[12] Symbian Ltd. offers licenses to other manufacturers to use Symbian OS in their devices, much in the same way that operating system vendors charge a per-device license for each copy of their operating system included on OEM machines. Symbian supports other popular technologies, like WAP, Bluetooth, GPRS, and SyncML. It's worth noting that there are essentially two types of standards that can emerge: dominant-author type and communal type. Symbian is definitely of the former type, and this usually (though not always) implies that the standard will be up-to-date and fairly well accepted. Although it costs money to license the standard, even smaller organizations can benefit from the reduced development time and decrease in interoperability issues that a standard like this offers.

An interesting feature of this operating system is that the authors decided to use a heavily example-based approach to explaining and distributing it. There are two complete "reference designs" that Symbian uses to explain Symbian OS and educate developers. The two reference designs, code-named Quartz and Crystal, are models of completely functional wireless information devices (Figure 3.7 and Figure 3.8). Quartz is a pen-based, tablet-style, pocket-sized device,

---

[12] *The Symbian Platform*, 3.

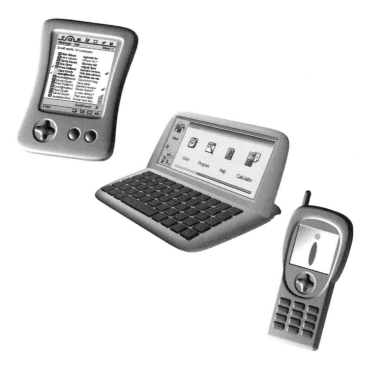

FIGURE 3.7 *Symbian OS reference designs, Quartz and Crystal. © 2001. Reprinted with permission from Symbian (www.symbian.com). All rights reserved.*

while Crystal is a keyboard-driven, Clamshell-like device. Both have at their core the Symbian generic technology that provides universal feature components for any device that supports the platform and which include the following:

- A multitasking kernel
- Data management
- Graphics
- Multimedia
- Security
- A messaging engine
- Browser engines for WAP and Java

- Data synchronization
- Worldwide locale support

Symbian OS has full support for strong encryption and certificate management—both of which are critical for the survival of any wireless device in today's information-rich environment. Furthermore, it supports worldwide locales through the use of Unicode characters by supporting Unicode consortium recommendations for international locales, and it has a text input framework designed to accommodate large character sets (like Chinese).

FIGURE 3.8 *A Symbian OS powered device. © 2001. Reprinted with permission from Symbian (www.symbian.com). All rights reserved.*

EPOC

EPOC (now called Symbian OS) is a C++ based operating system that was originally created and implemented by Psion for use in their line of handheld PDA devices. Symbian OS has a rich set of APIs, which means that programmers using either C++ or java, which Symbian OS supports, do not need to learn an entirely new programming language but merely become familiar with the APIs. One distinct advantage of Symbian OS for mobile computing devices is that it has been designed from the ground up to be event-driven and interactive, instead of procedural.

Since the focus of this book is not software development, we will not go into any further detail about Symbian OS; just be aware that it is the core of the Symbian platform.

OnStar

Although OnStar is really a conglomerate of services rather than a single technology, it has been included here because it is an example of mobile computing that will become increasingly popular in the very near future. The OnStar service, which is provided in many automobiles manufactured by General Motors, is touted as a "personal assistance" technology, since it encapsulates services like emergency roadside help, vehicle tracking, electronic communications, and other safety and convenience features. One arguably strong feature of OnStar is that the control console for all of the myriad services consists of only three buttons. Generally speaking, the user need only push a single button to activate OnStar; this connects the user via an onboard cellular system to a human "adviser" who then assists the user with their inquiry.

Since some forms of electronic information services, like cellular telephones, have been linked to automobile accidents,[13] bringing any new technology to the automobile must be considered with extreme caution. Some people have speculated that the increase in accidents linked to cell phone use stems from its physical constraints (and for this reason, only hands-free cell phone systems are being allowed in

---

[13] See *www.nejm.org/content/1997/0336/0007/0453.asp.*

automobiles in many states). Note, however, that no conclusion can be drawn yet about the real danger of cell phone use while driving; it could be the physical overload of juggling a phone and the steering wheel, the cognitive overload of having a conversation, or a combination of both, as mentioned earlier.

SyncML

SyncML (a contraction of "Synchronization Markup Language") is both an open industry initiative and a technology. The SyncML initiative is sponsored by Ericsson, IBM, Lotus, Matsushita, Motorola, Nokia, Palm Inc., and Starfish Software. The actual SyncML protocol is designed to provide a means of data synchronization standardization, since no current standard of this nature exists. Trying to sync the data on your Palm PDA to your colleague's other-brand PDA would normally be an impossible mission, for example, but SyncML provides the means by which you can accomplish just this.

As you might guess from its name, SyncML is an application of XML. This means that SyncML has a DTD, or document type definition, that describes how SyncML works. If you have any experience working with XML or SGML, you'll find this particular DTD very easy to read and understand. Several other DTDs complement this core DTD; for example, the device information DTD enables the exchange of device-specific information, like available memory, screen resolution, and so on. This protocol will obviously be handy when conveying data between heterogeneous devices.

Bluetooth

Although it sounds like the name of a pirate, or even some sort of exotic tooth decay, Bluetooth is essentially a technology aimed at replacing wires of all sorts, cutting users free from the copper and plenum leashes that keep them chained to a desk or wall. Ericsson was the original creator of Bluetooth; now the Bluetooth Special Interest Group, founded in 1998 and consisting of such promoter companies as Ericsson, 3Com, IBM, Intel, Lucent, Microsoft, Motorola, Nokia, and Toshiba, leads much of the direction of the technology.[14] (In case you're wondering, this new technology that seeks to "unite" devices was actually named after Danish Viking king Harald Blåtand, who united Norway and Denmark in the tenth century. Blåtand's surname translates to "blue tooth." Evidently he was very fond of eating blueberries, which gave his teeth the trademark hue.) The basic premise of Bluetooth is that devices built around this technology can interact with one another when they are near. For example, when you take a laptop to a client's site, you might like to print a document to their printer for their perusal. It's usually a bother, however, to find an Ethernet cable and plug in your laptop. A laptop and printer with Bluetooth inside could autonegotiate wirelessly, and thus save you a lot of time and hassle.

Another example of the capabilities of Bluetooth would be the electronic organizer (like a PDA) that can wirelessly and automatically beam business cards back and forth at a conference. In a similar vein, crates of merchandise could be supplied with a small electronic manifest with a Bluetooth chip and an electronic packing list. A Bluetooth-equipped inventory system could then automatically register the entire enclosed inventory at the time of delivery.

It is currently projected that Bluetooth will make it into mainstream products by 2002. The heart of the technology is a tiny wireless radio chip that will cost virtually nothing—perhaps U.S.$5 or less. The chip will enable communication between almost anything that you could embed the chip in: clothing phones, headsets, toys, remote controls (Figure 3.9).

Physically, Bluetooth operates in the radio frequency 2.4 GHz ISM band. Bluetooth can operate at one of three power levels, each designed for a different range of applications:

---

[14] See *www.bluetooth.com* and *www.bluetooth.org*.

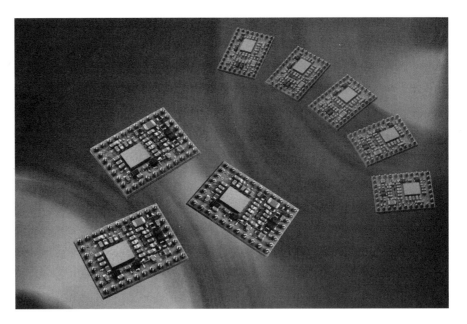

FIGURE 3.9 *Some Bluetooth chipsets. © 2001. Reprinted with permission from Ericsson Microelectronics AB. Photography Studio Photo. All rights reserved.*

- Power Class 1 is designed for long-range (~100 m) devices, with a max output power of 20 dBm.

- Power Class 2 is geared toward ordinary-range (~10 m) devices, with a max output power of 4 dBm.

- Power Class 3 is targeted to short-range (~10 cm) devices, with a max output power of 0 dBm.

In the Bluetooth world, there will be many ad-hoc networks that will come and go as users and their devices move from location to location. These tiny, transient networks are called "piconets," and they are one of the cornerstones of the Bluetooth philosophy. Technically, a piconet is any network consisting of one master Bluetooth device and one or more slave devices. There can be at most seven slave devices on any given piconet, so clearly the emphasis is not on scalability. This paradigm is optimized for small-scale personal networks.

Given the transportability of this technology, it is very likely that two piconets may collide at some point. The solution to this problem is the scatternet, an intersection of two or more piconets. A device that functions as a slave in one piconet can actually serve as either a master or slave device in other piconets at the same time. Although the implementation of this capability is beyond the scope of this book, let it be noted that the basic principle that allows it to work is time division multiplexing.

XML

XML, as previously stated, is a metalanguage that is a hybrid subset of its larger, more complex parent, SGML, and some of the Internet-savvy features of HTML. As in SGML, it is not possible to author documents in XML per se, but you can use the XML guidelines to create a markup language, also known as an application of XML. Since XML is completely concerned with content and provides no means of specifying the appearance or presentation of data, it is an excellent choice for a platform-neutral vehicle for data. XML lends itself to being transformed into other types of markup through the use of XSL.

The XML specification is governed by the World Wide Web Consortium, but input for the specification was given by many organizations and businesses that are members of the consortium. At the time of writing, the XML specification was at revision level 1.0, which has been considered the stable version since February 1998.

THE PROBLEM WITH DISPARATE TECHNOLOGIES

Suffice it to say that with the plethora of new types of devices, each of which has a unique set of idiosyncrasies, limitations, capabilities, and audience, creating Web content is no longer a simple matter of making pages that work in Microsoft Internet Explorer and Netscape Navigator. Until some sort of standardization is reached—either through brute-force market dominance or communal standards consensus—it will be nearly impossible to keep track of every possible combination of hardware/software that a user might potentially use to access your content. Although the situation may seem daunting, it is not hopeless; we will just have to rethink our current delivery architecture so as to accommodate the new myriad modes of content access.

The Universal Translator

Let's say that we are running a Web site. (Not an unlikely scenario, given the fact that you are reading this book.) Let's further assume that we have been given the unenviable task of making sure that our Web site is accessible and usable by people using Palm PDAs, BlackBerries, and Nokia Web-enabled cell phones, because our marketing department's gurus have assured us that 99 percent of our audience will be using one of these three modes of access. After a brief bit of investigation, we find that each device has abilities and limitations that are mostly orthogonal—they have little overlap—so that we will need to treat each device as a special case and present content appropriate for each device.

At first, it seems logical that we should be able to create four distinct versions of our Web site and simply put the appropriate content for each device under a different URL. This notion is quickly quashed, however, when we realize the immense amount of effort it takes to synchronize two sets of content—much less four (one for traditional HTML/ desktop PC/browser, the other three for the three devices). A bit of head scratching later, we realize that this is a job for automation—that the appropriate content should be generated automatically rather than all by hand. We know that there are three places that this can happen: at the Web server itself, at a proxy server, and at the client device.

Since it is unlikely that we'll get the device manufacturers to comply with our design—any such robustness in a PDA would come at the cost of immense software bloat, a feature that is an unaffordable luxury in small devices—we eliminate that possibility up front. The remaining two options both seem logical, but after carefully weighing the options, we find that a proxy server seems to make the most sense.[15] Even this resolution, however, leaves several problems unsolved. Namely, if the proxy server is responsible for understanding the type of requesting device and issuing the right sort of content for that device, the server software needs to understand exactly what sort of limitations and capabilities the device has in order to effect the correct data transformation.

A simple HTTP request header contains information about the browser that's doing the requesting, which can, in turn, reveal the sort of device that is underneath. This involves a lot of guesswork, however, and may not always result in an accurate assessment. A better technique is therefore needed. There are, in fact, at least four different proposals in development that address this exact problem:

- The W3C composite capability preferences profile (CC/PP)
- The WAP user agent profile (UAPROF) standard
- The SyncML device information (DevInf) standard
- The Universal plug and play (UPnP) standard

Each of these four proposals seeks to define a way for a server to understand the limitations of a device that requests a document; each proposal has strengths and weaknesses. Let's take a look at each one in turn.

TheW3C Composite Capability/Preferences Profile (CC/PP)

The World Wide Web Consortium is known for its contributions to the mass of standards for Internet and Web specifications—most notably, the HTML specifications, the XML specification, and many others you may not have heard of. CC/PP is one of its more recent

---

[15] This is arguably the best solution. Depending on an awful lot of variables, it might make more or less sense to go with a proxy-based translator; however, this particular scenario is being presented here for didactic purposes.

submissions and is essentially a sort of metalanguage; however, it does not actually provide a universal vocabulary for describing the capabilities and limitations of devices, but rather supplies a framework for *creating* languages that describe such vocabularies. Sound confusing? Think of it like this: XML isn't a markup language; it's a metalanguage that provides rules for creating markup languages. CC/PP isn't a device specification language; it's a metalanguage that provides rules for creating device specification languages. Unfortunately, what we really need is the actual device specification, and that is outside the scope of the W3C's work. So, for the moment, CC/PP leaves us in the dark—sort of. Read on.

The WAP User Agent Profile (UAPROF) Standard

The WAP user agent profile, a standard being developed by the WAP consortium, is actually an application of CC/PP. UAPROF therefore addresses the problem inherent in CC/PP. The goal of UAPROF is to enable end-to-end delivery of a user agent profile containing capability and preference information about a device, a server, or even a network. This information is usually abbreviated CPI, for capability and preference information. CPI can contain data about, but not limited to, the following:

1. Hardware characteristics
   - Screen size
   - Color capabilities
   - Image capabilities
   - Manufacturer
2. Software characteristics
   - Operating system vendor and version
   - Support for MExE
   - List of audio and video encoders
3. Application/user preferences
   - Browser manufacturer and version

- Markup languages and versions supported
- Scripting languages supported

4. WAP characteristics

   - WML script libraries
   - WAP version
   - WML deck size

5. Network characteristics

   - Bearer characteristics such as latency and reliability

UAPROF is designed in such a way that various nodes along the delivery pathway can add elements to the CPI. For example, network latency information can be "tacked on" to a CPI during transmission, which could help a server make an informed decision about whether to deliver a large-format image or a more economical one. This makes it similar to a degree to multilayered architectures like TCP/IP, where each layer of the network stack can append header information to the original data payload. Thus, UAPROF has the potential to enable an intelligent form of delivery over existing infrastructure.

Unfortunately, this fairly comprehensive standard is only useful if you're using WAP; it's unclear when or if it will be extensible to other types of transmissions. We can, however, certainly use UAPROF as a guideline for imagining a purely open design that would work in a variety of applications and architectures.

The SyncML Device Information (DevInf) Standard

As mentioned earlier in this chapter, SyncML is designed to enable a universal synchronization method between many disparate devices, such as PDAs, laptops, and pagers. Part of the SyncML synchronization process includes a handshake, during which two devices that have never synchronized before exchange capability information. Instead of utilizing CC/PP to facilitate this exchange, the capabilities and preference information, called "device information," is exchanged directly using a proprietary XML. Although SyncML provides some useful tools for synchronizing data between two devices, its domain is essentially limited to exchanging calendar, contact, and other similar information. Device information itself is left out of the picture, meaning that SyncML wouldn't be the best choice for a universal vocabulary, either.

The Universal Plug and Play (UPnP) Standard

This standard, headed up by Microsoft, is more concerned from a document standpoint with interdevice connectivity than it is with interdevice compatibility. Hence, for our purposes, it's also out of the running.

So Now What?

In summary, at the time of this writing, no one has yet authored a CC/PP-compliant language that truly meets the need for a universal capabilities and preferences description language for device independence. In fact, it's not yet provable that such a language can exist, given our constraints. Perhaps you shall be the pioneer who will invent it!

Let's dream for a minute that we have come up with the ideal CC/PP application that has allowed us to create universal CPI profiles that can be exchanged over a variety of network types. Once we have that piece of the puzzle, how do we create a system that can utilize the information contained inside those profiles? XML is probably the best starting block, since it separates informational content from any sort of presentation or formatting; XML makes a lot more sense than HTML, which would possibly be awkward or impossible to directly convert. So, data stored in XML format can be seen as a neutral, non-device-specific language.

In a three-tier approach, our system would consist of an XML server, a proxy server/translation engine, and the client. A typical transaction would look something like this:

1. Client device makes request to URL.
2. Request is intercepted by proxy server.

3. Proxy server unwraps the request, which should contain a unique identification code that identifies the device type and software installed or that exchanges the entire CPI profile as part of the header.

4. A unique session identifier is assigned to the client in the server's reply; this session ID is used in all subsequent transactions during this session. The server maps the ID to the CPI profile stored in memory or in a lookup table stored on disk or on the network.

5. The proxy server issues a request to the XML server for data.

6. The proxy server transforms the XML document using the rule set for that CPI, which could either be stored somewhere (written by the hardware/software vendor) or dynamically generated if the CPI is robust enough.

7. Transformed data is sent to the client in a reply—and is cached in case a device with the same unique identification code subsequently requests the document within a given time-out period. (Data is not cached if a no-cache pragma exists.)

This system is similar to the one described in the *Web Site Usability Handbook*, although that process was not quite operationalized to this degree. Since that time, several companies that claimed to provide this functionality have come and gone. As of this writing, at least one of these companies is still standing: HiddenMind, which merged with AnyDevice in June 2001. This company provides a middleware product that generates output in a proprietary language that is interpreted by a client program residing on the portable device itself. More information is available at *www.hiddenmind.com*.

CHAPTER SUMMARY

Many different technologies are used to deliver wireless content over a variety of physical networks. Each of the many variables introduced by this diversity can have an impact on a system's overall usability. The usability specialist needs to have at least a rudimentary understanding of the underlying technologies and their inherent strengths and weaknesses. A significant improvement in wireless network applications will be the implementation of device-independent content retrieval and delivery systems.

HANDS ON

1. Pick three devices you have in your environment, or that your colleagues or friends or family have, and make an inventory of the technologies that each utilizes.

2. Next, analyze each technology for strengths and weaknesses. Based on what you come up with, would you anticipate the device/system to generally be usable or not? How does this compare to the user's perception of the device(s)?

3. Of the technologies listed in this chapter, how may are open standards, and how many are proprietary technologies? What are the strengths and weaknesses of each type?

4

USABILITY TECHNIQUES

Want to know a secret? If you're a completely impatient sort, this chapter is where the majority of the hands-on techniques of this book reside. While much of the rest of this book provides background and guidelines on the subject of usability, this chapter is all about practical application. As you begin your quest to improve the usability of your pervasive computing systems, you will need a fairly complete array of techniques to help you along the way. Fortunately for usability specialists, even though information appliances are relatively new to the scene, the methods for testing their usability are not. You have at your disposal many time-tested and well-known techniques that will allow you to create a comprehensive plan for usability throughout the design and release cycle of your device/system/content. These techniques come from many sources. Many of them are principles stemming from human factors psychology. Others have been developed as part of the software and GUI testing tradition. Taken together, these techniques will allow you to ensure that your product accomplishes the things you intended, while staying user-friendly.

Some of the usability techniques that you may find handy include the following:

- The field study
- The interview

- The questionnaire
- Prototyping
- Focus groups
- The cognitive walk-through
- The heuristic evaluation
- Usability testing

Out of all of these, we will primarily cover one technique in depth: the heuristic evaluation, which has been adapted here for assessing the usability of information appliances. The methodology for applying these heuristics, as well as in-depth coverage of the other techniques, is outside the scope of this book. Although a working list of heuristics will be presented in this chapter, you will need to have a basic understanding of how to implement them as part of a heuristic inspection. If you are unfamiliar with this process or need a refresher, please refer to Appendix B, General Usability Testing.

This chapter will also briefly address a couple of other techniques that are particularly useful in the context of wireless Web usability testing: the field study and focus group. These two techniques were not covered in much detail in the *Web Site Usability Handbook,* as they had limited utility in the scope of "traditional" PC/browser Web usability. It is a different story, however, in our current arena.

USABILITY HEURISTICS

Now that you've seen an overview of the different sorts of technologies that are available to deliver content to pervasive computing devices, it's time to establish a set of usability heuristics, or "rules of thumb." A set of heuristics are absolutely necessary for developing a comprehensive usability testing plan, since they set overall parameters and design goals for the system you are developing. These heuristics can also be used to perform a sort of budget analysis of the usability of any system, called a "heuristic evaluation" or a "heuristic inspection." A heuristic evaluation is usually performed by several usability specialists at a time. Unlike classical usability testing (which is also a critical part of usability analysis), this method does not require in-depth, real-world task analysis performed by "real" users. According to Jakob Neilsen, who is credited with the invention of heuristic evaluation of Web site content, this method usually turns up about 80 percent of all usability problems with a system—and at a fraction of the cost of true usability testing. In fact, almost any usability problem can be traced to a violation of one or more of the usability heuristics (assuming that the heuristics being used are comprehensive).

In this chapter, we will take a look at the heuristics that apply to wireless, mobile, and pervasive computing devices and will develop an understanding of how they impact the usability of such systems. You will probably notice that some of the heuristics covered here come from Jakob Neilsen's original set of ten usability heuristics,[1] while others are derived from design requirements that are specific to PCDs. Taken together, they will enable us to approximate a comprehensive system for inspecting usability. In the chapters that follow, we'll take a look at several devices that belong to each class of device mentioned in Chapter 1 and will apply these heuristics against them and the content they provide.

Please keep in mind that these heuristics alone are not sufficient to exhaustively test your system's usability. The heuristic evaluation is simply one technique out of an array of many that need to be used to assemble a truly comprehensive test plan. If you are on a tight budget and can only engage in a limited amount of usability testing, however, the heuristic evaluation is what you will want to focus on.

Also provided in this chapter is a usability checklist that draws from the heuristics and from other sources. This checklist can be used in several ways: as a blueprint for thinking about the system before it has been developed, as part of the usability inspections/heuristic evaluations of

---

[1] See *www.useit.com/papers/heuristic/heuristic_list.html.*

usability evaluators, or as a guideline for self-reported user assessment of the system.

The checklist has also been provided in electronic form on the CD-ROM so that you can easily customize it and use it in your own comprehensive usability plan.

BASIC HEURISTICS

The following section covers heuristics that you may already be familiar with from previous usability experience. This set of heuristics comes primarily from Jakob Neilsen's original list of heuristics, although the particular interpretations presented here may or may not reflect Neilsen's own.

These heuristics, which stem from basic human needs, are not just applicable to mobile computing devices but to any system with which a human must interact. If a system violates any one of these principles or is lacking thereof, then the system is probably unusable.

Visibility of System Status

Have you ever clicked on a link in a Web site only to have to wait for what seems like an eternity for something to happen? This is not only a common scenario but is also one of the most common sources of frustration for users of Web browsing technologies. Users need some sort of feedback that lets them know that their command is being processed— that, in fact, "something is happening"—and that they don't need to click again. Many poorly designed shopping interfaces have caused woe to users who've clicked multiple times on the "Process Order" button— just one example of real fiscal damage that can be done by a system that does not provide adequate feedback to the user. The real problem here, however, is the cumulative frustration that this sort of brokenness causes end users.

It's always critical to provide some sort of feedback to your users to ensure them that they aren't just waiting for nothing (Figure 4.1 and 4.2).

FIGURE 4.1 *An example of one way to provide system status information to the user.*

This becomes even more important when designing content for mobile computing devices, given their even greater latency due to the primitive nature of our wireless infrastructure and lack of robustness and bandwidth. One of the PCD-specific heuristics covered next directly addresses this situation and suggests one way of coping with it.

In traditional GUI development, the state of the system can be conveyed in many different ways. Let's take as a first example a typical PC-style Web browser, like Netscape Navigator or Microsoft Internet Explorer. Both of these browsers feature a display area in the lower-left portion of the browser window itself, commonly known as the status area. This area is generally reserved for the browser to display the current status of any current or pending HTTP transactions, such as "image loading," "DNS lookup," or "connection in progress." It is possible, however, to override this message and display a custom message by using a client-side scripting language such as JavaScript or VBScript. Many well-meaning Web designers embraced this feature as soon as it

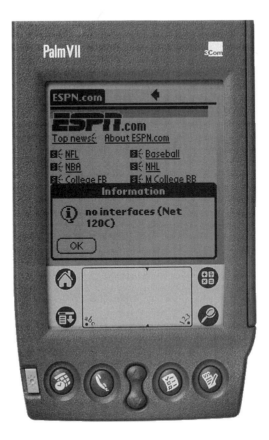

FIGURE 4.2 *In this example, the interface is not letting the user know what's going on, which can cause problems.*

was available and began cooking up their own custom messages. Unfortunately, since many users rely heavily on this area of the screen to keep track of what's happening with their connection, custom error messages, or even worse—custom messages that tend to annoy more than inform—simply impede the use of the browser.

This sort of status area is suitable for displaying nonessential system information; a pop-up window is better suited to the display of critical messages. A console window—a dedicated tiny slice of the screen that would display error and status messages—is another optional message delivery system, although it would not be suitable for many small handheld-class devices.

System status need not only be communicated visually; in fact, a system should have the flexibility to inform the user of system status via multiple means—using alert sounds, for example. This can be the case for many classes of devices. In the case of a device that is primarily speech driven, for example, an audio message could be delivered. If you use this technique, however, you must exercise caution and make sure you do plenty of user testing before you go "live" with the system, as signaling every condition that might produce an error with a spoken message could be overkill.

One final technique worth discussing in this category is the use of constraints. A constraint is a cue of some sort (or, in some cases, the absence of a cue) to the user that a particular feature is unavailable, such as the "graying out" of an item. This simple cue shows the user what they cannot do, thus communicating a form of system status to them. Note that the concept of graying out is not necessarily extensible to audio interaction. The closest equivalent is a spoken menu that simply omits unavailable options.

Use User's Own Language

Using a user's own language has a couple of meanings. First, it means the obvious: use whichever human language the user has proclaimed as a native or primary language. We've all experienced the hassle of having to specify the language we want to conduct our transaction in each time we use our ATM card—a situation that could be avoided if banks went to the minimal trouble of encoding each user's primary language on one of the tracks on the magnetic stripe on the card. Future devices should be able to "know" this sort of thing based on some established standard and be able to communicate that language to other devices in any given micronet. Note that current automatic translation programs leave much to be desired. Since each language has its own idiosyncrasies, it is not possible to programmatically translate efficiently between any two arbitrary languages. The bottom line is that you should use a human translator for your systems or you will end up with some really bizarre (and probably frustrating) translations.

"All Your Base Are Belong to Us"

You may have already heard about the "All your base are belong to us" phenomenon, but it's worth repeating here for those who haven't. In 1989 an English translation of a Japanese game named *Zero Wing* was released by Sega Genesis into parts of Europe. The game, which featured what was quite possibly one of the most mangled translations in the history of the world, eventually gained popularity in the United States—even though it was never officially released here—based on the hilarity of the opening sequence. The exchange featured dialogue between crew members of a starship—the mechanic, the captain, and the operator—and an interstellar madman known by the name of "Cats."

> **In A.D. 2101**
> War was beginning.
> **Captain:** What happen?
> **Mechanic:** Someone set up us the bomb.
> **Operator:** We get signal.
> **Captain:** What!
> **Operator:** Main screen turn on.
> **Captain:** It's you!
> **Cats:** How are you gentlemen!!
> **Cats:** All your base are belong to us.
> **Cats:** You are on the way to destruction.
> **Captain:** What you say!!
> **Cats:** You have no chance to survive make your time.
> **Cats:** Ha ha ha ha.
> **Captain:** Take off every "Zig"!!
> **Captain:** You know what you doing.
> **Captain:** Move "Zig."
> **Captain:** For great justice.

The moral of the story is that when you translate your Web content, skimping on the translation is only an option if you want your content to become the laughingstock of the entire Internet. This obscure video game that no one plays anymore is admittedly getting vast amounts of free press because of its outrageousness, but it is generally not advised to seek PR by opening up yourself and your company to ridicule.

The second meaning of this heuristic is that it is critical to use the terminology that the user is used to, not jargon that makes sense to you. Many systems are essentially unusable because the designer selected "cute," "artistic," "poetic," or just downright jargon-filled nomenclature for the system. It is vital that you develop a user-oriented vocabulary before designing a system so that you know what users are used to calling actions, objects, problems, and so on. By implementing users' own vocabulary, you will save on lots of potential headaches later.

This principle is also extensible to the manner of syntactic interaction between the user and the system. That is to say, the use of "natural language" should make an interface easier to use, since the human does not have to think in terms of the computer. This can make certain areas of interaction, particularly query-and-answer sessions, much more productive.

Leverage Users' Existing Schemata

Say you've just come home from the MegaMassMarket with a brand-new five-disc DVD changer that was on sale for a great price. You open the box, plug the player into your home entertainment center, and ... try to figure out where to load the DVDs. It seems that this particular product won a design award because it artfully hides the changer drawer underneath the system. No problem; you drag the player out of your entertainment center, divine the correct procedure for removing the disc magazine, load it up, put the player back on the shelf, and ... try to get it to play. The designers of the system, who all graduated from a world-renowned design school, have determined that the only way to true illumination is to encapsulate everyday suffering into a set of new, improved icons and controls for DVD players. The icons look nothing like "standard" play/fast forward/stop icons. After an hour of fumbling around with the controls (which are not documented, since the real fun in any interface is exploring the controls, through which true illumination is gained) you manage to guess which button does what. This is not an easy task, since all the control information displayed on the LCD panel (located on the side of the device, to make it more sleek looking) is written in Aramaic. Finally, you get the DVD to play and ... the image is upside down on the screen. Of course! Because standing on your head while watching a movie increases blood flow to the brain, thereby enhancing the viewing experience.

While slightly contrived, this example illustrates the effects of failing to leverage users' existing schemata. The fact of the matter is, there are so many widely used conventions already in place in the world, that there really is no need to reinvent the user interface. Virtually any interface you can imagine will have already been implemented in a standardized fashion. Most operating systems that utilize a GUI, for example, have published standards that document exactly how GUI widgets should look and act. There is no such set of standards for the Web, however, which is a source of trouble.

The fewer new navigation-critical concepts you introduce to the user, the more usable your system will be. By not toying with standards you will also avoid the very real problem of interference, a condition in which the user's past experience becomes a barrier to learning your new system. For example, learning keyboard shortcuts for a new program, while unlearning the shortcuts from a previously used one, can result in many hours of frustration.

User Control and Freedom

Ever have one of those days when everything you do on a computer just seems to go wrong? Like the time you accidentally lost weeks' worth of work by overwriting the folder that had all of your important documents in it? Even though a dialog box popped up to tell you that you were about to overwrite existing data when you dragged an empty folder with the same name as your work folder onto your desktop, you were really tired so you didn't pay attention to the dialog and just clicked "OK." The computer assumed you knew what you were doing and went right ahead and ended up obliterating about twelve weeks' worth of data. Where's the "undo" button for that? There isn't one, unfortunately, and short of working some arcane magic with a data recovery utility (or, if you're really fortunate, you might have a program installed that lets you easily undelete files), you lose. In a case like this, the computer has backed you into a virtual corner. You are no longer in control of the system; it has achieved control over you.

Many surveys show that users with a minimal amount of experience with a given system often feel helpless, "in the dark," and out of control. Poorly constructed error messages, such as those that programmers might use for software debugging, can confuse and frustrate an end user who does not have intimate knowledge of the software source code and can lead to increased anxiety, depression, and general ill-being in the user. In a perfect system, every action should be undoable. The underlying premise is that the human user should always be in control of the system, with the ability to see what's happening and to change important settings fairly easily.

Note that this principle is at odds with another principle of usability: simplify everything as much as possible, but not more than is possible. If you create a true "black box" that exposes no configuration details or glimpse of the system's inner workings, the system should be simple to operate. However, since the world is not perfect, it follows that black boxes may not be, either. Users need to be able to customize things to a certain degree, and they need to always be able to control what happens to them and their work. Striking a perfect balance between the black box and a totally transparent system can be tricky, and the only thing that proves to be useful to this end is testing—trial and error. If you reveal the fact to the user that a deleted file is really still there, but that its entry in the directory has been removed and the file deallocated from the file table, you have revealed some of the cogs inside your mysterious and wonderful machine. This is usually a path to unusability.

Consistency

Probably one of the single most important design principles for usable systems is to be consistent. This can be applied at multiple levels. First, a system should, at the bare minimum, be consistent within itself. That is, navigation constructs should not change across different parts of the system. If the selection of a check box button in one part of the system indicates that a feature is active, this should be the standard throughout the system. All too often, inconsistency is simply the result of careless or uninformed design. In other cases, it is the result of a designer trying to win an award for the most clever and artistic deployment. Keep your system consistent, and your users will have much less relearning to do. This also equates to happier users—and, it follows, less work for you in the long run.

Consistency can also be seen as a wide-scale concept. When Amazon.com established its paradigm for online shopping, many other companies followed. Although you might derive a certain smug satisfaction from offering some fancy navigation system that uses three-dimensional object trees presented in a Java applet, you'll do much better to use a system that other people already know. This principle is echoed in the heuristic "Leverage users' existing schemata."

Error Prevention

Good error messages that make sense to the user are always going to be necessary, since bad things can happen in any minimally complex system. Far better than great error messages, however, is the principle of error prevention. Error prevention is a feature that takes a lot of work and a lot of trial and error. Here's how it works: design a prototype of the system, then allow test users to interact with it until you have a suitably large sample, and catalog the errors that they make. Find out through an informal interview what led users to make their erroneous moves. Take this information back to the drawing board, and implement constraints that make it harder (but not impossible— remember that humans occasionally need to do "illogical" things with a given system, hence the heuristic of user control and freedom) to perform potentially erroneous actions. This may simply involve the holding down of a modifier key or some combination of actions that a user whose brain is on "autopilot" is unlikely to do. (How many times a day do you yourself click "OK" without actually reading what the dialog says?)

Recognition versus Recall

Humans have many sorts of memory. Some are more expensive in terms of using cognitive resources than others. Keeping large groups of facts accessible to the memory—the value of π to 100 places, for example, or the call signs of every radio station in North America— requires a large amount of cognitive power. With regard to wireless content, it can be very taxing on a user to remember that certain form transactions on your site are irreversible, while others are not. Phenomena like forgetting, interference, fatigue, stress, pressure, and distraction can cause humans to forget this sort of information when they need it the most.

Anyone who has ever taken a multiple-choice test knows that it is usually much easier to pick the correct answer out of a handful of incorrect ones than it is to recall the answer from memory. This phenomenon reflects the fact that humans rely on recognizing learned information in their environment as well as storing it in their mind. Dr. Donald Norman, whose *Design of Everyday Things* is probably one of the best works you can read on the topic of recognition versus recall, describes this distinction as "knowledge in the head versus knowledge in the world."

We see this principle in use every day: in street signs, the letters painted on keyboard key caps, iconic instructions for using a gasoline pump to fill our cars, and so on. The secret is to strike a balance between knowledge that is stored in the head (memorized information) and information that is externalized (labels, dialogs, and so on). Too much reliance on memorized information makes a system difficult to learn to use (at least initially; these systems often boast enhanced productivity rates once the system has been committed to memory). Too much reliance on external information, on the other hand, makes the interface cluttered and also hard to use.

Flexibility of Use

Go back and reread the quote at the beginning of Chapter 3. A good tool is often used for purposes that the inventor never dreamed of. A good system should also be flexible enough to be used in novel ways. Many would never have dreamed that they'd use their Palm PDA as a remote control for their home entertainment equipment, for example, but they do. Users are able to program macros to turn the television and receiver on, adjust the volume, set the equalization to the program of their choice, and play a CD—all in one keystroke. When it comes to using systems, moreover, no two people go about getting things done in the exact same way. It's amazing, for example, how many different ways there are to accomplish the same goal in UNIX via the command line— and how each user will religiously defend their way as the "right" way! People form habits in work and in play, and if you fail to take this into account in your design you might be in for trouble.

Since users' levels of experience with systems can vary, this leads to the necessity of having multiple "views" of users. Essentially, users can be broken into four strata, based on their experience and comfort level with a given system:

1. **Novice user:** Has little to no experience using system. Must often consult manual, online help, or the like. Enjoys minimal use of functionality of system.

2. **Intermediate user:** Is familiar with many aspects of system. Consults the manual infrequently. Is able to perform most tasks with ease.

3. **Power user:** Knows the system very well from an end-user perspective. Actively seeks ways to optimize performance by using hidden "accelerator" features. Almost never consults manual.

4. **Expert user:** Not only knows how to use system but also understands its inner workings. Adds to functionality of system through software add-ons, customized tweaks. Pushes envelope of system capability. Participates in mailing lists devoted to system.

Sensible Error Messages

Older operating systems like MS-DOS are infamous for their opaque and mysterious error messages (Figure 4.3). Even the Macintosh, which normally provides helpful error messages, is a culprit in this crime of poor design. If you're a Mac user, you are doubtless familiar with the "bomb" that sometimes pops up on the screen—usually after you've been working for hours on a really important document

FIGURE 4.3 *An example of a bad error message.*

without having saved your changes! The bomb is usually accompanied by a useless error message that describes an error code, such as "error type 10." Well, what is an error type 10? Is this supposed to be part of the user's vocabulary? Indeed, no. This is jargon, and it does not belong in a final product. At the very least, the default should be that the system delivers no jargon-filled error messages, only plain human language ones. The user could then toggle on programmer's diagnostic codes if needed.

All too often, meaningless error messages are the result of the software engineer's failure to remove debugging messages they've embedded in their software projects to help them figure out where a program is failing or where potential bugs might be hiding. Often these error messages contain numerical codes that an engineer can trace to a table, which in turn contains more useful diagnostic information. Leaving this sort of error message in the shipping product, however, is usually a guarantee of unusability.

Ideally, error messages should explain what happened in terms understandable to the user (Figure 4.4). One of the most important heuristics in usability is to use the user's natural language; this is particularly true with regard to error messages. After all, a user is most in need of good usability when a system isn't performing as expected.

Most users don't need to know the precise state of internal system registers, memory allocation problems, and so on. In an event where the problem state is caused by some deep underlying OS bug, the system should provide a mechanism for creating a "core dump" that can be e-mailed to support technicians for further debugging. In this age of interconnectivity, programs can be designed to proactively do just this. If a refrigerator can e-mail a technician with a warning of a failing compressor, surely a wireless Web device should be able to e-mail a memory dump to a technician when things go wrong. Remember that good service is also a part of usability—after all, it's impossible to use a system if it's broken.

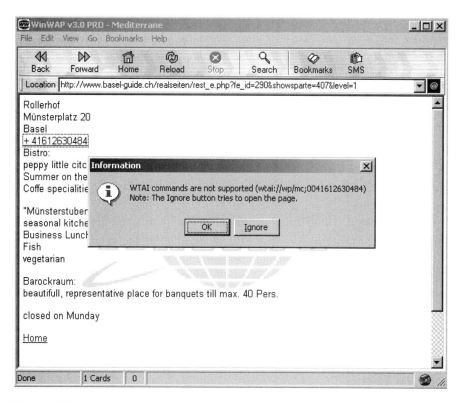

FIGURE 4.4 *An example of a "good" error message.*

Good Documentation and Help

As a usability specialist or designer, you will find that sometimes, despite the best possible engineering and usability work, a system will be too difficult to use without some sort of documentation. This is rarely the case with wireless applications, since most wireless application binaries are too small to become overly complex. This may change in time, of course, so it's important to remember that high-quality documentation can be crucial.

The part of this heuristic that is more immediately applicable to wireless applications is the "help" half. Designers can take advantage of the OS API for online help included with most wireless devices to assist the user in understanding the functions of particular features (Figure 4.5). It is

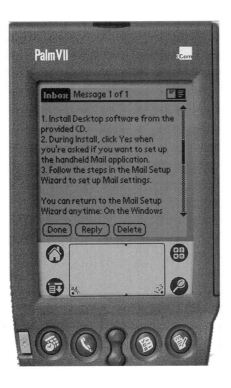

FIGURE 4.5 *An example of built-in OS level help.*

also possible to author your content to include help features such as feature documentation or troubleshooting. Writing good help features and documentation is outside the scope of this book, but it is critical to the success of a system, particularly a complex system.

PCD-SPECIFIC HEURISTICS

In this section we'll cover the heuristics that are specific to mobile devices and other sorts of PCDs. Internet content designers now have to contend with a plethora of new design considerations, including environmental variables such as location, ambient noise, network outages, radiation from devices, and so on. Even if you aren't designing the actual device itself, these heuristics can guide you to a more usable product.

Nomadic Capabilities

This heuristic principle is based on the notion that PCDs should be adaptable to their environment; one example given earlier is that a mobile device should be able to update its own system clock based on its location in the world. Being nomadic also means that any functionality of the device available in one location should, as near as possible, be available elsewhere. This means that a device that uses the GSM service in one place should be able to use CDMA in another (Figure 4.6). This should be transparent to the user so as to provide seamless functionality.

The quality of being nomadic also means that the device should carry with it enough information to be able to participate on micronetworks;

FIGURE 4.6 *This wireless device is nomadic, allowing the user to be nomadic also.*

in other words, the device should use a standard API over a standard wireless protocol to announce itself (or register itself) with any local small area network. This ensures that mobile devices will be able to interact with other local resources such as printers, other mobile computing devices, and integrated environmental components.

There are several technologies that can enable this principle in any mobile computing application. Among them are Bluetooth and Jini, both of which are specifically designed to address the notion of devices being nomadic.

Safety

Does your device/system irradiate your users with unsafe amounts of microwave energy? How many other activities will your user be involved in while using your system—driving, eating breakfast, listening to the radio? One unfortunate trait of many mobile computing users is their tendency to try to speed up all factors of their life by multitasking, even when it is known to be unsafe to do so. This means that you may be in line for litigation if someone wraps their car around a tree because they were struggling with the GPS feature of your new system. There is no way, of course, that you could personally offer advice to all your users on how to safely use your system. Even if you could, there would be no guarantee that the user would listen. Nevertheless, it is your responsibility to produce as safe a device/system as possible.

Ergonomics

This principle goes hand-in-hand with the previous one. Your system has to be ergonomically sound, meaning that it must cause as little strain as possible on the user—and certainly must not cause any type of physical injury from repeated use. Principles of ergonomics have been well studied and can be summed up as follows:

- Avoid making the user maintain a fixed posture/position for prolonged periods of time.

- Avoid making the user exert extreme force for any task; use other sorts of constraints if necessary.

- Avoid making the user engage in highly repetitive tasks (this can lead to repetitive strain injury).

- Take extreme user traits, as well as average ones, into consideration.

- Design for flexibility and adjustability.

- Minimize potential causes of physical and emotional stress as much as possible.

Self-Recovering Capabilities

Lots of things can go wrong in a network of sensitive electronic devices. When you add the wireless factor and the need to maintain state to the equation, you have a formula for bad news. The wireless world is non-deterministic, however, and interruptions of service do happen. It is critical, therefore, that pervasive computing components be robust against such outages and that they be able to recover from even the nastiest, least convenient break in connectivity.

Well-designed databases have featured this sort of robustness for years; in fact, the concept of "rollback and commit" comes from database technology. A similar technology has to evolve for wireless Web-based transactions due to the unreliability of the current infrastructure. Suitable techniques exist that implement ASP (Active Server Pages), and many middle-tier architectures; however, there is a need to integrate the ability to abandon a partial or botched transaction and to resume any interrupted transaction when connectivity resumes.

To be self-recovering also means that the system must never enter a condition in which it is "totally crashed"—no blue screens of death or NFS (Network File System) wedges. As mentioned previously, having to reboot a consumer electronic device in order to make it behave is not acceptable. An information appliance should be able to endure just about any error condition or unexpected input without going to an unstable state. Since each additional line of code in a program has a nonlinear impact on the potential bugginess of its functioning, this means that information appliance code has to be lean and mean.

Pervasiveness

One of the biggest selling points of mobile computing is its mobility. You can take it with you; you're no longer bound by category-5 shackles or power cord tethers to a Promethean work stone. The Palm PDA and the BlackBerry, for example, are very popular devices that took a very simple concept and made it mobile. The fact that technology is getting smaller, coupled with the fact that more and more everyday devices are becoming "wired," makes a logical path for technology to be pervasive: to be everywhere at once. If you're a fan of science fiction, you have probably dreamed of futuristic environments where everything is "alive" electronically. In his book *What Will Be,* Michael Dertouzos imagines a world in which electronic genies will direct him to a snazzy and coordinated outfit as he's getting dressed in the morning. Although Dertouzos's dream has yet to come true, the technology he describes would be pervasive in the sense that autonomous systems embedded in various appliances and common objects could coordinate through a small area network.

The unqualified benefits many see in the new technology's ability to be pervasive should not necessarily be taken at face value, however. Many experts and "futurists" take the position that humanity can be made better—that human suffering can be ended and the need for work become obsolete—by embedding silicon everywhere. Do you believe this? Can a window blind that is controllable via TCP/IP really do anything to reduce the amount of disease in the world?

Ease of Integration

One of the major factors in the longevity of any appliance is the degree to which it can integrate with existing and future technology. This is certainly true of information appliances; in fact, many standards have been established to enable developers to ensure compatibility between their products and those of others. Bluetooth, for example, addresses the problems of small area network intercommunication between devices. SyncML provides us with a means by which to synchronize data like contact information (names, addresses, phone numbers, e-mail addresses) with any other device that understands SyncML. Devices that use the existing GPS infrastructure are guaranteed some degree of compatibility with information that has been designed to work within the GPS framework.

It is clear that the usefulness of any device is contingent at least in part upon its adherence to known standards and its ability to integrate with other devices. You can bet money, however, that there will be organizations/companies that take a starkly different approach to this principle: the dominant-author, incompatible-with-anyone-but-us approach. These vendors use market leverage to call a closed-source, proprietary product "standard." Although this tactic is currently all too common, it remains to be seen how this particular market will play itself out over the coming years.

Simplicity

Less is more. Information appliances are not meant to be Swiss army knives of 1,001 functions; they are supposed to be simple devices with a limited focus and a user-friendly interface. Devices that aspire to be PCs are going to fail unless they are, in fact, PCs. Consider the popularity of the Palm PDA, for example. Although the legions of hard-core Palm enthusiasts/programmers have vastly increased the amount of applications available for the platform, the device does not attempt to replace the PC. Rather, it subsumes some of the functionality of the PC and some of the functionality of other traditional tools. One goal of pervasive computing is to allow the survival of specifically focused devices that can coexist and interchange data with other PCDs via small, personal area networks, or piconets.

In an age where the growth of technology vastly outstrips the ability of human users to adapt to and become capable of using the technology, there is much to be said for good, old-fashioned simplicity. Engineers often try to pack too many features into an interface, either because it makes sense to them or because marketing asked them for too much. Such "creeping featuritis" can undo a good product. A twist on the concept of simplicity is that of adaptive interfaces, also known as "smart" or "intelligent" interfaces. Such an interface "learns" from the user's actions over time. An example that you're probably familiar with is the menuing system found in most current Microsoft products, especially Microsoft Office. Features that have never been used or are infrequently used are hidden from the user. This keeps extraneous line noise out of the field of vision of a novice user. Expert and power users, however, can access the more sophisticated features by manually activating them once, whereupon they are added into the normal menu. This sort of approach utilizes a fairly straightforward algorithm, but it seems to be generally effective overall.

Predictability

Using a handheld device while trying to drive, navigate an airport terminal when you're late for a flight, or carry a child on one hip can be challenging. The actual nature of many information devices makes them difficult to use if a large amount of manual input is necessary. Designing your system to predict what the user might enter can greatly simplify matters for the user. This goal can be accomplished through a variety of techniques of varying levels of sophistication:

- **Very simple techniques:** Using default text in form text input elements, having hyperlinked "canned" GET queries, and providing template information in forms

- **Moderately sophisticated techniques:** Remembering users' previous queries or information they have typed in similar forms before (similar to Microsoft's "autocomplete" feature in Internet Explorer)

- **Very sophisticated techniques:** Using neural nets to predict likely navigation trends based on previous behavior; user profile modeling software that customizes interfaces based on user savvy (à la intelligent user interfaces)

Accessibility

Accessibility, or the ability of a user to use a device/system when they are either in suboptimal using conditions or have a physical disability that might otherwise prohibit them from using a device, is a critical part of usability. Accessibility is important enough that the World Wide Web Consortium (W3C) has dedicated an entire working group to the study and implementation of accessibility techniques to the Web. Take a look at *www.w3.org/WAI/* to get a feel for what they are doing in this area.

USABILITY CHECKLIST

In addition to a standard heuristic evaluation, a usability checklist, which is similar in concept but different in execution from the evaluation, is often employed. The checklist can be used by either a usability specialist as part of a routine inspection or by end users as part of a guided critique. You may derive other points for the checklist that are pertinent to your particular application but that aren't covered here. This is to be expected, and the system is flexible enough to allow integration of new points.

ON THE CD

A copy of the checklist is included as a Microsoft Word document on the CD-ROM. You are permitted to modify the checklist and use it for your own purposes with no restrictions. Each point of the checklist will be reviewed in detail in the remainder of this chapter to assist you in using it.

Audio Output

Quality

❑ The system is equipped with a speaker system that can reliably reproduce the entire spectrum of sound that the system has been programmed to generate.

❑ Sound does not distort when volume is turned up to maximum level.

❏ Sound does not distort at extreme ends of the reproducible spectrum.

❏ Audio outputs are provided to accommodate assistive devices like headphones and/or ear pieces as well as an output to external speakers if applicable.

❏ The audio system is able to faithfully reproduce all critical audio characteristics of human speech.

Level

❏ The system can produce adequate sound pressure levels (SPL) to overcome ambient noise from environmental sources.

❏ The system has an easily accessible volume control.

❏ The system does not have multiple (potentially interacting) volume level controls.

System Feedback

❏ The system provides nondistracting, nonirritating sound effects to indicate noncritical system information like completion of a task, informational message dialogs, etc.

❏ The system provides attention-getting sound effects for critical events (prompting on irrevocable actions).

Audio Input

Speech Input

❏ The system is equipped with a microphone that can reliably pick up all critical components of human speech audio, if system is voice controlled.

❏ The system does not distort speech input due to proximity effect.

❏ The system is equipped with adequate off-axis noise rejection characteristics to help isolate the speaker's voice from ambient noise.

Manual Input

Flexibility

❑ The system can adapt to left- and right-handed modes of utilization.

❑ The system can be equipped with an alternate manual input mechanism for users with limited manual capabilities.

Handwriting Recognition

❑ The system uses a well-known system for handwriting recognition (avoids use of new, special-purpose handwriting input alphabets).

❑ The system is capable of recognizing a wide variety of characters, including those outside of ISO8879 (Latin-1) encoding.

"Virtual" Keyboards

❑ The system avoids using "virtual" keyboards (on-screen), especially those intended to be actuated through touch typing.

❑ If the system uses a virtual keyboard, the keyboard performs with a minimal (optimally zero) number of errors generated by key proximity, incorrect hysteresis, etc.

Buttons and Controls

❑ The system uses buttons and other controls that are clearly labeled and that are easy to use in a variety of environments.

❑ Hardware controls are kept to a minimum without sacrificing clarity or ease of use.

Interactive Widgets

❑ The amount of manual input needed to drive the system is minimal, relying primarily on check boxes, radio buttons, buttons, and other types of GUI widgets, rather than textual input.

❏ Where possible, prompts for user input are predictive and offer pre-prepared answers for users so as to eliminate as much manual interaction as possible.

Display

Use of Color

❏ If system has a color display, the content/operating system does not rely on color cues alone to depict important information.

❏ The system features an option for high-contrast color display for people with visual impairment.

❏ The system does not use an "angry fruit salad" approach to color; color is used sparingly and color schemes have been soundly designed.

Viewing

❏ The screen is readable from as wide an angle as possible.

❏ Screen glare is minimized through polarized coating or other similar process.

❏ The system makes use of the highest resolution display affordable for the project so that on-screen information is easier to read.

Fonts

❏ Easy-to-read sans-serif fonts are used if the resolution of the screen device is low (< 150 pixels per inch).

❏ The system allows the user to increase/decrease the font size.

Ergonomics

❏ Display resolution is adjustable, allowing parts of the screen to be "zoomed" for people with visual impairment.

Safety

EMF

❑ The device does not emit harmful amounts of radiation via electro-magnetic fields.

❑ The device supports peripheral input/output devices that allow the transmitter/receiver element to be removed from the proximity of the user's head and other vital organs.

❑ The device supports decreased signal output based on distance to transponder stations (à la cell phones).

Environmental Conditions

❑ The device was tested in real-world conditions to ensure that its use does not interfere with other critical tasks.

❑ Use of the device is easy in all possible environmental conditions; factors such as backlighting, audio levels, manual input methods have all been tested for ease of use and safety.

Learnability

Training time

❑ The system is quick and easy to learn—if possible, without the need of a manual.

❑ The system leverages existing schemata to effect decreased training time.

Retention

❑ The system is easy to remember, even after a significant amount of time (i.e., greater than two months) of nonuse.

❑ The system provides adequate cues to help a user navigate (recognition versus recall).

Tutorial

❏ Wherever applicable, the system includes a tutorial to help the user learn the system.

Consistency

Look and Feel

❏ The system maintains a consistent look and feel throughout.

❏ The navigation style does not change from area to area.

❏ Consistent icons are used throughout the system.

❏ The system draws from well-known interface standards, rather than reinventing from scratch, to leverage existing user knowledge.

System Behavior

❏ The system responds to user interaction in a consistent fashion; alerts, warnings, informational dialogs and the like are standardized throughout.

❏ If the system is audio/speech oriented, vocal alerts, informational dialogs, and the like are presented in a consistent fashion/voice.

Parsimony

Screen Real Estate

❏ The system makes effective use of the limited amount of screen real estate (if applicable).

❏ Each interface/screen contains only items that are absolutely necessary for task completion.

❏ Extra features are hidden but easily accessible for power users.

❏ Icons are not used unless absolutely needed, and then universal standard icons are used.

Features

❏ The system implements only the features that are truly useful and needed to accomplish tasks (avoids "creeping featuritis").

❏ The system is dedicated to a minimal set of functions instead of taking a multifunctional approach.

Hardware Controls

❏ The system uses a minimal set of hardware buttons, sliders, etc., to accomplish tasks.

❏ The system effectively implements "soft controls" whenever possible.

Feedback/System Response Time

Online versus Offline

❏ The system clearly indicates when it is functioning in an offline fashion (due to signal loss, etc.).

❏ The system is able to function normally in an offline state using cached data.

❏ The system is able to resynchronize in a reliable fashion when connectivity is restored.

Automation/Control

Freedom versus Predictive Behavior

❏ The system provides predictive input in as intelligent a manner as technology will afford.

❏ The system allows for user override of the predictive input feature.

❏ The system allows at least a small amount of customization of predictive behavior (only auto-enters predictive input in form elements named "first_name," etc.).

Standards

❏ The system adheres to widely used standards for all protocols, markup languages, storage media, data representation, and interfaces.

❏ The system uses a minimal amount (preferably none) of proprietary components outlined in previous point.

❏ If system implements a new proprietary component, it is open source or available under Gnu Public License (free) so that others may derive compatible systems.

Bandwidth

Limit Resource Requirements

❏ Content for system requires as little bandwidth as possible.

❏ Bandwidth-hungry features like images, video, and audio are used sparingly.

❏ A mechanism is provided for offline caching of commonly used information (a.k.a. "hoarding").

CARD SORTING REVISITED

The *Web Site Usability Handbook* frequently refers to a technique called "card sorting," which can be used for deriving logical groupings of Web site content items based on what the user believes are strong similarities (as opposed to what the designers and management believe should go together). For example, a usability study conducted in 1998 found that 80 percent of the test participants had failed one particular task because they could not believe that the item they were searching for belonged in the area of the Web site it was located in. The problem was that the designers had been instructed about how to logically group information, but no one had ever asked the users what made sense to them. In a case like this, a card sort was the cure. When a new group of participants was asked to perform a card sort with the troubled content, they came up with a working hierarchy that had a zero percent failure rate with subsequent trials.

The card sort methodology cannot be covered here in detail, however, the following information should prove to be very helpful. Although, until recently, there were no real statistical models for making inferences about the results of a card sort—you pretty much had to just "shoot from the hip" and use your best judgment—a relatively new statistical technique called "cluster analysis" has been found to be well suited for analyzing card sort data. Cluster analysis is used to organize information about variables (in our case, the cards in a card sort) in such a way that relatively homogeneous groups, or "clusters," can be formed. In theory, clusters formed in a card sort or a similar technique should have the following traits:

- Group members should be internally homogenous that is, very similar to one another.

- Group members should be externally heterogeneous, that is, they should not be like members of other clusters.

Those statistical purists out there should know that even though cluster analysis is pretty straightforward and flexible, it is also a fairly new technique and is not supported by a comprehensive body of statistical literature. So, most of the guidelines for using cluster analysis are mere heuristics; true scientists will probably argue that it's best not to use the technique. Yet cluster analysis is certainly better than educated guesswork, and it affords the usability specialist a quantitative vocabulary for expressing similarities in clusters of information items. The bottom line, however, is that data talks; even though the results of a card sort may make it painfully obvious to you that a design needs a certain change, trying to sell a VP on the idea may prove difficult without supporting data. The results of your cluster analysis will probably not withstand the scrutiny of MIT statistics professors, but if they enable you to make your Web content more usable, it really doesn't matter. Whatever works, works.

THE FIELD STUDY

The point of the field study is to observe users interacting with your system in a "natural" environment. You can perform a field study before you ever begin design on your system; for example, to see how a competitor's system holds up under the duress of usability trials. This can be instrumental in shaping your initial design goals for your system and can give you the opportunity to develop a user-centered vocabulary for the types of tasks that your users are likely to perform. You can also perform a field study of your system to get a realistic picture of how your system will work when used by "real" users.

When we're studying the effects of location, motion, and other factors on the usability of wireless and portable computing devices, it's critical to actually see the devices in use in a real-world environment. Unlike the traditional PC/browser environment, in which the number of possible variables is large but manageable, a portable computing device can go virtually anywhere, which exponentially increases the number of potential variables. While software emulators give us a good idea of what to expect while rapidly prototyping our system, it isn't usually sufficient for a production system. Hence, the field study is one of the most important tools you can use.

The exact manner of implementation can vary. Since it is unlikely that you, as a test moderator, will be able to tag along with a user while they go out into the world and use their PDA or cell phone, you will have to rely a bit on self-reported data. Sending your test participants out with devices of the targeted platform, a list of task scenarios, and a self-scoring sheet can be a fairly effective technique and can allow you to conduct a trial with as many people as you can afford devices for.[2]

An alternate approach would be to send out several moderators with small groups of participants who would each be given a different set of

---

[2] Note to vendors: It would only benefit you to make your devices available in a loaner program or as inexpensive rentals to usability firms for precisely this reason. If designers are able to make highly usable content for your platform, that's cost-effective insurance for your company and product.

tasks. If you had three moderators and nine participants, for example, each moderator would take three participants and there would be three sets of tasks, labeled A, B, and C. Each group would have one participant with set A, one with B, and one with C. This would allow you to gather a decent amount of data and would also remove any possibility that participants might copy each other to arrive at the task success goals. It would also help eliminate the potential for participants to feel performance anxiety about other participants finishing the set before they do: you could simply explain to the participants that each set is different and that they were randomly assigned.

There are several things to consider when deciding what to have people do during the field study. First, you should not have participants do anything that could potentially be hazardous to them; in particular, *don't plan a task that involves participants driving a vehicle and using your system.* This may sound ridiculous to you—either because you would never do such a thing in the first place, or because you think it's critical to do so since real people drive and use electronic gizmos. Whatever the case, it cannot be stressed enough that doing so would put yourself, your company, your user, and the lives of bystanders in peril!

Eliminating the scenario of driving still leaves you with many other choices. Do you want to watch users in their "natural" environment? Then you would probably need to do the self-reported variation of this study, in which participants just "act normally" and aggregate data over time: a day, a week, whatever.

Self-Reported Data: The Pitfalls

There is always the very real chance with self-reported data of lowered data confidence. People have a natural tendency to give a positive slant to self-reported data; after all, no one wants to look incompetent or incapable. This potential for slanted responses is a real concern, since it may be impossible to tell if you're getting accurate data. In studies using small numbers of participants it can be particularly hard to ferret out unreliable responses, since there will be few data points for comparison. Some sort of validation should therefore be built into your testing. In research design, the term "validity scale" is used to represent the measurement of how likely it is that the participant is reporting bogus data. A common technique for dealing with this problem is to insert tasks that test the degree to which the participant stretches the truth; for example, tasks for which there is no solution or for which the solution takes a known minimum amount of time. Another common variation is to include a question twice by rewording it and positioning it elsewhere in the test. The starting state and the goal state of the tasks should be the same.

If you want to test the performance of the system under a variety of conditions, you may set up an "obstacle course" for participants that takes them through several locations exhibiting varying levels of ambient noise, signal reflectivity/absorption, and so on. In a case like this you might consider a modified focus group (see below). Either way, you have the option of having a test moderator go along. As mentioned previously, it's almost always best to have a monitor along, since a user may not recognize that certain subtle details are critical. Furthermore, much of what is revealed via the user's nonverbal communication during the trials will be lost forever if a monitor isn't present.

The Focus Group

A focus group is typically a small gathering of people, moderated by one or more usability specialists, who discuss in a lightly guided fashion the pluses and minuses of a given product or service.

A FEW FINAL WORDS ABOUT USABILITY TECHNIQUES

If you're like most people who are reading this book, you are familiar with the term "multitasking"—not in the sense of computers being able to do multiple, parallel tasks, but humans. Most people, for example, engage in other activities while talking on the telephone. With cell phones, this can be next to impossible to do because they can't be cradled between the head and shoulder the way a "real" phone can. If you've ever tried using a headset or an ear piece/microphone combination, you know that it can be more trouble than it's worth. Fortunately, it is possible to buy a cell phone that is larger than the standard size. This is not always the case with other types of devices; for example, devices based on the Palm OS basically come in only one form factor. are also other problems with small devices. In one online discussion thread,[3] visually impaired people complained that cell phones with tiny buttons are almost impossible for them to use. Bigger buttons make devices of all types easier to use for a variety of people—not just the visually impaired. But the paradox is that as devices get smaller and smaller, the buttons also have to shrink. Is it possible that a device can shrink to the point that it loses some of its functionality? In many cases, this is true.

Of course, shrinking a device also means that any associated power supply must also shrink. This results in diminished battery life, which equates to more headaches for the user. At the time of this writing, battery technology is still fairly primitive; there are no ultra-long-life tiny batteries. Running out of battery is a definite barrier to usability. Hence, the incredible shrinking computer isn't always the right thing for all occasions; a balance between utility and aesthetics should be maintained.

Well, what about faster? Faster is always better, right? Of course not. Keep in mind that as the speed of a processor increases, it becomes more and more difficult to keep that system in a state of crashlessness. Faster CPUs are prone to crash, just as a car driven at high speeds is more likely to crash. A crash in the middle of an important wireless transaction can spell disaster. Imagine the doctor who uses a Palm PDA to prescribe a drug for a patient over the wireless network. If the PDA crashes in the middle of the transaction, the dosage information might be mangled and could potential lead to a fatal overdose. This is not a fantasy

---

[3] See *www.afb.org/message_subject.asp?messagetopicid=60.*

scenario; doctors everywhere are beginning to use such devices for this exact purpose.[4]

The point here is not to assume that just because something is smaller, faster, or has more features, that it is necessarily better. It takes a lot more than just throwing silicon at a problem to yield a significantly superior and more usable system.

CHAPTER SUMMARY

The usability specialist can select from many different tools to measure and improve Web content usability. Not all tools are alike, and no one tool can stand alone; tools work best when used in combinations. Among the most powerful techniques for measuring wireless Web usability is the heuristic evaluation. A powerful tool for building usable systems from the ground up is the checklist.

HANDS ON

1. Pick three usability techniques that are not covered in this chapter, and discuss how those techniques would best be used within the context of wireless usability.

2. Perform a heuristic evaluation of a site of your choice on the device of your choice. Be sure to have at least two other colleagues participate as experts. The *Web Site Usability Handbook* also includes more detailed instructions on performing a heuristic evaluation.

3. Set up a card sort using IBM's EZ-Sort application, and try running through the sort yourself. Get a few other colleagues to run through the sort. Use EZ-Sort to perform cluster analysis on your resulting data set. What kind of inferences can you make based on the results?

---

[4] For an example, see *http://wireless.newsfactor.com/perl/story/7278.html*; there are also several links to similar stories.

USABILITY TOOLS

It can be just as daunting to test the usability of the myriad newly available devices that can surf the Web as it is for the users to use them. After all, if you have to ensure usability on seven different devices, you're going to need access to all seven for testing. While this has traditionally been easy for Web developers—entailing just the downloading and installing of all the browsers a user might browse the site with—it's not so easy to test with multiple devices.[1] Unless your organization has a huge budget, it's unlikely that you will be fortunate enough to own each of the newest electronic goodies you'll want to test against. The fact that these devices tend to change slightly over time (just enough to give consumers an incentive to buy more, and enough to give usability specialists fits), makes it even more cost prohibitive to own all this technology. That's why the software-based device emulator can be a critical addition to your arsenal of tools.

EMULATORS ARE YOUR FRIENDS

Most companies that develop PDAs and similar handheld mobile computing devices are kind enough to develop and release (usually for free,

---

[1] It pays to also have an arsenal of old browser installers on hand. Never assume that anyone has the latest and greatest technology, because you may be unpleasantly surprised.

sometimes for a fee) a software emulation program that allows you to mock up content on your PC. This allows for rapid, distributed testing, since everyone on the team will be able to have a copy rather than having to share one device. It also means that when an update is made to the real device, it will be fairly inexpensive (or free) to upgrade your tools to the latest version. You might even want to keep multiple versions of the tool on hand, just so you can check backwards compatibility. In short, if you can't afford to purchase a sample of every device you're writing content for, the next best thing is to acquire an emulator. In most cases, you have no excuse not to have emulators for each platform you're testing.

Caveat Emptor

Although emulators can be extremely useful, there are some profound limitations to using emulators for usability testing, and it's critical that you understand these limitations before you invest time and energy into a comprehensive usability plan. First and foremost, it is impossible to accurately test some of the most important usability variables using emulators for wireless handheld devices. Some of these areas are as follows:

- **Ergonomic considerations:** Since the "device" being tested is a virtual device, not a physical one, you'll miss a lot of important data about how users will physically interact with it, and thus with your content.

- **Bandwidth:** Most wireless devices will use some sort of radio-band frequencies for data communication with a wired gateway somewhere. Many conditions can affect wireless bandwidth, even above and beyond the typical factors that affect wired data communications (like congestion, downed routes, server availability, and so on). Wireless bandwidth can also depend on such variables as weather and atmospheric conditions, signal reflectivity of surrounding buildings and other geographic artifacts, and radio frequency interference from nearby devices and RF sources.

- **Signal availability:** As many variables can affect bandwidth itself, so can they affect whether or not you can even get a signal at all. Furthermore, since wireless connections are rarely seamless, moving from one cell site to another can cause unpredictable hiccups in service. It's probably impossible to say whether your system recovers from such interruptions without the real device. Since some wireless services may only be available in limited areas, this can cause additional problems that are not addressable through emulation. It's always critical to understand the implications that availability can have on your application.

- **Software modeling accuracy:** Depending on the architecture of your system, you may or may not be able to model the behavior of your emulator to perfectly replicate your system. This can lead to unpredictable bugs that might occur only in the emulator or only in the real system.

With all this being said, the fact remains that emulation software is still an excellent tool for the rapid prototyping of content, and for at least one level of usability troubleshooting. It's also often the only way you can simulate your system if you're on a tight budget. Remember, it's better to do some usability trials with an emulator that might not be a perfect reference than to do nothing at all—and thereby allow your paying users to do your "debugging" for you!

Obtaining Emulation Software

Most big-name system vendors have an arsenal of tools available for developers to use in order to craft content and applications for their devices. In some cases, the tools are easily obtainable without the need to sign nondisclosure agreements or pay a fee. Some companies, however, will require that you enter into a contractual agreement, will charge a fee (and usually these fees are not minimal), and will ask for lots of your private information for their own purposes. Common sense would seem to dictate that companies should make emulators freely available to usability specialists; after all, they are the ones who will suffer if no one can use the content on their devices. The companies could still charge a fee for access to the sophisticated tools, software development kits (SDKs), and API references that usability specialists usually don't need but that programmers/developers do. Many companies currently have some sort of emulator available. Although it doesn't make sense to list them all here, since by the time this book goes to press many of the links and models of products may likely have changed, fairly up-to-date information on obtaining emulation software can be obtained at *www.usablesites.com/pcd/tools.html*. A brief description of some of the emulation software available from major companies at the time of writing, and the terms for using it, follows.

Nokia

Summary: Nokia, the Finland-based cellular telephony giant, has an entire Web site dedicated to developers. You can find all sorts of downloads here, ranging from technical white papers to emulators to SDKs (Figure 5.1).

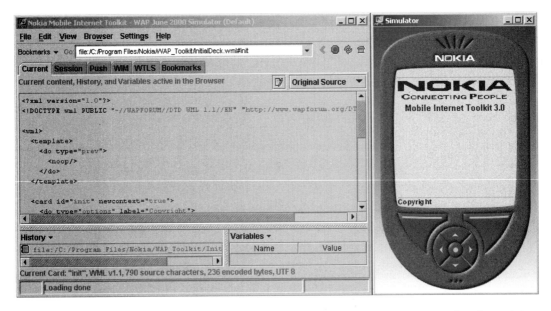

FIGURE 5.1 *The Nokia cell phone emulator lets you preview Web content. © 2001. Reprinted with permission from Nokia. All rights reserved.*

Terms: At the time of this writing, Nokia requires that you become a "registered user," which involves filling out a form that asks for lots of personal data.

WebTV

Summary: This Microsoft subsidiary provides the WebTV emulator free of charge on the developer section of their Web site. The emulator is available for Windows and Mac OS platforms, and seems to work pretty much the same on both.

Details: The WebTV emulator gives you two widgets to use: a remote control that simulates the one that ships with a real WebTV unit and a television-like console that mimics what you'd see on a real WebTV screen. It is worth mentioning that this emulator has been around for a while without having been given any really significant updates.

Terms: It is freely downloadable.

Palm

Summary: These purveyors of best-selling PDAs offer a variety of development tools; getting to them, however, requires jumping over several hurdles, a description of which follows.

Details: Getting this emulator to work takes some effort, since you need to cobble together three pieces. Once it's assembled, however, you get a fairly lifelike Palm on screen. You can customize the emulator to different Palm-compatible devices by changing out the skins and the system ROMs. A description of these components follows:

- **The emulator engine:** This is the core of the emulator and provides the interface between the host operating system and the Palm "virtual" interface.
- **Skins:** A group of additional cosmetic interfaces used to simulate the various styles of Palm-compatible devices. The skins also provide the virtual hardware buttons that differ from one Palm variant to another (including Handspring devices and, potentially, other Palm OS licensees).

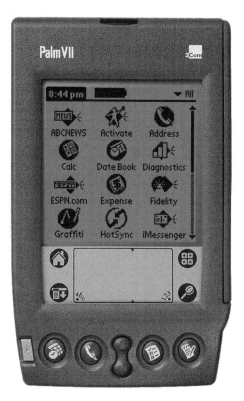

FIGURE 5.2 *The Palm OS emulator. © 2001. Reprinted with permission from TealPoint Software. All rights reserved.*

- **ROM images:** The most important part of the system, this is the file that actually contains the Palm OS in the form of a binary image.

Terms: The emulator engine and the skins are freely downloadable. To get the ROM images, however, you must become a "Palm partner" by applying for membership. Membership application involves supplying some personal information and possibly paying a fee. At the time of writing, fees range from zero to U.S.$20,000 annually. A free membership is also offered, but it only allows access to a fraction of the developer areas; access to other areas requires filing additional membership applications. To finally get at the ROMs, you have to join the Development Resources Seeding Program, which requires you to download a

PDF form and mail a signed copy (no faxes or e-mails are permitted) back to Palm. This process is much more involved than that of other companies, but since Palm is an important platform, you'll probably need to do it (Figure 5.2).

BlackBerry

Research in Motion (RIM) produces several small pager-like devices that work a little like a PIM, a little like a PDA, and a little like a pager. They provide a complete SDK, part of which includes an emulator for whichever device SDK you download.

Terms: You have to apply for a free account; this process is minimally invasive.

GoAmerica's BlackBerry/Go.Web Simulator

GoAmerica is, at the time of writing, one of the largest providers of wireless Web access in the United States, providing connectivity in many major metropolitan areas. One of their applications, Go.Web, allows users of a variety of portable computing devices, like the BlackBerry, to

FIGURE 5.3 *The BlackBerry/Go.Web emulator. © 2001. Reprinted with permission from Research in Motion Limited. All rights reserved.*

access e-mail and Web sites in a wireless fashion. GoAmerica provides a Go.Web emulation application that is encapsulated in a BlackBerry emulator (Figure 5.3).

Terms: It's free to download, although you do need to register in order to access the SDK download page. One caveat: If you're behind a firewall, this emulator may not work for you. Evidently, the emulator needs unrestricted access to and from network ports 2000 through 2256 and uses ephemeral, dynamically allocated ports to communicate with the demo server at GoAmerica's wireless gateway.

This particular emulator has some interesting features: it lets you adjust some real-world factors, such as battery state (strong, weak—even dead!) and wireless signal strength (Figure 5.4). Being able to simulate these

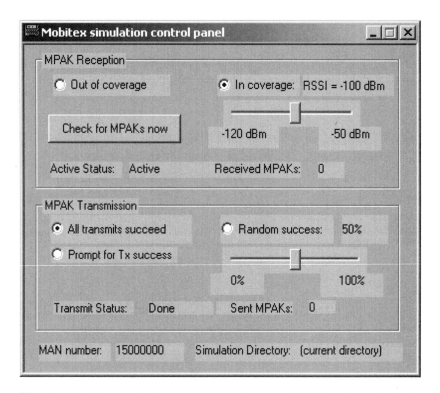

FIGURE 5.4 *Adjusting simulated signal strength on the Go.Web emulator. © 2001. Reprinted with permission from Research in Motion Limited. All rights reserved.*

variables is a huge plus in using any emulator, because otherwise you're not really emulating reality; you're experiencing an artificial situation.

Updates to Emulators

Be sure to look at the Usablesites.com Web site mentioned earlier for updates and more information on emulators from these and other vendors, since new additions come out about as frequently as new devices. Frequently, the emulation software will be modular enough that all you'll need to update are the ROM images of the operating system itself, and most emulators allow you to maintain several ROM images and configurations at a time. This is a boon for testing purposes.

OTHER TYPES OF TOOLS

Emulators are certainly an important part of your usability testing arsenal, but they aren't always enough to give you the full picture. Following is a listing of some other helpful tools, both hardware and software. These aren't all strictly necessary in your testing lab, but having them handy can make your life a lot easier.

Hardware

ELMO DT-100AF Document Camera

This handy little device is not named after the Sesame Street character, but is just as likable nonetheless. The DT-100AF is a tiny camera designed specifically for portable desktop use (Figure 5.5). Normally, this camera is used for capturing video and still images of paper documents, but it actually works great for capturing the display of cell phones, PDAs, and other devices for which you couldn't otherwise get screen shots. The camera is NTSC (the predominant video standard in the United States and a few other countries) compatible; other formats (like PAL, which is used in most other parts of the world) may or may not be supported. The camera is externally controllable via a built-in RS-232 interface and an included wireless remote, and has composite

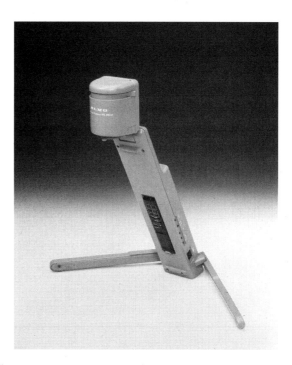

FIGURE 5.5 *The ELMO DT-100AF document camera. Image courtesy of WYNIT.*
© 2001. Reprinted with permission from Elmo-USA. All rights reserved.

RCA output and S-Video (which works well in capturing directly to a laptop equipped with video capture software—perfect for a mobile lab). The device is also autofocus, so there's little hassle in setting it up.

The Elmo DT-100AF can be purchased through WYNIT, Inc. (phone: 315-437-7617). At time of this writing, the approximate retail price of this camera is U.S.$1,650.

Software

ScreenShot Hack (Palm)

ScreenShot Hack (Figure 5.6) is an application for the Palm platform that allows you to get a screen shot of a Palm OS device (http://linke-soft.com/english/screenshothack/). This shareware program, which costs

FIGURE 5.6 *The ScreenShot Hack.*

U.S.$10 to register, is pretty handy if you want to allow test participants
to capture the screen state at various points during field studies. It comes
with a converter utility for Windows98/NT/2000 that allows you to
convert the Palm OS format picture to something more conventional.
Mac users can apply the famous graphic converter software from
LemkeSoft instead.[2]

Sloppy (Java Application)

Sloppy, a Java application, allows you to simulate a slow connection
over your existing LAN. (After all, most designers have their equipment situated on just such a network, and it isn't always feasible or
easy to have an analog POTS line run for the purposes of simulation.)
The way it works is to create a pseudo-proxy server on the Web server
machine, but you connect to it on a port different from the standard
port 80. All input/output through this proxy port is throttled down to
whatever bit rate you set in the configuration file. At the time of this

---

[2] Available at *www.lemkesoft.com/.*

writing, Sloppy is a fairly new development without a lot of support, but it works fine. You can find Sloppy at *www.dallaway.com/sloppy/*.

EZ-Sort (Windows Application)

IBM has come up with a free little utility called EZ-Sort (Figure 5.7) and a companion application called EZ-Calc that do card sorts electronically instead of with paper index cards. EZ-Sort lets you enter in descriptions for sorting card titles, and then allows you to run the application for the test participant, who can then organize the cards as they see fit. EZ-Calc performs some nifty statistical routines to help you derive meaning from what the user did. These utilities are presently freely downloadable from *www3.ibm.com/ibm/easy/eou_ext.nsf/Publish/649*.

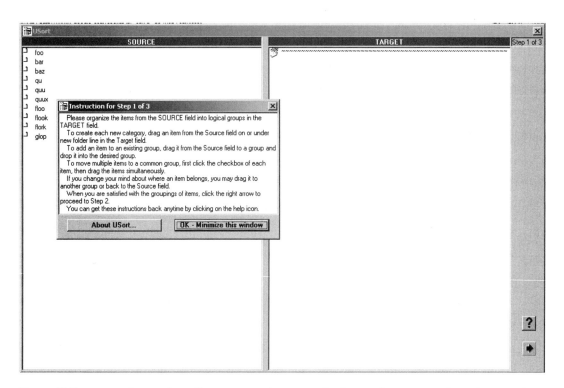

FIGURE 5.7 *EZ-Sort for Windows allows you to make statistical inferences from your card sorts by using cluster analysis. Courtesy of International Business Machines Incorporated.*

CHAPTER SUMMARY

There are several software and hardware tools that can accelerate a usability specialist's "dirty work," such as data analysis and multiple device platform content preview. Many of the tools are free or relatively inexpensive, which reduces the need for a large usability budget.

HANDS ON

1. Sign up for the developer programs on a couple of wireless vendors' Web sites. Order the Software Development Kits (SDKs) for their products.

2. Install the SDKs and especially the emulators. Get the emulators up and running.

3. Preview the content of a site of your choice. Do a simple walkthrough of the site via the emulator, and make notes of any usability barriers you come across.

6

ACCESSIBILITY GUIDELINES

Portable computing devices have the potential to make life easier for all of the human users who will invariably go out and buy them in mass quantities. The newest techniques in production, emerging technologies, and innovation involved in crafting wondrous products like PDAs, cell phones, and other modern tools will enable engineers to assist users in everyday tasks. We are very close, in fact, to achieving the reality of Star Trek–like instruments that could allow people with disabilities like color deficiencies, blindness, and impaired motor function to attain goals that other humans take for granted.

In all likelihood, however, history will instead repeat itself. Manufacturers will not take into account the Americans with Disabilities Act, passed in 1990 in light of the fact that, at that time, an estimated 43 million Americans had some form of disability.[1] Designers will overlook the fact that many studies suggest that about 8 percent of all males and around 1 percent of all females have some form of color deficiency. Marketing executives will ignore the fact that not everyone experiences the same range of physical mobility. And the technologically capable part of

---

[1] See *www.dinf.org/ada/ada_preamble.htm*.

145

the human race will choose not to utilize amazing new technologies in a way that would make everyday life easier for the millions of people with disabilities.

Technology for technology's sake is an empty thing. With the possible exception of experimental technology, only technology that allows humans to be humans has any true value. The goal of this chapter is not only to make you aware of the current methods for assisting persons with disabilities to use computing technology, but to make you aware of how you can increase the accessibility of your own creations. Computers are getting smaller, faster, and cheaper; palm-sized PDAs contain sufficient computational power to run a variety of functions that could serve as full-time augmentative or assistive services. Why not make it your own task to ensure that your creation supports accessibility on all levels?

WHAT IS ACCESSIBILITY?

Although the topic of accessibility was given a fairly comprehensive introductory treatment in the *Web Site Usability Handbook*, the basics will be reviewed here for the benefit of those who are encountering the concept for the first time. Within the context of usability, accessibility is essentially defined as the ease with which content, a device, or a system lends itself to be used by persons with a diverse range of physical conditions. Over the past few years, the World Wide Web Consortium's Web Accessibility Initiative group (WAI)[2] has been instrumental in promoting guidelines and standards of accessibility on the Web. Given the rate at which the number of personal computing devices is growing and the prominent role such devices are taking on in day-to-day activities, it is crucial that these systems also adhere to some common accessibility standards.

It is worth noting that, in many cases, simple "common sense" accessibility techniques can make using a system easier not only for those with

---

[2] See *www.w3.org/WAI/*.

disabilities, but for nondisabled people as well. In fact, there really is no functional difference between designing for people with disabilities and designing for those who are simply using the system under unusual or suboptimal conditions. In many cases, accessibility is not synonymous with physical disability, although the two are commonly linked. The bottom line is that the myth that "accessibility doesn't matter, since so few people have disabilities" should be eradicated.

It is very difficult to find any information at all on the topic of accessibility for handheld electronic devices; it is to be hoped that, before long, this situation changes. There are, however, several guidelines you can heed for making your content more accessible, a variety of which follow.

ASSISTIVE TECHNOLOGIES

One of the most important guidelines for maintaining accessible content is to make sure that you've planned for the integration of assistive technologies into your system. Over the years, many devices have been designed to help people with disabilities like paraplegia, vision impairment, and hearing loss interface with and use computer-based technology. Often a computer can be an open window to the world for someone with disabilities; it can be a means of gainful employment, a mode of communication, and a way of networking with others. Assistive technologies help make this a reality for millions of users worldwide. Assistive technology (AT), simply put, is the collection of interface devices and software tools that make it easier or even possible for users with disabilities to use computing devices and related peripherals. According to the Individuals with Disabilities Education Act (IDEA), AT is ". . . any item, piece of equipment or product system, whether acquired commercially off the shelf, modified, or customized, that is used to increase, maintain, or improve functional capabilities of individuals with disabilities."[3] This clearly is vague enough to include both hardware and software components. In the following section, we'll take a look at some of the most common sorts of assistive technology devices

---

[3] 20 U.S.C. Chapter 33, Section 1401 (25).

in use today. Although few, if any, portable computing devices integrate any of the features found in these AT components, it is hoped that as designers you will benefit from these examples.

A vast array of assistive technology devices may be found at *www. infogrip.com*. They seem to stock pretty much anything from alternative mouse pointers to cheek-activated switches to the Gemini communications system. The Gemini is a unique portable computing device that has been designed specifically for the assistive technology market.

ACCESSIBILITY AND THE LAW

If you maintain a Web site for the United States government, then you need to be aware of the legislation that will impact you significantly. In 1998, the United States congress amended the Rehabilitation Act to require all Federal agencies and organizations to make their electronic information accessible to people with disabilities. The amendment, commonly known as Section 508, is geared primarily towards Web-based electronic documents, and requires that government Web sites adhere to the standards for accessibility that are set forth in the amendment.

The Section 508 guidelines are really just a subset of the World Wide Web Consortium's WAI content authoring guidelines, and some have argued that simply being Section 508 compliant does not ensure complete accessibility of a Web site. Whether you work for the U.S. Government or not, it is a good idea for you to make sure your site is 508 compliant.

Mouse Emulators/Alternatives

Not everyone who needs to use a computer can physically use a mouse. Persons with impaired motor function, paralysis, or the loss of use of one or both hands may not be able to use a standard mouse. In light of this fact, several manufacturers have developed systems that allow mouse-like functionality via an alternative input system. One of the most common systems is the head-mouse style, in which a gyroscopic

FIGURE 6.1 *The HeadMaster from Prentke Romich. By using sipping and puffing actions, the user is able to manipulate the straw-like piece like a mouse. © 2001. Reprinted with permission from Prentke Romich. All rights reserved.*

device mounted on board a head-worn system can be used to track motion and allow input. One of the more common mouse alternatives in use today is the HeadMaster Plus from Prentke Romich.[4] (Figure 6.1) Most devices of this sort support mouse clicking through what is commonly called "sip and puff": the user either sips or puffs through a straw-like sensor to actuate a mouse click, allowing "mousing" to be accomplished without the use of the hands.

Other sorts of mouse alternatives include joystick-style input devices that can be mounted to a wheelchair or other surface to provide stability. This sort of device obviously assumes the use of at least one hand. Most of these devices work just like a gaming joystick. However, there are some hybrid devices, like the Jouse, also from Prentke Romich, which is integrated into a desk-mountable, extendable swivel arm and

---

[4] See *www.prentrom.com.*

features a sip-and-puff actuator on the end. The user can use their mouth or chin to move the arm to guide the onscreen pointer.

Keyboard Emulators/Alternatives

The same groups of people who might find a mouse alternative to be useful may also need an alternative to a standard keyboard. Dr. Stephen Hawking, one of the most brilliant minds to ever be a part of the human race, is a perfect example of a user with a particular need for an alternative to conventional input technology. Dr. Hawking uses a combination of assistive input devices, including a wheelchair-mounted PC that runs software called Equalizer from Words Plus, Inc.[5] This software allows him to assemble lectures and even books with absolutely minimal amounts of physical actuation—he merely has to press a switch to stop the cursor that roams across words on the screen (see description of switches that follows). In this fashion Hawking is able to painstakingly assemble his writings, which are then translated into a speech. Hawking writes papers for print publication using the TEX system, a document markup and formatting language invented by Donald Knuth, which is the de facto standard in academia for scholarly papers. Many, however, find this system difficult to use even with the full use of both hands.

Most modern operating systems include some form of on-screen keyboard that allows complete alphanumeric input with only a single-button input device. Microsoft Windows 2000 Professional has an accessibility menu that allows the user to access an on-screen keyboard, as do other information devices, like the Palm PDA. This sort of feature can make a huge difference for a user that doesn't have use of both hands, or all fingers. An onboard screen, combined with a mousing alternative like a head-worn mouse, can provide nearly 100 percent functionality to users in this context.

Other forms of keyboard alternatives include chord keyboards, which are simple devices but allow fantastic results. A chord keyboard enables

---

[5] See *www.words-plus.com*.

the user to effect complex sequences of typing with simple combinations of keys. A typical chord keyboard has far fewer keys than a standard 101-key device. Using chords can enable people with a variety of physical conditions to churn out text at fairly high rates. For example, the BAT one-hand chord keyboard (Figure 6.2) allows a user to type away with just one hand. The keyboard itself can be further augmented by software that allows the use of macros and other accelerators.

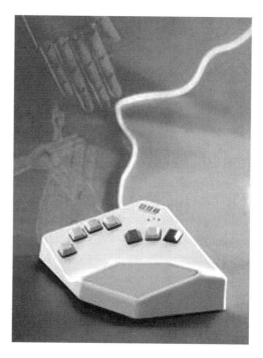

FIGURE 6.2 *The BAT one-hand keyboard. Image courtesy of BAT. © 2001. Reprinted with permission from InfoGrip. All rights reserved.*

Voice Synthesis

The dream of computers that can interact with human beings in the same fashion as a human being isn't new. Speech synthesis—or enabling a computer to "talk" with a human—has been the subject of study since at least the early 1970s, with much groundwork in the area having been done even earlier. The fact that many speech synthesis programs still render speech that sounds like a drunken frog is due to the complexity of the human voice mechanism and the difficulties of rendering these nuances in a digital format. Nevertheless, speech synthesizers that create acceptable-quality output have been available for decades, but not always at an affordable price.

Voice synthesis is a prime example of an assistive technology. People with some form of visual impairment can benefit greatly from devices like the Kurzweil Text Reader, which can take an ordinary printed text and read it out loud using a combination of optical character recognition (OCR) and text-to-speech (TTS) software. By using a speech synthesizer as an auxiliary or a primary output device computers can read aloud text information instead of displaying it on screen. Interactive telephone systems can provide computer-driven, dynamic speech output that can be entirely conjured up at run time instead of relying on prerecorded, "canned" digitized human voice samples. This sort of flexibility vastly increases the usefulness of such systems and, of course, also increases their accessibility.

The speech synthesis product being developed by Bell Labs,[6] which sounds decent, can run on a commodity PC with no special hardware. However, there are currently no plans to transplant the functionality of the software into silicon (which would yield a highly useful add-on for virtually any information device), since the software requires copious amounts of memory in which to run.

Before Digital Equipment Corporation was purchased by Compaq, it used to make a family of devices called DECtalk (Figure 6.3), which were platforms for speech synthesis that included dedicated hardware and software. A lot of assistive technology that is installed in user sites currently relies on DECtalk, and fortunately, it appears that Solectron's subsidiary, Force Computers, has purchased the rights to DECtalk and is continuing to develop it and offer it to the public through OEM resellers. Force Computers has a DECtalk demo site at

---

[6] See *www.bell-labs.com/project/tts/voices.html.*

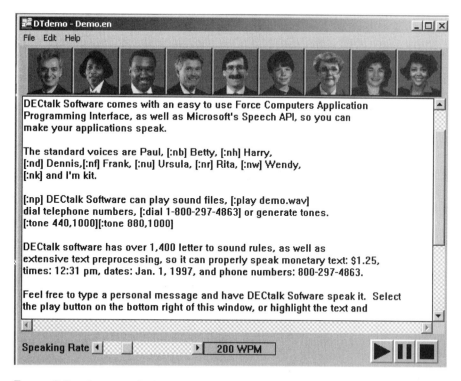

FIGURE 6.3 *The DECtalk demo.*

www.forcecomputers.com, if you'd like to see it in action. If you have ever used a Macintosh, this demo probably won't amaze you, as the speech quality is about the same as the speech that has been built into the Mac OS for ages now.

It's pretty easy to understand how a person who is completely blind could benefit from speech recognition. Many blind individuals have, in fact, been using this sort of technology for decades, although up to now it hasn't ever been really portable. Let's try and imagine a mobile speech-recognition device that does not currently exist but that easily could in the very near future. Our system is simply a next-generation Palm PDA-like device that has hardware expansion capabilities, say, for example, a Visor and an optional snap-in speech synthesis pack that can "mirror" text that would ordinarily be displayed on the screen. Applications that use a special XML-compliant language for tabular data would get the additional benefit of being "read" in a fashion that makes sense to the listener, since the markup language specifies the logical structure of the data in the table (as opposed to the very poor current practices of visual-only tables). Of course, getting data into the device would be another matter entirely, but that will be covered shortly.

Speech Recognition

If you think about the fact that in the twenty-first century, humans still put information into computer systems by taking ideas in their raw form, converting them into structured sentences, and then transforming the sentences into binary sequences of data by mechanically pounding on little plastic keys, it should be readily apparent that there has to be a more elegant—or at least a more efficient—way of going from thought to digital representation. Although we haven't yet figured out how to take raw thought and encapsulate it in a meaningful way, what we can do is eliminate the process of converting speech-thought into kinetic key-pounding form by going straight from speech to digital form. This is the purpose of speech recognition software.

Problems with Speech Recognition

Anyone who has used speech recognition software knows that it's an imperfect technology at best. There are numerous opportunities, for example, for the software to transcribe a similar-sounding word that is spelled differently, thus obscuring the user's intended meaning.

From a purely acoustical standpoint, speech-driven technology can be undependable in real-world environments where there is a lot of ambient noise, so any design that uses this approach must utilize a means to overcome this barrier. It's also important to realize that an off-the-shelf speech recognition device that can deal with any voice with any dialect or accent is purely mythical at this point. Most applications have to be "trained" to become accustomed to an individual user's speech idiosyncrasies.

Privacy and Speech-Driven Technology

The issue of privacy with speech recognition is also worth noting. If you're trying to fill in a sensitive document that asks for age, income amount, social security number, and so on, you probably don't want that information being read aloud and heard by all your neighbors. So it isn't immediately obvious if the cost of loss of privacy is outweighed by the convenience of this alternate input method, particularly for devices that are going to be frequently used in public. Besides the lack of privacy that a speech-driven interface might create, as a designer you also have to keep in mind the privacy of other humans near the user. Speech-driven interfaces that are used in such a way as to not generate noise for bystanders can be very useful and harmless to others. As a designer, you must constantly weigh these factors before committing to a design.

Magnifiers

A magnifier is an on-screen feature that allows the user to greatly magnify text so that it is easier—or possible—to read. Most popular operating systems have this feature integrated and accessible via a control panel or other similar application. Since most portable/wireless computing

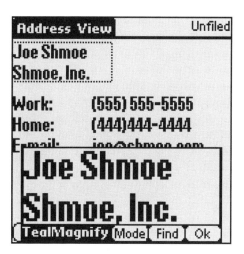

FIGURE 6.4 *TealPoint Software's TealMagnify for the Palm OS. © 2001. Reprinted with permission from TealPoint Software. All rights reserved.*

devices have small displays to begin with, it's often not possible to enlarge text on screen and maintain a usable system state. This is a real problem and the only real solution may be for handheld devices with slightly larger screens to become available.

Most recent versions of Microsoft Windows come with a set of accessories, under the category "accessibility," that includes a screen magnifier. Additionally, TealPoint Software, the creator of the popular TealDoc Palm OS application, has produced TealMagnify (Figure 6.4), which is a Palm OS magnification utility.

One other magnifying option is the use of head-worn systems that can either display a miniature screen on the lenses of glasses or project an image directly onto the retinas. Both techniques have the effect of generating a very large virtual screen. For example, in the case of the i-glasses from I-O Display Systems,[7] the user sees a virtual eighty-inch screen floating eleven feet in front of them. A small device coupled with such display technology could enable a virtual workspace equivalent to or better than a typical CRT-style display (Figure 6.5).

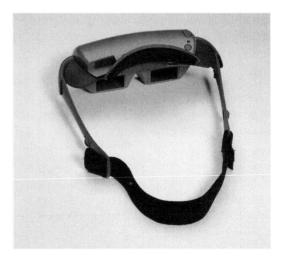

FIGURE 6.5 *The image of the SVGA i-glasses from i-O Display Systems © 2001. Reprinted with permission from I-O Display Systems. All rights reserved.*

---

[7] See *www.i-glasses.com/Store/iglasses_lcx2.php3.*

FIGURE 6.6 *Microvision's direct retinal scanning device. © 2001. Reprinted with permission from Microvision. All rights reseved.*

The display that produces an image directly onto the retina has the additional advantage of allowing the user to still have their "normal" visual field, as the computer-generated imagery is overlaid onto their range of vision. Researchers at the Human Interface Technology Lab at the University of Washington largely pioneered direct retinal image scanning (Figure 6.6). Their work has been launched into a commercial product by the Microvision company.[8]

Switches

Persons with disabilities may not always have a particularly wide range of body motion by which they can activate pointers and other input mechanisms. A person with a large amount of paralysis, for example, may only be able to partially flex one hand or may be able to shift another body

---

[8] See *www.mvis.com/retscandisp.htm.*

part just enough to activate a button. Switches fulfill this role and can be used in sets of several points of operation—or, in some cases, as a single point of operation. A switch, in AT terminology, is usually a large button, often with a cable attachment to a PC but optionally wireless, that is used to activate a mouse click or another programmable task. There are many different types of switches: the most common is button-like, but there are also string switches, which are activated by the user tugging on a string that's attached to the device itself.

Augmentative Communicators

It is not uncommon for people to be unable to communicate verbally for a variety of reasons. An augmentative communicator is essentially a device that affords such a person an alternative way to communicate with others. A common type of such a device is a body-worn tool that has been preprogrammed with "canned" words and phrases that are "spoken" aloud via built-in speakers whenever the user presses a button

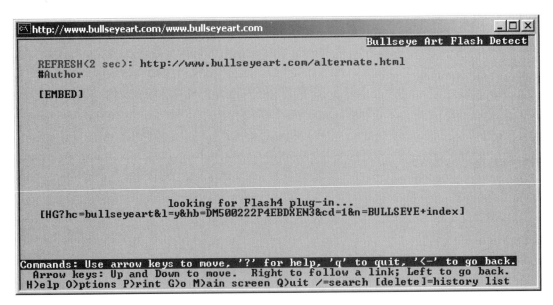

FIGURE 6.7 *Here's a speed bump in the Information Superhighway. If your site uses Flash for anything other than embellishment, it will be totally inaccessible and unusable by handheld users. Note that Macintosh IE users also are left out in the cold. © 2001 Bullseyeart.*

or a switch. Simple phrases and words like "yes," "no," and "help" can be recorded ahead of time and played back when needed. Unfortunately, most of the devices available can only generate a handful of words due to their small amount of memory. Common toys like MP3 players, however, contain sufficient resources and computing power to be utilized as a vastly improved augmentative communication device.

Automated Accessibility Checking

Fortunately, people who are interested in making sure that their Web content is accessible have an array of tools at their disposal. One very popular tool of this sort is Bobby, which is an automatic accessibility checker (Figure 6.7). You can try Bobby out by going to http://www.cast.org/bobby.

You begin by typing in a URL that you want Bobby to check and then selecting submit (Figure 6.8). Bobby will then return a marked-up version of the Web page, complete with information about potential

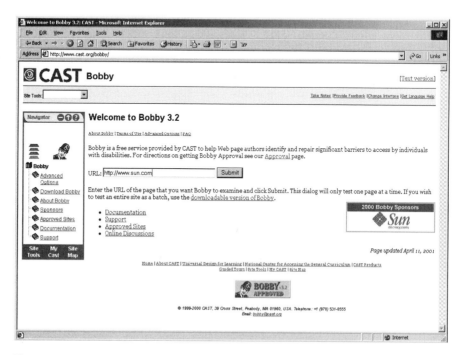

FIGURE 6.8 *The Bobby home page. © 2001 CAST.*

accessibility violations on the page (Figure 6.9). In addition to Bobby, there are other accessibility tools available to developers. Many HTML editing suites come with accessibility features built in, like Macromedia Dreamweaver.

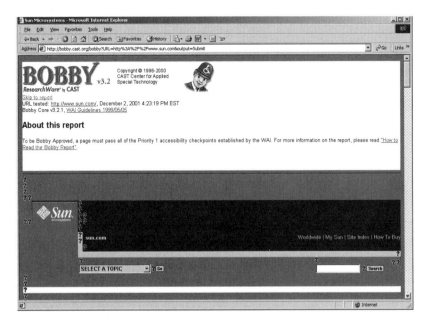

FIGURE 6.9 *The result of submitting the URL www.sun.com to Bobby. Site content © 2001 Sun Microsystems; Bobby annotation © 2001 CAST.*

DESIGN GUIDELINES

If you're the type of person who enjoys checklists, here's a helpful one for you. The Center for Universal Design at North Carolina State University has produced a document entitled "The Principles of Universal Design," which seeks to highlight high-level design principles that enhance accessibility of all things, not just electronic devices. This list has been included here, with permission from North Carolina State University. You should consider building yourself a similar checklist based on the design guidelines found at the W3C's WAI Web site, since that superset of Section 508 contains all the important accessibility guidelines needed for Section 508 Compliance.

THE PRINCIPLES OF UNIVERSAL DESIGN

The design of products and environments to be usable by all people, to the greatest extent possible, without the need for adaptation or specialized design.

The authors, a working group of architects, product designers, engineers and environmental design researchers, collaborated to establish the following Principles of Universal Design to guide a wide range of design disciplines including environments, products, and communications. These seven principles may be applied to evaluate existing designs, guide the design process and educate both designers and consumers about the characteristics of more usable products and environments.

The Principles of Universal Design are presented here, in the following format: name of the principle, intended to be a concise and easily remembered statement of the key concept embodied in the principle; definition of the principle, a brief description of the principle's primary directive for design; and guidelines, a list of the key elements that should be present in a design which adheres to the principle. (Note: all guidelines may not be relevant to all designs.)

Principle One: Equitable Use

The design is useful and marketable to people with diverse abilities.

Guidelines:

1a. Provide the same means of use for all users: identical whenever possible; equivalent when not.

1b. Avoid segregating or stigmatizing any users.

1c. Provisions for privacy, security, and safety should be equally available to all users.

1d. Make the design appealing to all users.

Principle Two: Flexibility in Use

The design accommodates a wide range of individual preferences and abilities.

Guidelines:

2a. Provide choice in methods of use.

2b. Accommodate right- or left-handed access and use.

2c. Facilitate the user's accuracy and precision.

2d. Provide adaptability to the user's pace.

Principle Three: Simple and Intuitive Use

Use of the design is easy to understand, regardless of the user's experience, knowledge, language skills, or current concentration level.

Guidelines:

3a. Eliminate unnecessary complexity.

3b. Be consistent with user expectations and intuition.

3c. Accommodate a wide range of literacy and language skills.

3d. Arrange information consistent with its importance.

3e. Provide effective prompting and feedback during and after task completion.

Principle Four: Perceptible Information

The design communicates necessary information effectively to the user, regardless of ambient conditions or the user's sensory abilities.

Guidelines:

4a. Use different modes (pictorial, verbal, tactile) for redundant presentation of essential information.

4b. Provide adequate contrast between essential information and its surroundings.

4c. Maximize "legibility" of essential information.

4d. Differentiate elements in ways that can be described (i.e., make it easy to give instructions or directions).

4e. Provide compatibility with a variety of techniques or devices used by people with sensory limitations.

Principle Five: Tolerance for Error

The design minimizes hazards and the adverse consequences of accidental or unintended actions.

Guidelines:

5a. Arrange elements to minimize hazards and errors: most used elements, most accessible; hazardous elements eliminated, isolated, or shielded.

5b. Provide warnings of hazards and errors.

5c. Provide fail safe features.

5d. Discourage unconscious action in tasks that require vigilance.

Principle Six: Low Physical Effort

The design can be used efficiently and comfortably and with a minimum of fatigue.

Guidelines:

6a. Allow user to maintain a neutral body position.

6b. Use reasonable operating forces.

6c. Minimize repetitive actions.

6d. Minimize sustained physical effort.

Principle Seven: Size and Space for Approach and Use

Appropriate size and space is provided for approach, reach, manipulation, and use regardless of user's body size, posture, or mobility.

Guidelines:

7a. Provide a clear line of sight to important elements for any seated or standing user.

7b. Make reach to all components comfortable for any seated or standing user.

7c. Accommodate variations in hand and grip size.

7d. Provide adequate space for the use of assistive devices or personal assistance.

Please note that the Principles of Universal Design address only universally usable design, while the practice of design involves more than consideration for usability. Designers must also incorporate other considerations such as economic, engineering, cultural, gender, and environmental concerns in their design processes. These Principles offer designers guidance to better integrate features that meet the needs of as many users as possible.

CHAPTER SUMMARY

Accessibility is the degree to which the content of a system can be observed and comprehended by users that might be in any of a variety of contexts. As the average age of the world's population increases, it is predicted that the percentage of people with some form of disability will increase. It is a myth that accessibility only benefits users with disabilities; it benefits all users of a system. The principles of usability are straightforward and do not require any special tools to implement.

HANDS ON

1. Perform an accessibility audit of a Web site. Simply take the guidelines listed in this chapter and measure how closely, on a scale from one to five, the site's content follows each guideline.

2. Become familiar with accessibility tools like Bobby (http://www.cast.org/bobby/); run the tools against content of your choice. Make notes of the things that the tools report as accessibility barriers. Which of the guidelines do each of the barriers violate?

3. Become involved with the W3C's WAI groups by following the instructions at http://www.w3.org/WAI/participation.html#pa.

CELL-PHONE-CLASS DEVICES

Each of the remaining chapters of this book will focus on a specific class of device so that we can explore their particular strengths, weaknesses, and applicable usability techniques using the three-layer approach developed in Chapter 2 (the physical layer, the logical layer, and the cognitive layer). You may notice that the physical layer frequently corresponds to accessibility, while the upper two layers roughly correspond to usability. This is not always the case but is a good rule of thumb. In some instances an attempt has been made to separate accessibility concepts from usability concepts, while in others it has not and equal weight has been given to both.

ADVANCES IN TELEPHONY

When inventor Alexander Graham Bell filed an application for Patent No. 174,465 on February 14, 1876, he probably had no idea that the invention of telephony would fundamentally change the world to the degree that it has. In fact, it's now difficult to imagine any society without a telephone somewhere. The telephone network was the first truly massive public electronic communication network in many countries, and to this day is one of the most pervasive. As the human race entered the digital age, the phone network expanded to allow for digital communications—both voice and data—over the public-switched infrastructure. Today millions upon millions of conversations consisting of both human voices and digital bits flow over the telephone network. And indeed the network itself, as well as the devices attached to it, continue to evolve.

The first attempts at a telephone were naturally very crude by today's standards. To call another person over the telephone network required human intervention in the middle: someone needed to "patch" a connection from the calling party through to the phone line of the person being called. Thus was born the role of the operator. Operators were experts at connecting calls across baffling panels of plugs and patch cables. (They were also adept at eavesdropping on conversations, much to the chagrin of many telephone subscribers!)[1] "Man-in-the-middle" compromises of security were not uncommon during the era of patches and plugboards; they are, in fact, still common today over both the wired and wireless networks.

One major disadvantage of the telephone network is that it requires the running of vast amounts of cable from point to point in order to create the myriad paths needed by data and voice switching equipment to route information traffic. Laying, marinating, and repairing cable is extremely expensive and requires a large percentage of the telephone companies' time and human resources. Such cables, moreover, are also prone to damage—such as when another utility company inadvertently hacks through a major fiber bundle, thereby cutting off communications to thousands or millions of subscribers (not to mention the times that the telephone company itself mistakenly disconnects one paying sub-

---

[1] It's worth noting that the need for security and privacy measures over public communication channels is not new, nor were telephone operators the first people to ever want to intercept transmitted messages. For a fascinating study of the history of codes, code breaking, and the struggle to hide the meaning of information, read Simon Singh's *The Code Book*.

scriber's DSL line to hook up another subscriber's line). All this cabling extends right down to the subscriber's handheld transceiver, which means that the user is inherently tethered to the communications device, thereby limiting the utility of the phone. In today's techno-nomadic culture, this situation is hardly acceptable.

In 1973 Dr. Martin Cooper, who at the time was employed by Motorola, filed a patent entitled "Radio Telephone System," which arguably represented the first documented description of a personal communication system employing a base station and a portable transceiver. Cooper used his prototypical system, which received a patent in 1975, to call up his competitors at Bell Labs, thus very clearly demonstrating that Motorola had "beaten" Bell in the cellular race (Figure 7.1). Dr. Cooper is usually regarded as the "grandfather of cellular telephony."[2]

FIGURE 7.1 *Dr. Martin Cooper with his prototype cell phone. © 2001. Reprinted with permission from Arraycomm. All rights reserved.*

---

[2] See *www.privateline.com/PCS/history8.htm.*

Since the time Dr. Cooper received his patent, the wireless network has steadily grown. At the present time, cellular telephony is ubiquitous, at least in those areas of the world that are considered "developed." The wireless network offers some significant advantages over the wired network. First, cumbersome cables are not needed, except to carry signals from base stations to nearby switching equipment. Second, the wireless network affords the user the freedom to move from place to place, even while a voice call or data session is in progress. Third, the cost of maintaining such a system is lower than that of a traditional system since several cost centers for the telephone company simply do not exist. Moreover, the raw cost of copper and/or fiber-optic cables is virtually excised, and the cost of repairing downed lines also vanishes. There are other benefits as well, but these are three major ones.

The wireless network has its share of problems, however. Anyone who has ever used a cell phone knows that the clarity of the signal is generally mediocre at best, poor to unusable at worst. Sufficient signal to complete or receive a call is often not present in all areas. Roaming fees accrued from traveling outside the "home region" can cause cell phone bills to skyrocket. Nevertheless, the cell phone is an immensely popular tool, and it is likely that the cellular network—or its replacement(s)—will continue to improve, eventually replacing the wired network as the de facto standard.

Recently, many cell phone manufacturers and cell phone service providers have collaborated to create a new class of services for cell phones, most of which revolve around what were traditionally PC-only Internet services, like e-mail and Web access. The combination of a portable information transceiver and access to the Internet results in a powerful system—at least in theory. In reality, most attempts to consolidate these two have resulted in imperfect solutions that frustrate rather than help end users. Our job as information usability specialists is to ensure that our content and systems are robust enough to not cause artificial problems for our end users, while solving the real problems that they bought the system to solve in the first place.

THE PHYSICAL LAYER

The form factor of the cell phone is a result of some tried-and-true human factors research as well as increasingly more fashion design. The cell phones popular in the U.S. and the U.K. are modeled after something James Bond might be seen carrying. Marketing campaigns portray cell phones as a highly personal device, to the extent that many phones can be augmented with custom faceplates to match the user's personality or sleek brushed-metal cases (Figure 7.2). Other phones have sophisticated-looking mechanisms for the mouthpiece, antenna, and LCD. In many of these phones, function has, to some extent, been sacrificed to form. This can be a severe problem, as we'll see as we begin analyzing the common cell phone from a physical standpoint. The limitations of this platform must be factored in when we consider our content, since we can actually do a good bit to improve the user's experience through clever use of the "resources at hand," so to speak.

FIGURE 7.2 *Cell phones are as much a fashion statement as they are a functional tool.*
© 2001. *Reprinted with permission from Nokia. All rights reserved.*

Buttons

One of the most common complaints about cell phones is that the buttons are too small—a result of overminimizing the device's size. Naturally, everything, including the buttons, has to shrink when the overall device shrinks. There are a number of user groups that suffer as a result of this aesthetic key-compression. People with any range of visual impairment have trouble using devices with miniscule buttons simply because it is difficult to read the labels on the buttons. The complaint has been made that the buttons often seem to have been designed by young, fully sighted designers who don't understand that others who may not share their physical resources are still interested in and need to use current technology. A discussion thread on the American Foundation for the Blind's Web site, *www.afb.org,* includes several messages from blind cell phone users who consider cell phone button size to be a major criterion in the decision about what type of phone to buy.

A simple but effective feature is to include a raised bump on the "5" key on the phone to give a tactile cue to the visually impaired about the location of the keys. Another technique that is usually suggested is a crude form of speech recognition, "voice dialing." Although the user can't have a full-on conversation with a cell phone, it is at least possible to dial in a hands-free manner. Voice dialing is an accessibility feature that not only benefits people with disabilities, but also benefits everyone else. Since dialing while driving is a potentially lethal mix, voice dialing makes it a little safer to use a cell phone in the car.[3]

The shape, feel, and response of cell phone buttons can be just as important as their size. Buttons that have a slight cup-shape are more conducive to alternate methods of actuation, such as with a mouth stick (a device used by persons with no use of their hands and/or arms). The keypad hysteresis (the degree to which it resists entering data until a threshold amount of pressure is reached) is also a determining factor

---

[3] But note that it can be argued that the act of having a conversation on the phone is just as dangerous, if not more so, than dialing the phone.

in how people with limited reach and strength interact with the device. If the sensitivity of the keys is too high, then users with limited motor control may spend lots of time having to correct mistakes. If it is set too low, some users may not be able to actuate them at all. Finally, backlighting the buttons can make them easier to use in low-light situations by people with and without vision impairment.

An obstacle to designers is the fact that, in order to enter text information via a standard cell phone numeric keypad, a user must often press a button several times to actuate the desired letter. In order to enter the letter "c," for example, the user must punch the "2" key three times to cycle through the letters to get to "c." This can mean that a ten-character URL can quickly expand into twenty-five keystrokes—which is, of course, very inefficient. Moreover, this does not account for URLs that might have special characters or mixed-case characters embedded. All of this amounts to cell phones being quite cumbersome for users to navigate in a traditional sense.

A number of approaches have been developed to overcome this obstacle, each of which is slightly different. We'll look at several of these later in the chapter.

The Telecommunications Act of 1996

One event that has the potential for seriously impacting design considerations is the Telecommunications Act of 1996. This act, which is an addendum and update to the Communications Act of 1934, outlines several requirements that cell phones must meet in order to be fully accessible to users with varied abilities. One organization, the Trace Center at the University of Wisconsin-Madison,[4] has drafted a plan for a cell phone that meets all of the criteria set forth by the act. An interesting twist is that the Trace Center has included with their cell phone design a guide that outlines how each of the phone's accessibility features can actually benefit everyone, not just people with disabilities.

---

[4] See *www.trace.wisc.edu/about/*.

This is an attitude that many of us in usability/accessibility must assume, since corporate types often don't "get" accessibility, just as they often don't "get" usability. Frequently, decision makers will verbally support the concept of accessibility, but, when it comes right down to it, will avoid allocating funds or resources to the effort. No CEO, of course, wants to communicate that blind people don't matter, but, in reality, actions often speak louder than words. Showing such people that the bottom line also benefits from the inclusion of accessibility features makes it easier to convince them of accessibility's importance.

One of the features that this prototypical phone (Figure 7.3) includes is an "EZ button" that allows a user to hear the label for any other button on the phone. Such a useful feature could be integrated at a nominal

FIGURE 7.3 *The Trace Center's prototypical telephone. © 1999. Reprinted from http//.trace.wisc.edu/docs/phones/, with permission of the Trace R&D Center, University of Wisconsin-Madison. All rights reserved.*

cost that would factor out over time. This concept could also be taken beyond this first step so that such devices could be made to substitute speech for all customarily visual-only feedback. This would enable a visually impaired cell phone user who cannot see the phone's display to know the strength of their signal, for example. The point is that a well-designed system should allow for multiple forms of feedback to ensure universal accessibility.

The Telecommunications Act of 1996 is one piece of legislation that will hopefully impact the industry at large in a positive fashion. In the Trace Center documentation for the prototypical phone device, there is a very handy chart[5] that shows how the telephone design meets all the accessibility criteria outlined in the act. The chart is a great reference for not just cell phones, but all handheld devices in general.

Data Input

Most cell phones have been designed with only the standard twelve buttons (the numerals 0–9, plus "*" and "#") and possibly a few other buttons for operational details (like an "end" button or a "call" button). When the user of a cell phone is only entering numeric data—like telephone numbers—the small selection of buttons is generally not a problem, especially given the fact that a number button always maps to exactly one and only one number. This sort of "numeric-only" interaction with a phone, then, isn't all that bad if your eyes are good enough to see the tiny buttons, and if your dexterity and motor control are sufficient to allow you to press them in an error-free fashion.

When the cell phone with standard keys adopts the responsibility of a Web browser, an e-mail agent, and a two-way pager, however, the role of the numeric keys becomes overloaded. Since letters and special characters need to be accessed in these scenarios, the user is often put in the position of having to hit a key multiple times to effect the production of

---

[5] Various versions of the chart can be found at *www.trace.wisc.edu/docs/phones/*.

a single alpha character. There are, however, easier ways of accomplishing the goal of text entry on a cell phone device:

- An alpha-style keyboard might be built into the phone.

- An external attachable keyboard might be provided.

- An on-screen "soft" keyboard, like that on a Palm PDA, might replace the cell phone's traditional keypad.

- An "alphawheel," which would allow the user to scroll rapidly through the alphabet, might be added to the phone.

- The phone might be programmed for predictive input: the software could "guess" what the user is about to type and then type it for them if they approve.

Some of these techniques have already been implemented in various products. For example, the Nokia 8000 series telephones frequently feature predictive text input, which can significantly speed up things. Several types of phones that have come and gone over the past few years have featured built-in keyboards—although these were generally not acceptable in form, since they either took up too much space, rendering the phone too bulky, or were in an awkward location. In general, building a keyboard into a cell phone is probably not a good approach. The detachable keyboard could be a good thing; the same innovation exists for PDAs, and the users of such keyboards are usually quite happy with them. Such an approach would tend to indicate a very high amount of usage of the phone in Web browser mode or e-mail mode.

An alternative type of data entry for cell phones is the "T9" method, which uses a sort of predictive text entry based on a customizable dictionary on board the phone or an external card. T9 is a system that was originally created by Tegic Communications, which was purchased by America Online in December of 1999. Prior to that time, T9 technology had been under development for twelve years as an augmentative communication system to aid people with disabilities. The way T9 essentially works is that you have to triple tap the first character of a word, but subsequent characters are predicted according to the most likely match in a dictionary based on the next key you press. So, for example, if you began by typing the letter "h," then hit the "6" key, instead of cycling through "m" and "n," the phone would go directly to "o," saving you a couple of clicks. However, this feature can be a bug under certain circumstances, such as when the user needs to spell a non-standard word.

The Fastap keypad from Digit Wireless is a recent innovation that addresses the clumsiness of entering alphanumeric data on a standard cell phone keypad by providing all the alpha keys in the same space as a standard numeric keypad—without making each button absolutely microscopic. The Fastap uses the space between the numeric keys for placement of the remaining alpha keys. The time savings offered by this design is substantial. Typing the phrase "Be home by 9!," for example, only takes a total of fourteen keystrokes on the Fastap compared to the twenty-seven required by the triple-tap technique.

The Fastap has also been designed according to the Universal Design Principles for Accessibility created by North Carolina State University's Center for Universal Design, which were included in the previous chapter. Although the device itself is tiny—it is the same size as the smallest Nokia phones we can get in the United States—it features strong tactile feedback for users with visual impairment. Moreover, the sheer fact that each key maps to a single character makes it possible to keep track of which letter is currently being entered. Finally, the alpha characters are laid out sequentially instead of in QWERTY fashion, which means that you can find any letter on the keypad simply by feeling along to the desired key. An added touch that might make this design even better would be an audible indicator of which letter has just been pushed.

The inventor of Fastap, Dr. David Levy, was, from 1987 to 1992, the chief ergonomics specialist at Apple Computer, where he headed up the ergonomics efforts for the original PowerBook series. Dr. Levy's vision for the Fastap came out of a clash of two graphs. As he put it, "On one hand, technological devices keep getting smaller and smaller. But device complexity keeps getting greater and greater. If you were to graph these two factors, you could predict that they would eventually meet." At the time of writing, several major cell phone manufacturers were planning to use the Fastap keypad in future cell phone designs. You can see more info about the Fastap at *www.digitwireless.com.*

Kyocera has blended the Palm PDA form factor with a cell phone in one unit. This means that the sort of "soft" keyboard found on a Palm PDA is also available on the phone, which could be quite useful. It's probably possible to create a cell phone with a small touch screen capable of similar input, even without all the other Palm-like capabilities.

Display

Many Web designers don't like it when they have to make sure that all their content fits into 216 Web-safe colors at a resolution of 640 x 480 pixels (or less, really, to account for usable screen real estate). Designers who must fit content into the tiny displays of most cell phones would be grateful for such abundant parameters! In the cell phone display world, everything is tiny, in a single color—black—and often with no graphics at all. Using a Web-enabled cell phone is currently a bit like taking a ride back in time to the days of text terminals. After all, such a phone is really just a glorified terminal of sorts. Although this is changing, it may be a while before sufficient bandwidth, display technology, and other factors come together to make a high-resolution, color cell phone display possible. One huge stumbling block for designers/developers is that they believe that Web-enabled cell phones should simply display a "miniature version" of the Web. This is a fatal mistake; as this book keeps stressing, *the wireless Web is not a miniature version of the Web.* Later in this chapter, we'll talk a lot about the differences in content expected by users of portable computing devices versus the traditional PC/browser combination. For now, suffice it to say that cell phone displays are, at best, tiny and generally ill-suited to displaying graphics due to their low resolution and small amount of available display memory.

While various wireless protocols allow for the inclusion of images, this feature is spotty at best. Limited bandwidth and minimal display capability severely limit what can be shown on the display. Therefore, designing with a text-only mindset is currently an adaptive trait for wireless content developers. One phone offered by cellular giant Nokia, the Nokia 7190 (Figure 7.4), offers a display that is a whopping 65 rows of 96 pixels large. This cell phone has been designed from the ground up to be WAP capable and is therefore geared towards displaying wireless Web content. Not all phones boast such a display, however, and even this display's size is a far cry from the 640 x 480 pixels in a worst-case traditional scenario.

One "limitation" of most cell phone displays is that they use only one color: black. Strictly speaking, this isn't terrible from a usability perspective since it rules out all the problems inherent in colorful design. These problems can include an often insufficient contrast between foreground and background, a lack of usability on the part of people with color deficiencies, and the challenge of maintaining consistent-looking color across multiple platforms.

FIGURE 7.4 *The Nokia 7190 phone. © 2001. Reprinted with permission from Nokia. All rights reserved.*

It won't be long, however, before most cell phones sport at least some color display. The availability, reliability, and cost of organic light-emitting diodes (OLEDs) should continue to improve, allowing OLEDs to subsume part of the arena once dominated by LCDs (Figure 7.5). Some products, like the Motorola Timeport 8767, are already using OLED technology in their displays. The Timeport only has three colors—red, green, and blue—which cannot be blended into other colors. Nevertheless, the Timeport is an early entry into the OLED color display market, and there's every reason to expect that in due time such displays will attain the same capabilities as their LCD cousins, while potentially consuming far less electricity.

FIGURE 7.5 *OLED displays are flexible and use a fraction of the energy required by LCDs. © 2001. Reprinted with permission from Cambridge Display Technologies. All rights reserved.*

Overall Size

Faster, smaller, cheaper. Faster, smaller, cheaper. That's the mantra of Moore's Law, and it is chanted in earnest among virtually all electronics vendors. Each new product release cycle, cell phones seem to shrink more. This physical smallness isn't always a winning benefit, of course—particularly if your users have to use the phone to navigate Web content. Think about it: cell phones are, after all, primarily phones. The cell phone's buttons and display can be small because with traditional use (making voice calls), you spend a small amount of time dialing and most of your time talking. Making the keys and other navigational items easily usable, therefore, isn't necessarily a priority to manufacturers. Engineers instead tend to focus their efforts on other goals, like integrating higher-quality audio/digital components.

Rapid Serial Visual Projection (RSVP)

With wireless Web-savvy phones, a great deal of time must be spent punching buttons, spinning alphawheels, and looking at the display in order to navigate. This shifts the importance of these input mechanisms—a fact that should be reflected in the item's design—but it can also be reflected in the software design and the content design. Circumventing the clumsiness of a tiny display, for example, can be accomplished through the use of a technique called rapid serial visual projection (RSVP). RSVP causes words that comprise a paragraph or sentence to be rapidly flashed on the screen, one at a time, so that the reader interprets each word as a meaningful single symbol rather than attempting to "oralize" the words. Since the technique discourages scanning back and forth through the text, higher reading speeds are generally achieved. Xerox's Palo Alto Research Center (PARC) has published a paper[6] that describes the Speeder Reader, which is a setup that allows a reader to navigate textual information in an efficient way that is derived from an automobile-driving metaphor. The PARC research has shown that it is possible to implement RSVP in a way that overcomes its traditional limitations—namely, its lack of an effective means of organizing hierarchical information (such as chapters in a book or pages in a Web site).

---

[6] See *www.parc.xerox.com/red/members/back/papers/speeder_2p.pdf.*

A similar interface could be implemented in handheld devices, specifically for areas of text that might otherwise be too large or cumbersome to display and scroll on a screen. It doesn't appear that this approach has yet been tried. Implementing such a feature would really only require software changes, as buttons that already exist on the phone could be used to navigate while in RSVP mode. Alternately, additional buttons on the side of the phone could be used—possibly with a pressure-sensitive strip to control the speed of text (like a gas pedal in an automobile). If a phone were outfitted with pressure-sensitive buttons, a built-in key rather than a special function, could be used for this purpose.

RSVP has been shown experimentally to greatly increase the number of words per minute a person can read, which is a bonus; but the real benefit is that it allows you to fit a lot of text into a small amount of space. Three researchers at the Software Usability Research Center at Wichita State University in Kansas found that RSVP works quite well in the context of small screen interfaces.[7] The results of a study they conducted in 2000 show that the participants found that reading text via RSVP in a small screen context was as easy and pleasurable as reading the same text in three-line mode (simulating a typical cell phone display) and in ten-line mode. This provides evidence that using RSVP could be a great screen real estate saver for small handheld devices.

Please note that RSVP is not appropriate for all modes of navigation in a device: it is assumed that this technique will be used primarily for reading large chunks of text, like the latest news, weather forecasts, and stock quotes, for example. It is possible to use RSVP for site navigation, although it appears that the efficacy of this technique has yet to be studied. Would users, for example, be able to use a navigation "bar" that was presented in a serial fashion? There are Java applets that scroll by news headlines and the like, allowing a user to select whatever story they'd like to read by clicking on its headline. It's possible that this might also work in conjunction with RSVP.

---

[7] See *http://wsupsy.psy.twsu.edu/surl/usabilitynews/2S/rsvp.htm.*

Other Size Factors

Without a doubt, small phones are easier to carry around than large ones; however, they are also easier to lose, more difficult to manipulate (smaller parts require a higher degree of manual dexterity to operate, as Fitt's Law predicts), and harder to see. All of these equate to usability barriers for you, the designer/developer. Yet it is hoped that, eventually, vendors will figure out that they can't pack ten pounds of features into a five-ounce cell phone shell. Web-enabled devices have to be a little larger, simply because of the need for a reasonable display and ease of operation. Note, however, that a new type of technology—the microdisplay—has the potential to eliminate this limitation. A microdisplay allows the user to see a "huge" virtual screen, while only requiring a physical display the size of a postage stamp.

THE LOGICAL LAYER

In the logical layer of a cell phone, we encounter the operating system that drives the phone and its various applications. Cell phones have been steadily accruing more and more functions: games have become commonplace, and scaled-down Web browsers are becoming more popular. A cell phone is really a tiny PC, with small amounts of "main" memory but not really any "secondary" storage (like a hard drive—although it would probably be easy enough to integrate storage devices like the Sony Memory Stick or the more generic compact flash into any phone). Since the OS that drives a cell phone is tiny, it is generally robust and not prone to crashes. This is a good thing, since consumer expectations for similar devices don't allow for hard-core failure of this sort. At the time of this writing, each cell phone is different; few phones share totally similar operating system environments. This will probably change in the near future, as many new doors will open up for the company that can attain such domination of the cell phone OS market. Microsoft and Sun are both currently vying for control over this area, and, at the time of this writing, Microsoft is poised to unleash Stinger, a combination of OS and cell phone, onto the market. Stinger will feature lots of Window-esque components, including a version of Microsoft

Outlook, as well as offering many features of conventional PDA-style devices, like synchronization.

Cell phones are currently a veritable Tower of Babel, since consistency across brands is virtually nonexistent. Nokia phones do exhibit an impressive amount of brand consistency; virtually all of their phones feature a very similar-looking interface so that once you've learned one of their phones, you don't need to relearn everything if you upgrade to a better phone. Although their better phones do include new features, all the old, comfortable things are still there. It will be interesting to see how the battle for domination of the cell phone OS market plays out: whether industry behemoth Microsoft will take over or vendors will maintain proprietary operating systems in their phones—or something completely different transpires (like a small company coming out with the "killer" cell phone OS).

Since there are so many variations in cell phone operating systems, it is impossible to adequately cover the features of a significant set of them here. Moreover, since it is unlikely that you are personally involved in the design of such an operating system for a major cell phone vendor, you will probably not have much input into the design process of such an OS. Nevertheless, you will still suffer if your application/content is run on a phone that is difficult to use! At the time of this writing, little to no information exists for creating usable content under the J2ME platform or Whistler. Java offers up a few sparse paragraphs of information on accessibility and usability in their *Java Look and Feel Guidelines*,[8] but volunteers nothing of substance.

For the moment, we have to look past these facts and address the issues that we *can* influence. In time it is likely that there will be a few dominant operating systems for portable computing devices, and it will then be feasible for usability testing to generalize to a significant number of phones.

---

[8] See *http://java.sun.com/products/jlf/ed1/guidelines.html*

THE COGNITIVE LAYER

Here's where your content or application sits. In reality, the application itself sits in the logical layer, and the manner in which the user interacts with it sits in the cognitive layer. A small semantic difference; we'll say it's all cognitive for example's sake. The methods used for evaluating the performance of the system at this layer are almost identical to those used for classical usability work: heuristic evaluation, classical usability testing, field studies, and so on. You'll have to decide based on your resources—budget, time, etc.—whether or not you can use real cell phones. You may have to opt to use emulators, but keep in mind that emulators don't effectively replicate real-world environments. You will certainly be in for a lot of unpleasant surprises if you only use emulators for testing, because when you go "live" your first users will effectively become your first real beta-testers. This can spell disaster! Emulators are great for rapid prototyping and development work, but they fall short in the testing arena.

There are several factors that can impact the usability of your cell-phone-based system, each of which you should be familiar with before creating a system for use in this context. The main points will be covered here in detail.

Signal Availability

When cell phone signal strength drops off, the services that rely on that signal also disappear. A number of factors can impact signal strength, including proximity to other sources of RF interference or high RF absorbency, a lack of digital service for phones that use digital signals, and weather and solar conditions. Furthermore, in some countries it is legal to install "cell phone killers"—devices that interfere with area cell phone frequencies, thereby making it impossible for users to make or receive cell phone calls. Two of the most important usability heuristics you can possibly apply in this area are feedback and visible system status. It's critical that your application/content be aware when service is no longer available—even if only momentarily—so that the user will know what's going on. Response time on the Web is a key issue in usability: people expect nearly instantaneous response or they feel that the system isn't working.

Most cell phones have a signal strength indicator that's part of the permanent display portion of the screen, and most users are aware that the little bars on the side of the screen represent the signal strength. A loss of signal doesn't necessarily have to equate to degraded performance in your wireless application. Currently, there does not seem to be a legal way (in the United States, at any rate) to simulate variable signal strength with a real cell phone to create realistic testing conditions. Several emulation programs allow you to simulate various levels of signal, but, as mentioned earlier, emulators don't always exactly predict reality. This is why it's critical to test your application/content under real-world circumstances.

Modes of Use

Internet-savvy cell phones are a sophisticated blend of various technologies. The way people use cell phones varies across the planet, and, arguably, users in the United States are far behind the rest of the world with regard to cell phone infrastructure and utilization. There are essentially three things that cell phones can be used for:

- Regular cellular telephony (human-to-human conversation)
- Web browsing and e-mail retrieval
- Text messaging (where available)

Since regular cellular telephony is really outside the scope of this book, it won't be covered here; Web browsing, e-mail retrieval, and text messaging, however, will each be looked at in turn. Web-capable phones are available in many parts of the world, with service that enables these features becoming increasingly available. Text messaging is currently much more predominant in Europe than in the United States, and Japan as a whole is generally much more advanced than the United States with regard to available features and services.

Web Browsing via Cell Phone Interface

Within the umbrella genre of Web-enabled cell phones, two specific categories exist at the time of this writing:

- Cell phones with standard monochrome displays
- Cell phones with built-in Palm factor displays

The browsing experience will differ according to the type of display that is used. Cell phones like the Kyocera Smartphone and similar recent releases by Samsung, which feature a color display and a system driven by the Palm OS, will have almost the exact same usability issues as a Palm VII or similarly equipped clone. This standardization makes for a slightly clunkier telephone but also reduces the Batman factor by one device. Let's begin by looking at the Web browsing experience with a standard tiny screen, such as the one found on a Web-enabled Nokia 7650 phone (Figure 7.6).

A tiny screen means that most traditional Web content won't look right; it may not even function at all. Many cell phones are WAP enabled,

FIGURE 7.6 *The Web-enabled Nokia 7650. © 2001.*
Reprinted with permission from Nokia. All rights reserved.

meaning that they can only receive and display data from a WAP server. It follows, then, that the content for this sort of device will have to be custom designed in WAP. This has a couple of significant implications for the designer. First, much work will have to be done to migrate existing HTML-framed document content over to a WAP version, and a lot will probably have to be shucked in the process. Here it's important to remember the first law of the wireless Web: The wireless Web isn't a smaller version of the Web. The functionality provided by the traditional Web and the functionality desired by users of Web-enabled cell phones should be fairly orthogonal. After all, these are two very different tools, and forcing one tool to do the job of another is never a good idea.

Web Browsing via Palm-Like Display

This is similar enough to straight-out PDA-style interaction that it does not merit an entire section. When designing for this sort of phone, it is

FIGURE 7.7 *The Kyocera QCP™ 6035 smartphone combines both PDA functionality and cell phone capability in one device. © 2001. Reprinted with permission from Kyocera Wireless Corp. All rights reserved.*

recommended that you review Chapter 8 of this book. In addition to Kyocera's smartphone (Figure 7.7), several other brands of phones that incorporate the Palm platform are available.

Text Messaging

The line between pager-like devices and cell phones is beginning to blur a bit, since many cell phones are beginning to take on some of the functionality of pagers. Initially, alphanumeric text messaging was common on pagers but unheard of in cell phones. The cell phone standard in many parts of Europe, where text messaging via cell phone has been an explosively growing area since the early 1990s, is GSM (Groupe Spéciale Mobile), which has a provision for a service called SMS (short messaging service). Since interacting with text messaging is really just limited to entering text, receiving it, and reading it, few facets are exposed to the tools of usability. We've covered the inherent limitations of the typical cell phone keypad. Reading text on a screen, if the text is presented in a serial fashion (no navigation within the text itself; e.g., no internal hyperlinks or other control aspects), is only a problem if there is no easy way to navigate through the text (forwards/backwards) or if the type is simply too small or otherwise illegible.

EXPERT INTERFACES VERSUS NOVICE INTERFACES

Although this book stresses the idea that predictive interfaces are a great idea and a crucial technique for improving the usability of a system with a potentially cumbersome interface (like a cell phone keypad), in keeping with the usability heuristic of user control and freedom, it's important to recognize that even the best-laid plans can sometimes work against the user in unexpected ways. According to the research findings of Rebecca Grinter and Margery Eldridge of the Xerox PARC and Xerox Research Centre Europe, respectively, European teenagers have evolved a sort of pidgin English that makes heavy use of contractions to accelerate text messaging via cell phones. In fact, in the study, the participants reported that predictive text input interfered with their operation during text messaging, since the hard-coded dictionaries on board the phones attempted to autocomplete text in an incorrect fashion, and such text was not capable of being deleted easily. In this case, a feature intended as an accelerator for novice users became a liability for expert users of the interface. The usability heuristic of user control and freedom states that users should be able to toggle a feature like predictive input on and off at will with minimal effort.

SOCIAL IMPACT

Cell phones have a very pronounced and interesting side effect shared by many electronic devices to a lesser degree: they can have a profound sociological impact when used in public. This effect is so profound, in fact, that it has led to the coining of the term "cell phone rage." This sort of rage can manifest itself in many ways. Take, for example, the anger expressed by the public when a twenty-three-year-old woman was killed at an intersection in Atlanta, Georgia, by a driver who had been talking on his cell phone and hadn't noticed her. How about the feeling you get when someone in a movie theater gets a cell phone call in the middle of an important scene—and then proceeds to talk loudly to the caller? Unfortunately, high technology does not instill a corresponding amount of common sense into its users, nor does it seem to elevate one's sense of basic human decency and respect for others. If anything, the cell phone is often a catalyst for people with bad personalities; it magnifies their lack of concern for anyone else in the world. Grinter and Eldridge found that one of the most compelling reasons that European teens use text messaging is that it allows them to avoid actual conversation, which is almost always laden with "normal" human societal filler like, "How are you?" "What's new?" and so on. Text messaging allows the teens to interact with one another in a terse fashion that would be considered rude and socially unacceptable via other conventional forms of interaction. It's as if the technical limitations of text messaging act like a shield to insulate the teens from potentially awkward interaction with other humans. So, ironically, a high degree of "connectedness" in electronic terms does not necessarily equate to a high degree of human connectedness; in fact, it often seems that the opposite is true. This could help explain the increase in depression shown to correlate with excessive Internet use.

As a usability specialist, there isn't much you can do about these societal factors. No sort of heuristic evaluation can help you prevent users from becoming increasingly disconnected from humanity as they become more involved with the artificial universe of the Internet; no usability testing will allow you to short-circuit the depression that can underlie chronic Web surfing. But it's important to be aware of these things. If this book leaves you with one lasting impression, it should be that you, the reader, would do well to adopt a larger sense of responsibility in your current assignment or job and begin to think about how your creations fit into the whole picture of humanity.

When a new technology becomes available, humans use it for everything; we're like children with a new toy. Consider the fact that when the properties of radiation became known through work by the Curies, it was common for clock and watch manufacturers to use the radioactive element radium in clock and watch faces to make them glow in the dark. Little did they know that exposure to this wonder of science would eventually be the cause of sickness and death. We already know that information overexposure has its own brand of negative consequences.

Chapter Summary

The telephone is one of the most significant communication tools in history. It has changed forms only slightly over time, and remains one of the most widely recognized high-tech devices in the world. Advances in cellular telephony have enabled system designers to offer other services over the cellular networks, including Internet connectivity. However, cell phone class devices do not replace conventional browsers, nor does wireless content replace traditional content.

HANDS ON

1. Download and install a wireless phone emulator, like the Go.America browser. Pick a random Web site and take a look at it through the emulator. Take notes on the things that appear non-functional.

2. Discussion: What positive impact might the widespread availability of Internet-capable cell phones have on society? What negative impact?

3. Design a small set of Web pages that are optimized for delivery on a cellphone. View the site with your emulator.

PERSONAL DIGITAL ASSISTANTS

Ever since the original Apple Newton MessagePad 100 was announced at MacWorld Boston on August 2, 1993, the tech world has been gravitating towards an ever-more-usable portable device that approaches the vision of the Newton's designers. The Newton was an ambitious device that unfortunately failed to generate the mass sales that Apple had originally hoped for.

Consider the fact that the Newton's handwriting recognition, which was satirized by the Doonesbury cartoon strip, was never actually intended to be a part of the Newton's design. According to Larry Tessler, who was the leader of the Newton Group at Apple, Apple's marketing team put some outrageous claims in the original Newton marketing material without ever consulting with engineering to make sure the claims were within the grasp of the technology of the day. Tessler was shocked when he saw that a draft of the first Newton brochure claimed that the Newton could "read your handwriting," and he subsequently insisted that marketing remove the fictitious claim. Marketing initially disagreed, but later complied. When the brochure was actually printed, however, the claim was not only still there, but handwriting recognition was listed as the Newton's number one feature! Tessler claims to have known that the

Newton was doomed the moment he saw the first brochure.[1] Marketing had shot the entire project in the foot by setting unrealistic expectations much too early in the game, and, as a result, despite remarkable improvements and colossal engineering feats, the Newton was sunk. Apple announced the demise of the Newton in February 1998. With its streamlined approach, the junior contender, the Palm Pilot, had dethroned the mighty Apple and taken the kingdom of PDA by storm.

While the Palm has been king of the hill for several years now, other contenders are milling about, hoping to snap up the market share that Palm has forged. Microsoft introduced its Windows CE (Compact Edition) operating system, version 1.0, in November 1996. Although it initially seemed to some that mixing Windows and small devices would never take off—WinCE at first seemed like Windows 1.0 all over again—the device has gained some ground, Microsoft is definitely hoping to take market share from the Palm OS. WinCE is undeniably a more full-featured operating system than the Palm OS, and it integrates fairly well with desktop versions of the scaled-down applications that run under it. The real question is whether users want that additional feature set—and its associated complexity.

Within the context of this chapter, it will be assumed that the two major platforms for the personal digital assistant form factor are WinCE and Palm OS, although there are others out there. Those folks who'd like to write and publish their own usability analysis of a favorite PDA system are encouraged to do so; we'd all benefit from it.

The Palm-style form factor for portable computing devices is extremely popular. According to a WAP survey conducted in July and August 2000 by the U.K. group Usability by Design, Ltd., 91 percent of respondents reported that they currently owned or were planning to obtain a Palm-sized PC.[2] This category was second only to cell phones; however, most respondents reported that if they had to keep

---

[1] See *www.techtv.com/screensavers/showtell/story/0,23008,3013675,00.html.*
[2] See *www.usability.uk.com/resources-wap.htm.*

only one portable computing device, it would be their Palm-sized PC. The same study also showed that the vast majority of respondents (80 percent) were male. This may or may not signify usage trends in this area, but it's probably an interesting statistic to have for a historical baseline.

THE PHYSICAL LAYER

As one would derive from the name, the Palm PDA is designed to fit in your palm. For the majority of "average-sized" people, this is indeed the case, and the form factor is generally quite comfortable. Palm founder Jeff Hawkins actually prototyped the now-famous Palm out of a small block of wood.[3] Hawkins was displeased with previous attempts at a handheld PC because they were too big to fit in a shirt pocket (which, as it turns out, tended to be one of the features most prized by many early male Palm owners). He crafted a block of wood to the approximate dimensions of an "ideal" palm computing device and carried it around to meetings. He'd also hold up mockups of screens for the device to get a feel for how the real thing might look. Although this sort of lo-fi prototyping might be exceptional, the output was certainly a winner. It just goes to show that usability experts should go to any length to make a better system. It clearly pays off in the end.

Physical size is plainly an important factor in determining the usability of a PDA: if it's too small, it becomes impossible or difficult to use; if it's too large, it becomes too cumbersome to carry around. (The HP Clamshell PC could be described as representing the worst of both worlds: it had the scaled-down feature set of a PDA with some of the bulk of a laptop. It was too big to carry in a pocket or clip to a belt, but too underpowered to replace a laptop outright.) Beyond the physical size, other concerns are weight and the actual dimensions of the device. Typically, the batteries in such a device will account for a high percentage of the total device weight. Advances in battery technology will help

---

[3] Eric Bergman, ed., *Information Appliances and Beyond*. (Morgan Kaufmann Press, 2000), 82.

push the weight down, but it will be a while before this area is significantly changed.

Several Palm-class devices have been able to break records in trimness and slimness, like the Visor Edge, which weighs in at just 4.8 ounces (149 grams) and which is only .44 inches thick (11 mm). A device that was any smaller would be likely to get lost, sat upon, or otherwise broken, because its owner wouldn't have any tactile sense of its presence. The Visor Edge, therefore, will probably be the benchmark for future Palm-class devices. Currently, color-display equipped models are larger, mainly because of the need for backlighting. Note that backlit displays are more prone to washout when the amount of ambient light is high, which means that color PDAs can pose an additional usability challenge. It's actually probably wise to avoid color altogether for Palm-friendly content, at least until a new generation of displays that don't rely on backlighting or similar techniques emerges.

Wireless Access

One area in which wireless computing suffers in general is in that of network access speed and reliability, neither of which is available to any large degree. To boot, there are technological barriers within the types of wireless modems used in most PDAs. Although wireless communication over cellular telephones happens largely in a digital fashion, the modems found inside most wireless-capable PDAs still use analog signals to transmit data.[4] In other words, your Palm or other PDA transmits a digital signal to your wireless modem, which then converts the digital stream into a modulated analog audio stream that is transmitted over the (oftentimes digital) cellular network. When the signal reaches the other side it is demodulated from an analog signal back into digital data. To say that this system is inefficient would be an understatement.

Typical theoretical top speeds for wireless data networks are in the 14.4 K range, which essentially takes us back several years in the technological

---

[4] See *http://faughnan.com/palm.html.*

time machine. This lack of high-speed access means that, to a degree, we are back in 1994, and that suitable design for portable devices must follow. This does not mean that the wireless Web is useless, however; it only means that it is a very different tool than the wired version and that designers have to adjust to make it work.

Display

PDAs typically have displays that are very similar, if not identical, to others in the same class. The average Palm PDA features a display resolution of 160 pixels by 160 pixels[5]—not a lot of real estate by most Web designers' measure. To a degree, the display and the input device in a PDA are one and the same—the touch screen serves both purposes. The typical Palm has a pressure-sensitive LCD that comes in four different variations: 4-level gray, 8-level gray, 16-level gray, and color. Input can be performed with either a finger or a stylus, depending on how accurate a selection is needed.

Several types of touch screens—including resistive, acoustic, and captive touch screens—are commonly available today. Currently, Palm devices use a resistive touch screen because they are the cheapest and the most robust of the three; plus, you can use a stylus with it (the other sorts aren't necessarily stylus-friendly). Resistive touch screens are made up of a glass or acrylic panel that is coated with both electrically conductive and resistive layers. The thin layers are divided by invisible separator dots. Once the device is switched on, an electric current flows through the screen. When a stylus or finger presses against the screen, the layers touch at the point where the pressure is applied, causing a change in the electrical current. This change in current signals a touch event to the CPU, as well as providing the coordinates of the pressed area. Resistive touch screens are robust because they have a fairly high resolution and aren't affected by foreign particles. On the other hand, their surface can be destroyed with a sharp

---

[5] Actually, the general rule of thumb is 150 pixels by 150 pixels. This accounts for "lost" screen real estate owned by the OS, etc.

point and they aren't perfectly transparent—they allow only about 80 percent of light to filter through, which has the effect of slightly obscuring what's underneath.

Glare is also a concern with this sort of screen, since plastic is also reflective. The WriteRight screen protector, a product made by Concept Kitchen,[6] is supposed to reduce glare on the screen, improve handwriting recognition, and extend the screen's usable life. It seems reasonable that Concept Kitchen could license their technology to PDA manufacturers, if only for glare reduction. Note that techniques for dealing with glare that are applicable to larger devices, like CRTs or tablet-sized PCs, may not work as well with smaller PDAs. Among the products offered by Palm for reducing glare are a top-hinged flap that offers some modicum of shade from the top but not from the sides. (Side flaps would make the Palm unholdable.)

Input

A distinguishing feature of PDA-style devices is the fact that they are predominantly stylus-driven. A pointing device is used almost exclusively for all input of information if the input is done directly on the device. Users of PDAs quickly discover that it's generally painful to enter large amounts of data (or even small amounts if you can't get the hang of Graffiti) on a PDA. Hence, most data entry is done offline, in the way of synchronization with a desktop or laptop computer. Several third-party companies make extension keyboards that fold up compactly for Palm devices. They usually cost almost what a bottom-of-the-line PDA costs, so such a peripheral may not always be cost effective. Moreover, the added bulk of the keyboard, even in the folded-up state, may not work for every user.

Use of a tiny PDA and stylus combination requires keen manual dexterity as well as use of both hands. This is unfortunate, since there is suffi-

---

[6] See *www.conceptkitchen.com*.

cient computational power in a low-end PDA to drive a variety of assistive technologies for users with disabilities, as well as for users in a variety of use contexts. The Handspring Company's Visor line of products includes the capability to enhance the functionality of their PDAs through upgrade cartridges. In theory, speech synthesis modules as well as voice recognition software could be fashioned to attach to a Visor. A current obstacle to this line of development is that both speech recognition and speech synthesis take up a fairly large amount of memory and CPU, and the average PDA doesn't quite have the horsepower to make it all work—yet.

Output

Most output from a Palm-style device will be to its tiny screen. This may render the device unusable by people with visual impairments. Even the use of a software "magnifier" has limited use when the entire screen real estate is a tiny 160 by 160 pixels. The average PDA architecture does not appear to allow for external displays to be connected. It should be possible, however, to use a Palm connector and serial adapter to link the device to an electronic Brailler (Figure 8.1). To date, no such Palm-compatible device appears to be available.

Although many PDA/Palm screens are difficult to read in daylight, some newer models feature sidelighting (instead of traditional backlighting), which vastly increases readability. When testing content that will be deployed on PDA devices, however, you should always make sure to include trials that examine the impact of daylight conditions. Typical trials that can test this axis of usability include reading comprehension exercises (not the kind you used to take in grade school; remember, people don't read Web content the same way they do other text). Such an exercise can involve requesting the participant to locate pricing information for five or six products, or finding other close-packed tabular data, in an outdoors environment where direct sunlight is likely. You should also have a control group perform the same search indoors to make sure that you're actually measuring the obscuring

FIGURE 8.1 *An electronic Brailler. © 2001. Reprinted with permission from Tieman. All rights reserved.*

effects of the sunlight and not the obscuring effects of the layout or other unknown variables.

Many PDAs feature IrDA (Infrared Data Association) infrared networking ports that can allow data transfer between two PDA devices, between a PDA and a desktop or laptop computer, or even from a PDA to a printer or other peripheral. This feature can actually constitute a serious problem from a security standpoint. If a PDA device is configured to automatically accept "beamed" content, it could inadvertently admit a virus-like program granting remote access to otherwise private data on an arbitrary user's PDA.

THE LOGICAL LAYER

The many different operating systems that a PDA might run include, but are not limited to, the Palm OS, Windows CE, EPOC, Linux, J2ME, and other proprietary systems like RIM pagers. Most, however, run either Palm OS, WinCE, or EPOC. At the time of this writing, Palm OS probably has the greatest share of the market, followed by

FIGURE 8.2 *The Palm OS.*

WinCE and, more distantly, by Symbian's EPOC operating system. According to the *Standard*,[7] a news service that provided information on the Tech world until it declared bankruptcy in September 2001, the Palm OS platform (see Figure 8.2) accounted for about 86 percent of all PDAs sold in the United States in February 2001.[8]

Unfortunately, this means that your job as a usability specialist is going to be tricky. Universal usability may only be a dream for the moment, since new devices come out all the time. Your best strategy is probably to choose

---

[7] See *www.thestandard.com/article/0,1902,23844,00.html.*
[8] Palm itself, however, accounted for only 62 percent of those sales; it looks like the decision to license the Palm OS is not increasing the overall Palm OS market share but is only eroding sales for Palm.

wisely which platforms you will support, and support those as fully as possible. Palm OS and WinCE are probably the best candidates at this point—at least until Microsoft is able to use their overwhelming desktop OS market share to overcome Palm.

Since the Palm OS and WinCE are generally heavily tied to a particular screen size, the content you design for one is probably not going to behave exactly the right way on the other. Most Palm devices have 160 pixel by 160 pixel displays; WinCE devices often have sideways quarter VGA (240 x 320) displays, like the Compaq iPaq. When designing for the Palm OS, if you keep the actual limitation of 150 pixels width in mind (due to the screen real estate that's taken up from OS components), you can be pretty sure that the same content will work with the PocketPC platform, running Windows CE. Of course, most designers will want to take advantage of the PocketPC's wider resolution and color capabilities, a tendency you'll have to keep in check (see Figure 8.3).

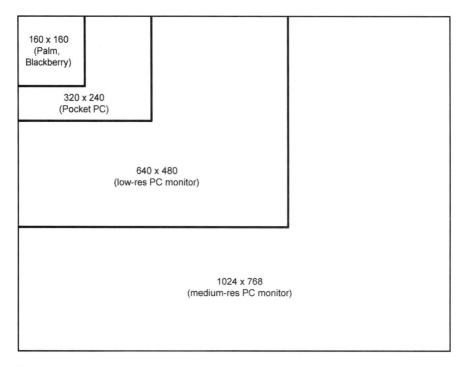

FIGURE 8.3 *A comparison of various screen resolutions.*

THE COGNITIVE LAYER

Because the screen of a PDA is so small, problems can occur when content originally designed for a much larger screen is displayed on it. Several options can reduce the risk of barriers to usability when enabling content for delivery on PDA screens; these have been assembled in the form of a checklist. Many of these points are also applicable to any device platform. One of the most important things you can do is to view all of your content using the Palm OS emulator, available from Palm. This application will give you a decent idea of what your content will look like on the real thing (Figures 8.4–8.7).

- **Avoid clutter.** It's easy to go hog-wild with embellishments, tables, and other design elements that beautify "normal" Web pages intended to be viewed via a PC/browser combination. These will

FIGURE 8.4 *Getting started with the Palm VII emulator requires a manual configuration adjustment if you plan on using your Internet/WAN connection for the emulator's connectivity. First, you need right-click on the emulator, choose "Settings," then "Properties…"…*

not properly scale down to the PDA, however. If an element isn't necessary to convey the critical information, remove it. This is in accordance with the usability principle of parsimony.

- **Make smart graphics.** Just as with graphics designed for RIM interactive pagers, it's important to use the appropriate sort of images if you must use them at all. Generally, you'll get the best and most consistent results with low-bit (4 or fewer per pixel) mono-chrome images. The usual process involves converting an image to grayscale, then to indexed color, and using as small a palette as possible. At the time of writing, there is not a plug-in for Adobe Photo-Shop or any other commercial software package that intelligently converts images to a format acceptable by PDA displays.

FIGURE 8.5 *... and then you have to check the box next to Redirect NetLib calls to TCP/IP. Until you perform these two steps, you will get mysterious error messages from Web Clipping apps that state "No Net Interfaces (120C)."*

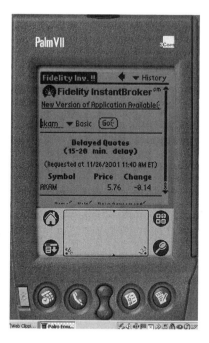

FIGURE 8.6 *This Fidelity Web clipping application displays stock quotes. Note that this application integrates a tasteful use of a branding-style graphic without hogging a large part of the screen. Also notable: the application is able to recognize when an updated version of itself is available. © 2001 Fidelity.*

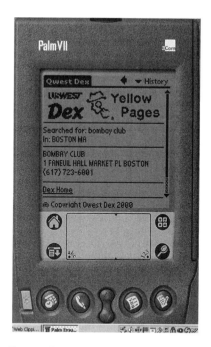

FIGURE 8.7 *One necessary quirk of many Palm Web clipping applications is that the "back" button is located at the top of the screen, near the drop-down menu that is usually used for categories. © 2001 Qwest.*

- **Avoid long pages.** This, again, is a "common sense" tip, but it is profoundly true for PDA-displayed content. As mentioned previously, the WAP/WML paradigm for documents is based on decks of small cards, each of which is tiny enough to be just about completely displayed on a single screen. In some cases, pages that exceed a maximum length may be truncated, which is not what you want to have happen. Consider using named links to allow users to quickly jump to the content they desire. PDA devices might be the one place where you can confidently create a depth-heavy design rather than a breadth-heavy design.

- **Forget puttin' on the Ritz.** Say you are sitting in an airline terminal and hear that your flight has just been canceled and that there are no further flights to your destination out of this airport for the day. You aren't going to care if the Sabre-savvy airline reservation tool on your Palm has fancy layout and impressive graphics; you'll only be concerned with figuring out how to get from here to there. A PDA-based interface that makes it easy to do that, even without any fancy look and feel, is going to score infinitely higher than a nonfunctional but design-award-winning interface. People who use PDAs to access Web content are rarely looking to find the best-looking sites on the Web; they are task-oriented and looking for quick information.

- **Use menu items to reduce text entry.** Obviously, much energy should be spent helping users avoid entering data by hand. You can get closer to this goal by using content design that relies more on check boxes, radio buttons, and drop-down menus than text entry fields.

- **Don't use tables for document layout.** Although it's difficult to avoid doing so when designing for traditional Web pages, it's not so difficult to avoid tables when you don't really have enough screen real estate to do layout wizardry in the first place. Do, however, use tables to format tabular data.

- **Use accelerators.** Users shouldn't have to enter the same text repeatedly. They should be able to keep their commonly searched-for items, for example, in a wallet-like list that they can drop down and choose from.

- **Don't use unnecessary HTML.** Keep your documents free from as much markup as possible. Stick to the bare-bones structural tags like "<H1>," "<P>," and so on. Not all PDA browsers will react gracefully if you throw an "<IFRAME>" in there. Most executable content, of course, like Flash Animation and Java Applets, won't work at all in a PDA browser; keep this in mind as you design.

- **Use the "HandheldFriendly" meta tag.** Be sure to include the "<meta name = "HandheldFriendly" content = "True">" tag in the header of documents that have been optimized for handheld delivery. Many browsers, like AvantGo, will not turn on JavaScript functionality, tables, or HSPACE and VSPACE attributes of image elements without the presence of this tag.

- **Pay attention to title elements.** Many PDA Web browsers truncate the title of an HTML document displayed in the title bar of the browser; try to keep titles to a maximum of fifteen characters just to be safe.

- **Avoid frames.** Most PDA browsers only support HTML 3.2. Despite the fact that frames were a de facto standard when the HTML 3.2 specification first came out (think version 3.0 browsers), frames and framesets were actually not a part of the specification. In any case, using framesets in such a tiny amount of space is just asking for trouble.

- **Avoid image maps.** Most PDA Web browsers can't handle client-side image maps. Many style guides suggest breaking a large image map into smaller images and reassembling them with a table. If you can, try and avoid this can of worms entirely; use text-based navigation instead.

- **If you do use color, use high-contrast schemes.** Since you can never know if your content is going to end up being viewed on a monochrome display (or, for that matter, with which bit depth) or a color display, you should always assume the worst-case scenario and choose a scheme in which the contrast between the background and the text is very high. View the page in grayscale mode to see if you can still read the text. If you can't, your color scheme needs to be fixed.

CHAPTER SUMMARY

Personal Digital Assistants are a new breed of portable electronic device that now have the capability to be outfitted with wireless Internet access. The two most popular types of applications are wireless email and Web browsers. Web surfing on a PDA can be a limited experience. At 160 pixels by 160 pixels, the maximum viewable area of a typical Web site is a tiny fraction of the designer's intended viewing area. Content that has been formulated for viewing on a PDA should be minimal, and have flexible layout to allow for the scaling that the PDA browser will perform.

HANDS ON

1. Download and install a PDA emulator.

2. Make sure that your Internet connection is set up properly to allow the emulator to work with the proxy server, if one is required. Note that the instructions for doing this will vary depending on the emulator you are using. See the vendor's developer Web site for more information.

3. Perform a heuristic evaluation of a Web site of your choice, as viewed through the emulator.

PAGER-BASED SYSTEMS

Pagers have come a long way since the early gray, heavy boxes you clipped on your belt. These early pagers had limited functionality and would only work within a very short radius of the base station. Today pagers have taken on multiline display screens capable of both alpha character and numeric data display. Their effective operating range has expanded dramatically, since the infrastructure for paging service has, in many cases, grown nationwide. Services offered via pagers have grown to include text messaging via e-mail, news updates and stock price information, and, in some cases, two-way communication allowing the pager wearer to respond to pages. The more sophisticated pagers become, the more the line between them and other, more complex, personal information devices blurs. In fact, it looks like the pager form factor may fade out in the not-too-distant future, since cell phones are absorbing some of their traditional functions. Why have two (or more) devices when you can have one that does the job of two?

In this chapter, we'll look at a variety of devices but will primarily focus on two different types of pagers offered by Research in Motion (RIM). While "traditional" pagers offer little two-way functionality, interactive pagers (Figure 9.1) like those offered by RIM allow the user to surf the Web and send and retrieve e-mail. This so-called BlackBerry service

FIGURE 9.1 *Wireless handhelds are becoming quite common in the workplace, since they often obviate the need to lug around a laptop just for e-mail.* © *2001. Reprinted with permission from Research in Motion Limited. All rights reserved.*

allows subscribers to fetch e-mail from several different sources, including Microsoft Exchange and Lotus Notes servers. For mobile workers, this is a true miracle: sales force members no longer have to lug cumbersome laptop computers around everywhere just to be able to receive and send e-mail. Web browsing is also possible through various services like GoAmerica's Go.Web service. It can be a real challenge to view a Web site on a display of the smaller, pager-like size, although text-only content is generally usable. The larger form factor, which approximates the display resolution of palm-sized PDAs, offers the designer a large canvas, albeit monochrome. These larger displays—even those that are optimized for 640 by 480 pixels—are still not really optimized for viewing Web sites. Since most vendors have settled on the de facto standard of 160 pixels by 160 pixels, you'll probably want to devote a separate section of your Web site to small-display devices, or else employ a three-tier architecture like the one described in Chapter 3 on content delivery technologies.

ADVANTAGES OF THE PAGER FORM FACTOR

If you're the sort of person who tries to avoid the Batman factor as much as possible, a pager-style mobile PC may be just the right thing for you. In short, they have one major advantage: size. They are typically smaller than other form factors, including Palm-style PCs and many types of Web-enabled cell phones. This is not always strictly true, of course. The Motorola Timeport series includes a couple of models that come close to the size of a Palm-sized PC and which are, in some cases, even heavier than a Palm.

So far, there hasn't been too much integration between popular Palm-style PCs and the paging network infrastructure, which has given this form factor the ability to adapt and grow in a market that is flooded with such devices as Palms and iPaqs. At some point, however, the two form factors may very well merge. After all, there's not a compelling reason *not* to integrate paging service into a Palm-style PC, and with the new cell phone/Palm-size PC hybrids coming out, this seems like a logical next step.

Most pager-style wireless devices have the same form factor as a regular alphanumeric pager. Typically, these devices have monochrome LCDs that can support from three to eight lines of text, generally with one fixed font size. Currently, two of the most popular series of pager-style devices are the RIM 800 and 900 series. In this chapter, the focus will be primarily on the RIM 850 and 950, since these more nearly resemble the pager form factor than the RIM 857 and 957, which are closer in nature to a Palm PDA form factor device (Figure 9.2). The technology and operating system is more or less the same in all RIM devices, but the form factor makes a big difference in usability.

FIGURE 9.2 *The RIM 850 Wireless Handheld™. © 2001. Reprinted with permission from Research in Motion Limited. All rights reserved.*

Pager-style PDAs tend to be noncomputationally advanced; they are not designed to do much besides receive and transmit information via the onboard radio frequency transceiver and display information on the LCD. Furthermore, they tend to have a minimal amount of main memory, since there is generally little need for more. The RIM 800 and 900 series interactive pagers feature between 4 and 5 megabytes of memory, plus a small amount of dedicated system memory. There is currently no form of secondary storage, although in theory it shouldn't be too hard to allow for compact flash or other types of storage.

There are currently two main wireless networks utilized by the RIM pagers for data transmission in the United States: the DataTac network operated by Motient and the Mobitex network operated by Cingular Wireless. Both are packet-switched networks optimized for wide-area wireless data communication. The Mobitex network utilizes two standards of wireless communication: GSM (Global System for Mobile communication), which is the de facto standard in most of the world, and TDMA (Time Division Multiple Access), which is an older standard that is dominant in the United States. GSM is a variation of TDMA. At the time of writing, RIM was beginning to offer BlackBerry service in the United Kingdom through BT Cellnet.

From a physical standpoint, the RIM 800 and 900 wireless handhelds come in two basic shapes: a larger, palm-sized PDA shape and a smaller, pager-sized shape. The smaller of the two shapes features a pager-like LCD screen that can display either six or eight lines of text, depending on the user's preference setting in the device's configuration utility. This has a design implication: the display "resolution" of six lines is really like the traditional screen resolution of 640 pixels by 480 pixels—it's the lowest common denominator. This means that you should design your content in such a way that the most important information appears within the first six lines of text and avoid filling this crucial space with images and other baggage. There is currently little data regarding user's tendencies to scroll versus not scroll (Figure 9.3).

FIGURE 9.3 *The RIM Wireless Handheld™ features a desktop space similar to that of the Palm: 160 pixels by 160 pixels, monochrome only. © 2001. Reprinted with permission from Research in Motion Limited. All rights reserved.*

Speaking of scrolling, a universal control called the trackwheel, or alphawheel, is used on the RIM pagers for the majority of navigational tasks. Depending on the context of what's being displayed on the screen, the trackwheel can move the cursor up, down, left, right, or any combination thereof. Note that many other devices—like certain cell phones—also use a trackwheel for at least some navigational tasks. Usually, the trackwheel is actuated by the thumb, and it is also usually located on the right side of the device. RIM does not appear to manufacture a "lefty" version of their interactive pagers, which may present a challenge to left-handed users.

ThumbScript: An Alternative to Standard Text Input

One major stumbling block of tiny devices is that the smaller they get, the harder it is to include the old-fashioned, oversized human interface elements that we're all used to. In Chapter 7, we took a look at the Fastap keyboard system, which allows designers to condense the alphabetic keyboard into the same space as a standard

FIGURE 9.4 *The ThumbScript prototype. © 2001. Reprinted with permission from Thumbscript Davaco PM&NT, LLC. All rights reserved.*

telephone keypad. Another alternative method of input is the ThumbScript, invented by Dr. Jeffery Smith (Figure 9.4).

The ThumbScript system is different from most input methods in that it does not use buttons that are labeled. Instead, a set of buttons that radiate outward from a central button are pressed in different sequences to create any given letter or other character. One benefit of this type of system is that since there are no labels on the keys, the same keypad can be used to map to many different languages; the concept of a native language for the keypad does not exist. The keys take advantage of Fitt's Law by leveraging the equal proximity of the keys to the central "home" key, reducing the theoretical time needed to travel from one key to another.

Since the functionality of the keyboard is contained in the driver software, the keyboard can quickly be mapped to any character set. To date, two Asian languages have been mapped to the Thumb-Script keyboard. It's worth noting that the ThumbScript system can also be effected on the main nine keys of the standard cell phone keypad (Figure 9.5).

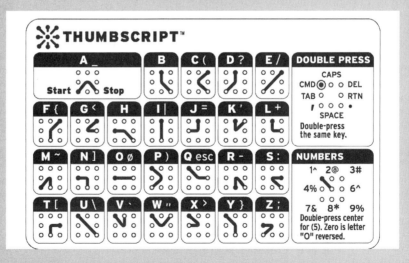

FIGURE 9.5 *The ThumbScript alphabet. © 2001. Reprinted with permission from Thumbscript Davaco PM&NT, LLC. All rights reserved.*

Computer Prototyping

If you are in the business of actually designing your own interactive pager, or, for that matter, any sort of wireless hardware, you should consider using computer-based prototyping to hash out the details of your interface design before you ever sink a single dime into hardware fabrication costs. It is prohibitively expensive for all but the most affluent manufacturers to generate many hardware prototypes. Instead, you should try mocking up the interface in a program like Macromedia Director, or even Flash (Figure 9.6). This will allow you to deliver a totally interactive system to test participants at a tiny fraction of the cost of hardware fabrication. Plus, you will be able to quickly implement fixes in software and reissue the prototypes for further testing.

If you're designing hardware, you can't really afford not to prototype a Web site. An electronic prototype frequently follows several initial pencil-and-paper sketches and possibly a cognitive walk-through.

FIGURE 9.6 *A mock-up of a pager-type information device. You can create prototypes that are almost fully functional in Macromedia Director or Flash.*

THE LOGICAL LAYER

RIM wireless handhelds all use the same basic operating system, a proprietary system optimized to run in the small amount of memory avail-

able. The OS is similar to most operating systems found on small
devices like this one and consists primarily of an application chooser
(Figure 9.7). System settings are accessed through an application, just
like any other feature of the pager. The OS comes equipped with a variety of common features you would expect in a PDA, like a calculator,
some games, and so on.

Navigating the RIM interactive pagers is fairly consistent from model to
model. For the purposes of this chapter, we'll focus on the Go.Web service offered by GoAmerica. In general, Go.Web supports HTML version 3.2; on RIM devices, HDML 3.0 is also supported, along with a
subset of WML 1.1. Here's a brief synopsis of features and availability at
the time of this writing.

FIGURE 9.7 *A view of the RIM wireless handheld's application chooser. © 2001.
Reprinted with permission from Research in Motion Limited. All rights reserved.*

Feature	Availability
Images	Available (requires configuration on the device)
Tables	Available (requires configuration on the device)
Forms	Available (multi-element selects are not supported)
Java applets	Not available
JavaScript	Not available
VBScript	Not available
Image maps	Not available
Frames	Available (Sort of: if there's no frames section to the page, the individual frame content links are shown instead of the frameset.)
WMLScript	Not available

Other Web Browsers for RIM Pagers

Several browsers are available for the RIM interactive pagers. Some support HTML, some support WML, while GoAmerica supports both, as well as HDML and MobileClips. MobileClips is a proprietary technology featured on BlackBerry devices that allows wireless application installation without the need for a docking cradle. Thus, MobileClips isn't really a content delivery vehicle per se. The following list summarizes the types of browsers available for the RIM interactive pagers.

- **AvantGo** (*www.avantgo.com*): Supports HTML
- **GoAmerica** (*www.goamerica.net/partners/developers/*): Supports HTML, WML, HDML, and MobileClips
- **Novarra** (*www.novarra.com/partners.htm*): Supports HTML
- **Neomar** (*www.neomar.com/developers/*): Supports WML
- **WolfeTech** (*www.wolfetech.com/main/*): Supports HTML

THE COGNITIVE LAYER

As you might expect, browsing the Web on a pager isn't always an easy task. The small display makes it hard to read even those Web pages that have been designed with small displays in mind. Only being able to see six lines of text at a time can make it difficult to navigate a site, especially if links are scattered all over the place. The user must also adjust to mousing around with the thumb-operated trackwheel.

The spotty nature of the wireless network that interactive pagers work over, furthermore, can mean long or delayed download times. Designing for this sort of device is a big challenge, even though the basic principle involved is quite simple: Keeping pages text-only, and with important links clustered tightly together, can make a Web site much more usable on such a device (Figure 9.8).

There are several things you can do to help ensure that Web pages accessed via one of the RIM devices are usable, some of which may seem like just common sense. Most of these points come from the Go.Web style guide, which is downloadable from GoAmerica's Web site. Probably the most sage advice is to use only text wherever possible and to keep that text as short as possible without compromising clarity. Additionally,

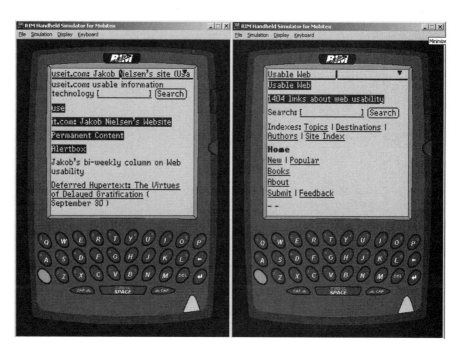

FIGURE 9.8 *Using the Go.Web simulator to look at several Web sites.*

always be sure to preview your material in the RIM BlackBerry emulators available from Research in Motion's developer program.

Guidelines for Accessing Web Sites Using RIM Pagers

Rely on Text More than Images

There isn't enough screen real estate to display tons of images on the RIM devices. If an image can be taken out of a page without significantly diminishing the usefulness of the page, remove it. If you must include images, make sure you do so sparingly, and observe the following guidelines. Make sure that any images you use are optimized for monochrome viewing. You may need to go back to the old-school techniques of building an image one pixel at a time.

Don't Make the User Scroll

It can be very frustrating for those using the six-line display RIM devices to have to scroll through page after page of information. Be sure to include named hyperlinks at the top of the page to allow users to

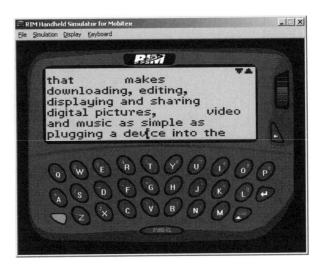

FIGURE 9.9 *An example of a page that has a broken feel to it because of the many line breaks.*

quickly go to the content they want without having to first wade through information they're not interested in. Also remember that line breaks and extra long lines can cause the page to display in a disjointed fashion so be sure to always preview your work in the emulator as well as the real thing before going live (Figure 9.9).

Optimize Display Graphics

If you must use graphics, optimize them for display on the RIM devices. The RIM 957 has a usable screen real estate of 150 pixels wide—and it's doubtful that you'll want to hog up all that real estate with a graphic. The smaller RIM interactive pagers, like the 857, only have a usable screen real estate of 132 pixels wide. The best format for images for a RIM is 2-bit grayscale GIFs that are the correct size already—images that are too large will be rescaled, which will probably negatively impact the image quality.

Currently, the RIM devices support GIF, JPEG, and WBMP image file formats. In case you are not familiar with WBMP, it is the wireless bitmap format that is often the only supported file format in WAP browsers. All WAP browsers that support images must support this format, so content that is intended for viewing on both WAP devices and the RIM interactive pagers should probably use this format. As of this writing, the WBMP specification is at revision level 0, although future revisions are expected. The following is a list of the general traits of a WBMP Level 0 image:[1]

- No image compression
- 1bit color, with black = 0 and white = 1
- 1-bit color depth (monochrome)
- The high bit of each byte is the leftmost pixel.
- The first row in the data is the first row of pixels.

---

[1] See *www1.wapforum.org/tech/documents/WAP-190-WAESpec-20000329-a.pdf.*

Note that if you're automating your output based on the client request-ing the data, you could use a package like Image Magick. To automate image output, you will need to do a little bit of CGI wizardry. Essen-tially, you will need to read the HTTP request header that the client sends when it asks for the Web page. By looking at the value of the vari-able "HTTP_USER_AGENT," you'll be able to determine if the client is a RIM interactive pager and can print out the right kind of image. The crude Perl 5 script provided here illustrates how to read in the "HTTP_USER_AGENT" variable and generate the correct image for a very simple page. This script does not do the actual conversion; it assumes that you have created both versions of the file ahead of time. Using a server-side conversion utility may provide extra flexibility, but it will also cost you a lot in the way of additional overhead for invoking so many Perl processes (or compiled C, or whatever). If your Web site has lots of images that are constantly changing, however, this approach might be right for you. Just be sure to have lots of computational power at hand.

```
#!/usr/bin/perl -w
# import the CGI perl module
use CGI;
# now create an instance of the CGI object
my $session = new CGI;
# declare a couple variables now, initialize them later
my $image_type;
my $suffix;
# Now find out what type of client is
# requesting this document
my $user_agent = $session->user_agent();
```

You will obviously need to run this script as an executable Web page from your server. The way you accomplish this will vary from server to server, but the one common configuration option is that you must enable files with certain suffixes to be allowed to execute. You may need to name the file something like "index.html" to get it to work. Also, your path to the Perl binary on your system may be located somewhere besides /usr/sbin/perl, so be sure to find out where it really lives and change the "shebang" line (the first line of the program) to reflect this. You will also need the CGI Perl module installed. It is outside the scope of this book to provide detailed instructions on how to do this, but you can find documentation at *http://stein.cshl.org/WWW/software/CGI/*.

It may be difficult to find open source programs that will allow you to create compressed GIF images, since UNISYS, who owns the patent for the LZW compression scheme used in the GIF format, charges a fee to anyone who uses the algorithm in their software, even if it's distributed at no cost. Hopefully, RIM will integrate support for PNG (Portable Network Graphic, a file format developed to replace both GIF and JPEG file formats) in the near future.

Use the "HandheldFriendly" Meta Tag

Yet another use for the "HTML <META> tag": Setting the following tag in the header of your documents will allow search engines, wireless devices, and other automated and manual services to understand that the page has been optimized for handheld devices: "<META name = 'HandheldFriendly' content = 'True'>"

It's a good idea to make sure that any pages you link to from a Hand-heldFriendly page are also HandheldFriendly pages, for obvious reasons.

This meta tag is also used in the creation of both AvantGo channels for the Palm and Palm Clippings. Information on creating custom AvantGo channels can be found at *www.webreview.com/2000/12_08/developers/12_08_00_1.shtml*. Note that the RIM pagers don't support AvantGo clippings, so this information is only applicable to the Palm platform (and thus is slightly out of place in this chapter).

Keep in Mind Maximum Page Length

Depending on the RIM device model the user has, the maximum page size is going to be either 50 K or 150 K—not very large for a page bloated with graphics, but plenty big enough for pages that are primarily textual in nature. Note that these are not the default page size settings, but the absolute maximum allowed after the size is toggled up through the RIM control panels. If a page received by the RIM device exceeds the maximum page size, the words "page truncated" will appear at the end point, where the truncation began.

Keep Important Information "above the Fold"

This old Web designers' adage has new meaning with pager-style portable computing devices: here the most important information should appear in the first six lines of text, since you can't be sure that users will have any more than this available at a time. Since it isn't always possible to completely adhere to this rule of thumb, it is important to at least observe the "inverted pyramid" style of writing. That is, you should always put the most important information at the beginning of a paragraph (or page, or screen, etc.), and place items of increasing detail/decreasing importance closer to the end. This way if users don't scroll very far they can at least get the gist of your information. Even savvy users who know that you're supposed to scroll often do not, if the first bits of content don't contain at least a hint of the information they are looking for.

Most users of pager-style portable computing devices are likely to use such devices primarily for text messaging, either via e-mail or another messaging protocol like SMS. It is unlikely that they will use this form factor heavily for Web navigation, since it does not lend itself well to this mode of use. While writing this book, the RIM 950 interactive pager was used frequently and it is truly a wonderful device for checking e-mail remotely. It can be extremely awkward to use for surfing the Web, however. That is to say, it can be very difficult to access Web pages that haven't been specifically designed for wireless devices. One test to use for a quick assessment of a device's Web-friendliness is to bring up the search engine *www.google.com.* If this Web site, which is almost completely made of text, doesn't work well in the device, it is unlikely that anything will.

So what do most people use the RIM interactive pagers for? According to Cahners In-Stat Group,[2] a Technology oriented news service, more

---

[2] http://www.instat.com

than 1.5 billion handsets and PDAs will be equipped with wireless data capabilities by the end of 2004. That's a lot of nomadic activity, and a very large portion of that activity will center on e-mail. It is also probable, however, that users will still want to access Web sites via interactive pagers. It is unlikely that many people will pleasure surf with this platform; rather, the nomadic pager-wielding businessperson will more commonly operate in the mode of known-item searching and retrieval of critical information, like stock prices, inventory information, and flight updates.

CHAPTER SUMMARY

Pager-style computing devices have become popular for a variety of reasons, but the most popular feature by far is wireless email. Most wireless providers also offer Web browsing capabilities through a limited number of pager models, but the experience of surfing the Web with one of these devices is limited at best. Content that is modeled for interactive pagers has the same sorts of limitations as cell phone displays. Using a "basic" version of your pages for use by interactive pagers can help ensure usability.

HANDS ON

1. Download and install an interactive pager emulator, like the RIM emulator from Go.America. Preview a site of your choice through the emulator.

2. Compare the same site when viewed through the cell phone emulator you downloaded in the exercises in Chapter 7. What differences are there between the two?

3. Discussion: What are the fundamental interactional style differences between Web content and email or instant messaging?

10

TELEVISION-BASED DEVICES

Although television-based computing systems, also known as "set-top boxes," aren't portable or wireless, a chapter has been included on this category of device because it is a form of ubiquitous computing, which is what this book is really all about. More and more Internet-savvy devices will come into the mainstream over the next few years, and the usability specialist has to be able to extend the toolbox of measuring techniques and usability skills to each new wave of device. It is impossible to predict exactly what sorts of new devices are going to come along, so this chapter will discuss examples of existing adaptations.

Interactive television has long been a dream of entertainment mavens and consumers alike. The whole notion of interactive television got off to a very slow start in the 1970s with an experimental service called Qube, which was only offered to a small group of test participants. The service was a revolutionary, but financially nonproductive, venture of Warner Amex Cable. Qube's two-way programs encouraged people to take part in whatever they were watching—the first instance of truly interactive electronic media. On one occasion in 1980, for example, viewers were able to use the system to call the plays for the Columbus

Metros, a minor-league pro-football team coached by John Dobbie. According to Dobbie, however, the game dragged on because it took so long in between plays to tabulate viewers' votes for the next play.[1] Interactive TV was, unfortunately, ahead of its time; the technology just wasn't ripe yet.

The 1980s and most of the 1990s saw little headway gained in this area, but it seems that the platform may finally be gaining some support and installed base. Big companies are speculating that the world of computer entertainment and information services will have a great degree of overlap, and before the two services potentially meld completely together, hybrid solutions will come about. One thing that has changed since the original Qube trials is that computing infrastructure has radically improved. While the supercomputers of the 1970s had about the same computational power as the CPU inside a child's gaming console, many features that were only dreamable back then are now a reality. Also in place is the necessary network infrastructure for tying together millions of viewers and for communicating updates to set-top boxes (Figure 10.1).

MSN TV

The original ancestor of Internet-savvy set-top boxes is probably MSN TV, which integrates Internet access with one of the most familiar information appliances in history, the television. This innovative offering was introduced to the public in 1995 by WebTV Networks, which was acquired by Microsoft in 1997. Although it is difficult to find reputable figures for the current number of MSN TV users, the number is significant and continues to grow.

Currently, Microsoft offers two forms of MSN TV, which are distinguished by the set-top boxes used for each level of service and their corresponding features. At the time of writing, these are the specifications of the two devices:

---

[1] See *www.dispatch.com/news/bus00/oct00/452954.html.*

FIGURE 10.1 *The Nokia Media Terminal set-top box. © 2001.*
Reprinted with permission from Nokia. All rights reserved.

Classic Receiver

- Made by Phillips Magnavox
- Key features: Internet, e-mail, chat,
  instant messaging
- 8 MB RAM, 2 MB ROM, 4 MB Flash
- 56 K-capable modem
- 150 MHz R5230 processor
- Wireless keyboard and remote control included

Plus Receiver

- Key features: Web picture-in-picture, TV listings,
  Internet, e-mail, picture e-mail, chat,
  instant messaging
- 16 MB RAM, 8 MB ROM, 2 MB Flash
- 56 K-capable modem

- 167 MHz R5231 processor
- Wireless keyboard and remote control included

The absence of any real sort of secondary file storage means that MSN TV can't be used for file downloads, nor can new applications be installed. Periodically, however, MSN "pushes" software updates to connected systems, a policy that has been the brunt of many an Internet discussion forum. The small amount of memory available means that the browser's cache can fill up quite often. According to a WebTV FAQ, the only real way to clear the cache effectively is to either switch users or turn the box off and back on again.[2]

For several years, it seemed like everyone was determined to make the Web function more like television: animated GIF files were the precursor to streaming video and other multimedia innovations for Web browsers. Innovators like Macromedia have brought file formats to the Web that allow for efficient, full-motion files that simulate life in Television Land. After all, both computers and televisions use CRT technology for output, which must make them at least cousins. Recent additions to the MSN TV product lineup include UltimateTV, which has nothing to do with the Internet, but rather has TiVo-like features, such as live program pausing, recording of shows, and other programming controls. It's not immediately obvious if this type of functionality will ever be integrated into MSN TV proper.

AOLTV

Perhaps the only rival to Microsoft's offering that stands a chance of survival is AOLTV, a product of media giant America Online. AOLTV integrates the Web, television, and AOL's patented look, feel, and service offering. The service is roughly the same price as MSN TV and offers many of the same sorts of features. Additionally, many familiar features from "regular" AOL service are available, such as

---

[2] See *www.geocities.com/ResearchTriangle/8795/faq.html#cache.*

Buddy List, instant messaging, and shopping. AOLTV is built upon the Liberate platform.[3]

At the time of writing, *http://developer.aoltv.com* had a link promising a PDF developer's guide but did not actually contain the document, which presumably contains information to help authors create usable content for the AOLTV platform. Related information has been assembled in the section of this chapter dealing with the cognitive layer. Unfortunately, AOLTV has not provided a suitable collection of authoring tools for developers and usability specialists. The only "tools" they currently offer are a small collection of HTML documents that perform limited, JavaScript-based functions, like checking to see if the current user agent (browser) is the AOLTV browser. AOL needs to implement an AOLTV emulator if they desire their service to be on a par with MSN TV. It is worth noting that currently AOLTV features only a handful of the media types that MSN TV supports.

THE PHYSICAL LAYER

Interacting with a networked TV is, as one would expect, like interacting with a combination PC and television. Output is based on familiar television standards: the TV screen, which inherently has lower resolution and overall quality than the average PC monitor. This presents a number of barriers to usability for both users and designers. This is not a surprise; having the convenience of Web capability on a "legacy" device comes at this price. Note that as high-definition television sets become more common and newer types of display technology emerge, the difference between TV sets and computer screens will blur, then dissolve. In the interim, however, designers must follow a set of fairly well-known rules to ensure that content will work for this format.

Input to a set-top box is generally guided via two input devices: the remote control, which borrows heavily from the television remote control

---

[3] See *www.liberate.com/*. Warning: there is a gratuitous use of Flash animation.

paradigm, and the wireless keyboard. Since constantly switching between the two devices is burdensome, the keyboard should only need to be used infrequently, like for the occasional URL or entering a large volume of text.

THE LOGICAL LAYER

So far, there is no common denominator for set-top box operating systems. Although the major players would love to gain control of this area, most boxes utilize a proprietary operating system. The interaction paradigm is pretty similar from device to device, since they all borrow from the concept of hyperlinks. Services like digital cable television use this paradigm for navigation; even hotel room television systems that aren't exactly "Web savvy" draw on this mode of interaction. It has, in fact, become so common to the average technology user that it is now second nature—and could stand as an example of the usability heuristic "Leverage user's existing schemata" in action.

MSN TV Emulator

One helpful feature of the MSN TV platform is the MSN TV emulator. The emulator, which is freely available from *http://developer.webtv.net/ design/tools/viewer/Default.htm,* allows usability specialists to preview content as it would be seen on a real MSN TV device and to troubleshoot problems without necessarily needing an actual MSN TV device. Binary versions of the emulator are available for Macintosh and Windows platforms.

Several things to keep in mind when using the emulator draw from the fact that an emulator is never exactly like the "real thing." The differences between the real MSN TV device and the emulator are summarized below. The golden rule is that you should always view your work on the real thing to weed out the problems that the emulator couldn't catch.

- **A television screen and a computer monitor are very different.**
  The resolution of a computer screen, which is what you will be

experiencing while using the emulator, is much higher than that of a television screen. The low resolution of a television screen can make it difficult, or even impossible, to read text under certain conditions. Additionally, colors do not appear the same on a television set as they do on a computer monitor, and it is possible for a color combination that works well on a PC monitor to be unusable when viewed on a television screen.

- **The Macintosh version of the emulator does not support SSL.** This means that you won't be able to view pages that use Secure Sockets Layer encryption, so your choices are to either view SSL pages on a Windows PC or to simply use a real MSN TV device. Note that MSN TV itself definitely supports SSL transactions.

- **The viewer doesn't support persistent cookies.** Although the real MSN TV device does support both session and persistent cookies, the viewer on both platforms only supports session cookies.

- **The Macintosh version of the emulator does not support audio.** Again, even though the MSN TV browser itself supports many different graphics formats, the Mac viewer does not.

- **MSN TV doesn't really support many image file types.** Even though MSN TV supposedly supports a lot of different file types natively, in reality the browser itself only natively supports GIF and JPEG image file formats. The MSN TV proxy servers transform other obscure file types into one of these two on the fly, then serve it up to the MSN TV client. If you are viewing files directly from your hard drive, the emulator will not have access to these proxy servers, and hence will not be able to open anything other than GIF or JPEG.

THE COGNITIVE LAYER

What do people expect from a set-top box system? Are they influenced by their experiences with regular television? It has been speculated that a large percentage of people who use set-top boxes as their primary means of Internet access have never used a PC before, and thus have little to no frame of reference with regard to traditional PC/browser combinations. They may not be as accustomed, therefore, to the concept of lag. Since most set-top box systems are an odd hybrid of one-way and two-way technology—upload, if not download as well, run over an external 56 K modem connection—performance is going to be substantially slower than service found in broadband solutions.

People also do not interface with set-top devices the same way they do with traditional PCs. The average set-top user sits at least ten feet away from the screen,[4] and interacts through a wireless remote control, which replaces the functionality of a mouse, and a wireless keyboard. Both of these facts have implications for design. The following list of design tips comes from the MSN TV authoring guide[5] and the ETV-Cookbook.[6]

Guidelines for Accessing Web Sites Using Set-Top Devices

Keep Links Together

It's a good idea to avoid scattering links across the page as a general rule, but in the case of set-top box surfing, this is particularly true. This is because the mode of navigation on set-top boxes is the selection box, which is like a URL cursor that the user moves around with the arrow keys on a remote control. Having links in one place greatly reduces the amount of time a user has to fidget with the remote to actuate the desired link.

Don't Use FrontPage to Author Content

In a humorous bit of irony, the MSN TV developer site includes a section that describes how to make HTML forms behave properly

---

[4] See *http://etvcookbook.org/extra/aoltv.html.*
[5] See *http://developer.MSN TV.net/.*
[6] See *http://etvcookbook.org/.*

under MSN TV. The author of the piece states that in examining some problem code, he discovered some embedded garbage inside the "<FORM>" tag. This "embedded garbage," of course, is actually Microsoft FrontPage clutter! The author explains that removing the offending junk code fixed the problem, and that the "secret" to having working forms under MSN TV is to have "good code." It is likely that this gem describing the incompatibility of one Microsoft product with another was written before Microsoft acquired MSN TV Networks in 1997.

Avoid Framesets

This is a no-brainer, but it's worth repeating: Set-top boxes have very little screen real estate to begin with; every little thing you do to use up screen space leaves that much less space for main content. The overhead and the quirkiness of frames, make them undesirable for set-top-compatible content. Note also that MSN TV actually converts frames into table cells, which can have some odd results. If you do use framesets, do not use nested framesets for the exact same reasons.

Keep It Small

You may hear various estimates of the "correct" usable screen size for set-top boxes. It appears that the average size that is agreed upon by vendors is 585 pixels by 380 pixels. This accounts for various screen elements that can exist on the most common platforms, as well as other screen elements.

Don't Use 400 and 500 Series HTTP Errors

For some mysterious reason, the MSN TV browser will not display any Web page that comes with an HTTP response code of 4XX or 5XX, which means that "404 NOT FOUND" errors will not show up in MSN TV. To work around this, you must instead use a "302 MOVED TEMPORARILY" error message that points to your 404 error page.

Remember the Modem

Most set-top boxes have a curse: they use a 56 K modem for at least a portion of their data transmitting and receiving. This means that, despite the fact that a set-top box might almost look like it is broadband, it's really a throwback to 1997 or earlier in terms of connectivity. Once again, you should limit the size of individual pages to 30 K to provide the user with a reasonable access time for your content.

Don't Rely on Java

Neither MSN TV nor AOLTV supported Java as of this writing, so don't expect your users to rely on Java applets for anything.

Use JavaScript 1.1

Both AOLTV and MSN TV support some form of JavaScript. The lowest common denominator between the two is JavaScript 1.1, which means that if you want to be cross-platform compatible, you'll need to avoid the neat features of JavaScript 1.2 and higher.

Use Supported Multimedia Formats

Both AOLTV and MSN TV can display and play an assortment of multimedia files. Here's a list of the formats that are common to both. Keep in mind, however, that the MSN TV system does not truly support any file formats natively besides GIF and JPEG; the MSN TV proxy servers translate other image file formats on the fly to either GIF or JPEG. This means that if you are opening a sample file directly from your hard drive using the emulator, you will be unable to see anything that isn't a GIF or JPEG.

Images

- GIF
- JPEG
- PNG

Audio

- WAV
- MIDI

Animation

- Animated GIF
- Macromedia Flash Version 3

CHAPTER SUMMARY

Integrating the television, which is one of the world's most powerful information devices, with the power of a PC and Internet connectivity, seems like a logical move. Despite the apparent symbiotic potential between the two, however, few vendors have managed to produce working, integrated systems. Viewing Web content on such systems can be substantially different than experiencing the same content on a "standard" PC/browser combination. By following design guidelines for this new media, you can create Web content that is usable on a variety of systems.

HANDS ON

1. Download and install the MSN TV/WebTV emulator.

2. Pick five sites at random, and visit those sites using the emulator. Make notes on things that appear broken or unusable.

3. Design a small Web site (with only 5–10 pages of content) according to the design guidelines given in this chapter. Take a look at it using your emulator. How usable is your content?

TABLET AND
PAD DEVICES

Ever since the crew of the Starship Enterprise punched up critical sensor information on a tablet-like electronic device, sci-fi buffs and tech gearheads alike have pined for just such a gizmo: an electronic data pad that combines the familiar form factor of a pad of writing paper or book with electronic computing power. One of the earliest user-friendly—and truly portable—laptop computers, the Apple PowerBook, was designed at least somewhat with this design goal in mind. The history of the tablet PC, in fact, goes back some thirty years to the Xerox Palo Alto Research Center, where famed computer systems guru Alan Kay came up with the idea for a revolutionary device—the DynaBook. The DynaBook was to include innovations such as a flat-panel display, wireless networking, and many other features that are only now being realized by current technology. In other words, PARC was well ahead of its time. Kay's initial design for the DynaBook never materialized, but it led two PARC scientists, Chuck Thacker and Butler Lampson, to create the landmark Alto computer (Figure 11.1). The Alto was deemed an "interim DynaBook" that would bridge the gap until technology caught up with the original design. The Alto, in turn, became the inspiration, at least in part, for the first Apple Macintosh.[1] To say that the Alto has had a lasting impact on the face of modern computing would be a major understatement. In fact, thirty years later, the brains behind Microsoft's Tablet PC included none other than Thacker and Lampson.

The tablet PC is, at least in theory, a design that should be immensely popular. In reality, however, it has mainly found its way into industrial and professional settings. There haven't been any real cases of phenomenally successful tablet-style PCs to date, and at least one company that bet the farm on the tablet, the late, Seattle-based ePods, has gone out of business. Several major vendors, including Microsoft, Fujitsu, and Sony,

FIGURE 11.1 *The Xerox Alto. © 2001. Reprinted with permission from Xerox Palo Alto Research Center (PARC). All rights reserved.*

---

[1] See *www.msnbc.com/news/562422.asp?cp1=1.*

are poised to dominate the tablet market, should one ever exist. For various reasons, the tablet hasn't picked up as much steam as its cousin, the PDA. In fact, at the time of writing, the tablet PC is a much-maligned item in the personal and home market. Most attempts at a tablet-style device have resulted in a cumbersome, underpowered contraption that simply doesn't deliver on its promise. Fortunately for fans of the tablet form factor, however, technology has finally caught up with the dream, and viable tablet PCs are making it into the mainstream.

Perhaps the true "killer app" of the tablet is in its incarnation as an electronic book. The effort, however, to create a single electronic device that could contain all the works of Shakespeare, for example, has so far been foiled not only by technological problems, but by sociopolitical issues—particularly those pertaining to the protection of intellectual property. Book publishers and distributors of recorded music are both very keen on making sure that they maintain their ability to protect the material they own. In truth, book and music publishers could vastly reduce their production and distribution costs via electronic delivery. To date, however, many attempts at electronic books have failed due to lack of customer demand. For e-books to be successful, there needs to be a good delivery device and appropriate digital rights management tools to protect copyrighted material both for the publisher and the author.

One semi-successful manufacturer of electronic books is Franklin, purveyors of the eBookMan (Figure 11.2). The eBookMan has some of the features of a Palm PDA but is geared heavily toward the online reading of e-texts. Franklin offers a host of public domain e-texts on their Web site, *www.franklin.com*. The eBookMan has lots of features that are similar to those found in the PalmOS, even though it's designed primarily to be an electronic book. In contrast to the eBookMan, the NuvoMedia RocketBook is just an electronic book, plain and simple. It is debatable whether either approach is superior. On the one hand, having a single device that can perform multiple functions means, in theory, that you are able to carry around fewer devices. On the other hand, multifunction devices rarely perform all functions to the full capacity that a dedicated device can.

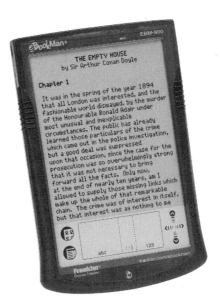

FIGURE 11.2 *The Franklin eBookMan. © 2001. Reprinted with permission from Franklin Electronic Publishers, Inc. All rights reserved.*

Although much of the physical makeup of a tablet-style device is similar to that of a laptop computer, there are some notable differences. First, most tablet-style devices have significantly less processing power than the average laptop. This is due to several factors. It usually follows, for example, that the larger the device, the faster the processor, and the more horsepower a PC has, the more energy it draws. Since it's critical for a portable device to have exceptional battery life (otherwise, it isn't truly portable), tablet manufacturers generally offer a small, RISC-type processor or something like the Intel StrongARM processor. The lack of processing power of a tablet-style device isn't generally a problem, since most people use these devices to do relatively noncomputationally expensive work, like word processing, writing e-mail, and quick Web browsing. It's unlikely that someone would do Fourier transformations or compile large applications on such a device; hence, users may never notice how slow the device could be under these conditions.

Most tablet-style devices do not contain disk-based secondary storage; rather, they use removable, nonmoving media like Compact Flash or the Sony Memory Stick . This cuts down on the overall weight of the system, since hard disks weigh a considerable amount. This generally also means that, unlike traditional desktop PCs that might have upwards of 60 gigabytes of available storage, the tablet-style device is unable to store large amounts of data. It's not uncommon for such a system to have a meager 32 megabytes of secondary storage, with even less for main memory. An exception to this rule is the Fujitsu Stylistic series of tablet PCs, which actually feature shock-mounted multigigabyte hard drives, as well as a healthy amount of memory. On the horizon is Microsoft's entry into the arena, which is supposed to replace the functionality of both a PDA and a desktop computer. Only time will tell if this device that attempts to straddle these two very different functional domains will succeed.

Recent innovations by companies like IBM—take, for example, their tiny Microdrive (Figure 11.3), which stores a gigabyte of data on a platter the size of a quarter—have made it possible for tablet devices to grow and mature considerably. The price of RAM has dropped phenomenally over the past six years, and the battery-thrifty nature of the TransMeta Crusoe® processors could contribute to a new tablet-style PC that's truly ready for prime time. The hitch is having to equip these tablet PCs with wireless capability that goes beyond the typical IEEE

FIGURE 11.3 *The IBM Microdrive. Courtesy of International Business Machines Corporation.*

802.11x wireless Ethernet—like the capability of wireless products like Metricom's Ricochet wireless modem service. This service allows you to connect to the Internet from anywhere within the Ricochet coverage area, at speeds of up to 128 kbps.[2] Sadly, Metricom recently announced that it was declaring Chapter 11 bankruptcy, so it is unclear if this service will continue.

LESS POWER + NO KEYBOARD = TABLET PC?

Perhaps one reason that tablet PCs haven't taken off more than they have is that they are typically underpowered compared to their desktop and laptop companions. There are several reasons for this, but they can be boiled down to two major factors: battery life and processor size. Most processor vendors make scaled-down versions of their desktop CPUs that are designed smaller so as to accommodate the size constraints of a laptop chassis. In a tablet PC, the display has to fit into the same chassis, which reduces the available real estate even more. Smaller CPUs tend to be less powerful than a full-sized version; this is the current physical law of CPUs. The second factor, battery life, is a constant theater for engineering warfare. Batteries don't stay charged forever, but consumers want them to last at least the duration of one commute, for some value of "commute." So far, CPU manufacturers have used very simplistic power-saving techniques to reduce the amount of power consumption in laptops. Spinning the hard drive down saves a lot of energy, since the hard drive is really the only moving part in the laptop. However, the CPU itself also consumes a lot of the battery, especially the faster the CPU runs. One technique used by manufacturers to conserve power in this area includes cycling the CPU speed down to one-half its normal speed—a crude approach that does not allow for a graceful transition from low speed to high speed. The Crusoe processor from TransMeta (Figure 11.4) actually has the ability

---

[2] At the time of writing, the coverage is scant and extremely patchy: many areas can only get 28.8 kbps connectivity. Nevertheless, many people who use the service swear by it.

FIGURE 11.4 *The TransMeta Crusoe processor. © 2001.*
Reprinted with permission from TransMeta. All rights reserved.

to continuously cycle its own speed up and down to any speed in order to meet the processing needs of currently running applications. This way, the processor uses only the amount of power it truly needs for any given task. This capability translates into a marked improvement of battery life and will enable vendors to integrate higher-speed CPUs into smaller devices.

Evidently, Microsoft is hoping to even the playing field by using the Crusoe processor in its Tablet PC. Microsoft is touting the Tablet PC as a desktop and laptop replacement as opposed to merely another device to have around. Another vendor, PaceBlade, is taking a similar approach but is also including some innovative features in their Pace-Book tablet PC that set it apart from the rest. The PaceBook, which is designed to be completely portable, can be used as a laptop (Figure 11.5), a desktop with LCD, or a tablet (Figure 11.6), thereby allowing it to replace these various devices. The company's Web site boasts six-to-eight-hour battery life.

FIGURE 11.5 *The PaceBook configured as a laptop. Note that the keyboard is completely unattached to the display unit; it is wireless. The case that holds the two pieces together also acts as a hinge. © 2001. Reprinted with permission from PaceBlade. All rights reserved.*

FIGURE 11.6 *The PaceBook as a landscape-mode tablet PC. © 2001. Reprinted with permission from PaceBlade. All rights reserved.*

THE PHYSICAL LAYER

Since there are several aspects of a tablet PC to consider when evaluating the usability of the system, this section has been broken down into corresponding components. Much of the design goal of a tablet form factor PC is to replicate the familiar writing tablet, which is much the same form factor that ancient civilizations used for scribing documents. Although some may question the relevance of this paradigm for the twenty-first century, there is, nonetheless, a healthy amount of interest among vendors in developing this sort of product.

Tablet PCs combine desirable aspects of laptop computers and PDAs. They are lighter and smaller than the average laptop, they can be held in one hand and actuated with the other, and they have far more horsepower than the average palm-sized computer. Newer tablet PCs have reasonable amounts of primary and secondary storage, which means that they can serve as more than just "dumb terminals," or thin clients. Of course, the key enabling technology in all of this is wireless networking. Without it, the utility of the tablet PC is greatly diminished. The most likely wireless connectivity for a tablet PC is 802.11 wireless Ethernet. The implication is that most tablet PCs will be used in an environment that has a fully wired LAN with distributed wireless network access points. At the time of this writing, it is unclear whether any tablet PC comes standard with a form of packet or cellular data connectivity. Since many tablet PCs feature PCMCIA slots, however, there is no reason why a user couldn't outfit a tablet PC with a radio modem of some sort for true nomadic capability.

Display

If we take the paradigm of the tablet PC as a sort of portable mega-book as valid, it becomes clear that we expect to be able to interact with this form factor in a similar fashion to that of a printed document. After all, the displays of many tablet PCs approximate A4 or U.S. letter size sheets, which theoretically makes them perfect for displaying electronic documents. Unfortunately, however, one severe limitation of tablet-style devices is their average display resolution is a measly 72–75 pixels per inch—a far cry from the 1200-plus dots per inch of a typical high-quality magazine (see Figure 11.7).

Although LCDs are vastly better for your eyes, comprehension, and brain than a traditional CRT-style display, their resolution still simply isn't that great. LCD panels are also extremely costly to manufacture because of their high failure rate during manufacturing. When you bought that fancy new LCD monitor, you were actually paying for about four of them, offsetting the cost of broken panels that didn't survive the manufacturing process. Depending upon the vendor, a panel is considered defective if it has more than two to nine "broken" PELs (picture elements). A PEL is simply one light-generating cell, equivalent to a pixel. If you have an LCD, you can probably detect at least a couple of broken PELs on your screen by blanking the screen using a screensaver or the like. If you look carefully, you'll see dots of color that stick out from the black. It's normal for a brand-new LCD panel of any kind to

FIGURE 11.7 *A prototype display by IBM that features much higher than normal resolution. Although you can't really detect the difference in resolution by looking at a picture of it in a book, the improvement in quality would be readily apparent by viewing it "live." Courtesy of International Business Machines Corporation.*

have at least two of these. As panels get older, more PELs are likely to get "stuck" this way.

Part of the bulk of an LCD panel is in the fluorescent backlighting needed to make the displayed image visible. This backlighting is also one of the major sources of power drain in the panel itself. Innovations like OLEDs may reduce the amount of power consumption needed to generate a high-quality, bright image, but at the time of writing this technology is still several years away from mass consumption.

On that note, there are several very promising developments that will bring computer display technology closer to textbook quality in the very near future. These are covered in detail in Chapter 13. Moreover, as manufacturing techniques improve in reliability, you can expect prices to drop and resolution to increase.

For the moment, we will assume that our users are going to be using a traditional LCD, and we'll look at problems that can be encountered when using this sort of technology.

Glare/Ambient Light

One major problem with LCDs is that much of the information displayed on the screen can be obliterated by interfering light. Glare off the tablet's display surface, sunlight, and bright artificial lights can all make it difficult to read text displayed on a screen. Unfortunately, there isn't much that can be done about this at the moment—unless you happen to be a manufacturer of displays and have some great new trick up your sleeve. Since portable computing devices can be used anywhere, environmental lighting is a major concern for usability specialists; we need to know how to build our devices so that they are robust enough to be usable in a variety of environments, including those in which there is direct sunlight.

Manufacturers have used several techniques to combat screen glare, and a variety of screen glare filters is available. The least expensive sort of glare filter is a simple wire mesh. These cost only pennies but profoundly impact the viewing experience, as you might imagine.

Antireflective coating features a marginal cost and marginal performance, as it can result in both a diminishing of the viewable light from the display itself and a reduction in the maximum angle of viewability. The top-of-the-line technology in glare reduction is the bonded quarterwave filter, which has a minimal impact on viewing and has excellent glare reduction capacity, but is very expensive. One factor to keep in mind within the context of glare reduction is that many types of LCDs consist of multiple layers of glass and/or plastic, each of which can act as a reflective surface. It is advisable to make sure that the so-called "first surface"—that is, the exterior surface that will first intercept light—is treated to minimize the spreading of light to the underlying layers.

Another technique for battling monitor glare that has been used with some success is the use of "shade wings," panels that attach to the sides and top of the display to shield the reflective screen from ambient light. This design could easily be incorporated into a tablet in the way of flip-top and flip-side panels that lock behind the tablet when not in use.

Input

One other feature that typically distinguishes the tablet form factor from that of the laptop is the lack of a physical keyboard. Eliminating the keyboard means that the display can be larger, which is usually a good thing. On the other hand, the lack of a keyboard means that it's a bit more difficult to enter information. Fortunately, most tablet-style PCs have a touch screen that supports stylus-driven navigation and input. A "soft" keyboard is a typical feature of this style of device. Although this type of tablet is suitable for point-and-click navigation and simple button pushing, it does not lend itself to long hours of text entry. Like cell phone devices, tablet PCs can benefit from predictive input since typing is somewhat laborious.

Since touch screens are notorious for eventually succumbing to "drift"—the condition by which pointing to one part of the screen erroneously actuates a different part—it's important to feature recalibration in your system. Depending on the operating system your device is using, this may be built in. Windows CE, for example, has a built-in stylus recalibration utility. It's quite possible to include a USB (Universal Serial Bus) port on even the thinnest tablet PC, which in theory means that you should be able to hook up an external USB keyboard if the need ever arises for extensive amounts of text entry.

A problem that is similar to drift is "shaky input," a situation in which a user's data input is affected by elements in their environment. This can occur under a number of circumstances; for example, while a user is typing on a moving vehicle. Some notebooks feature both a "cat tongue" pointer and a trackpad, presumably to provide maximum choice for the user. This design can backfire, however; since the trackpad is positioned near the place where users occasionally rest their hands, they can end up actuating the mouse in a random way by accidentally brushing the trackpad. This can cause the mouse to jump across the screen, drag-select text, and then delete it or overwrite it with the sentence the user happens to be typing—without the user being aware that anything unnatural has transpired.

Since mobile computing devices can be used in many places PC vendors never dreamed of their devices going, a whole new genre of environmental variables exists for usability specialists to think about.

The problem of drift brings us to another usability barrier with tablet-style PCs: minimum element size. Since using a stylus on a potentially incorrectly calibrated touch screen can present a real navigational challenge, it's important to always make sure that navigational screen items are large enough to be actuated easily. Text items like hyperlinks should be large enough to serve as a reasonably sized target. The same goes for images, which should also be regularly shaped so as to ensure maximum potential actuation area. A tiny five-pointed star, for example, would probably be pretty hard to click with a stubby stylus. A square with the same outside dimensions would be slightly easier to click, simply because of the increased surface area.

You may want to simulate an incorrectly calibrated system[3] for your usability trials. Stylus-driven systems do not permit the same sort of feedback to the user that JavaScript image rollovers (also known as "hover buttons") can afford in a mouse-driven system. This means that there are fewer mechanisms for providing a user with information about which hyperlink is about to be followed. There are ways of working around this in hardware, but they are not easily implementable in existing commodity tablet PCs.

Those of you who are sticklers for mathematical formulae will probably want to know how big the minimum element size is. There are, in fact, several means of computing these magical numbers, but the most important consideration here is that you avoid making things tiny for cosmetic or aesthetic reasons, and do real user testing to determine the "right" size for your users. Ultimately, mathematical equations that seek to describe the nature of humans can only be taken as guidelines, not as immutable laws of the universe.

It is also worth noting that the method of stylus interaction with the touch screen has a significant impact on selection error rate. According to Xiangshi Ren and Shinji Moriya, using a technique called "slide touch" can increase accuracy and reduce the mean time of selecting navigational items on a touch screen.[4] Essentially, the slide touch method of stylus input allows a greater degree of inaccuracy on behalf of the human, but yields greater accuracy on behalf of the device.

Handwriting Recognition

One of the features that is likely to come as standard tablet PC equipment, particularly on the Microsoft product, is handwriting recognition (Figure 11.8). There are many approaches to handwriting recognition;

---

[3] Although the exact method for doing this is outside the scope of this book, all you do is run the stylus setup utility and tap the screen in the "wrong" place—like just to the left or right of the crosshairs that appear on the screen.

[4] See *www1.acm.org/pubs/articles/journals/tochi/2000-7-3/p384-ren/p384-ren.pdf*.

FIGURE 11.8 *The Graffiti alphabet, a simplified handwriting input system that has been optimized for handwriting recognition systems. This approach requires far less "brains" than a flat-out universal handwriting system. © 2001. Reprinted with permission from Palm Image. All rights reserved.*

some work well, others fail. If you ever owned an Apple Newton, you are probably aware that the end result of the Newton's handwriting recognition software was less than stunning. However, the underlying engine to the Newton's character/word recognition was a marvel of modern technology;[5] it may be that it was simply too complicated to be effective for the types of actions likely to be performed by the average PDA user. The handwriting recognition engine in the Palm OS takes a completely different approach: you have to learn a proprietary alphabet that is stark in nature, which allows the recognition engine to work very well in a tiny amount of memory. Since resources are usually at a premium, efficiency is a virtue in this class of device. (Not to say that "bloatware" is ever excusable.)

Handwriting recognition, in theory, is a boon to users since it enables them to interact with a tablet PC or PDA in the same way that they would a writing tablet or sticky note. But is this *really* a benefit? Many people can type much faster, and for a lot longer, than they can write by

[5] You can find an excellent, if highly technical, exposition on the Newton's handwriting comprehension engine at *ftp://ftp.apple.com/research/neural/larryy/ANHR/ AIMag/Yaegeretal.AIMag.pdf.*

hand. Writing with a tiny stylus on a tiny screen can lead to all sorts of repetitive strain injuries and, at the very least, hand cramps. Handwriting should therefore only be seen as one alternative to typing, and one that is useful in a limited number of scenarios. Even on tablet PCs, you should limit the amount of text typing that is required of the user. Instead, use form elements for pregenerated choice selections. Permitting the user to customize your content is also a good idea, especially if commonly used queries or other input information can be predefined.

According to Jan Noyes,[6] the current state of both speech recognition and handwriting recognition is less helpful than it could be, mainly because the preconceived expectations of users do not match the reality of the systems they attempt to use. For example, when two humans speak to one another and one cannot understand the other, it is common to slow speech down, talk louder, or simplify sentences. This technique does not work with speech recognition, however, because it does not mesh with the algorithms used by the speech recognition engine. By the same token, if a human being cannot read the handwriting of another, steps such as writing in all capital letters are used to aid in legibility. Such a scenario, however, cannot apply in most handwriting recognition schemes, and so the user's expectations from experience with human interactions are not met.

Microsoft has chosen to take a new approach to handwritten data with their forthcoming Tablet PC: instead of forcing the user to have handwriting translated or "recognized," the user's handwriting stays as handwriting. As Microsoft put it, "Ink stays ink." The Tablet PC will also allow handwritten input to be stored and edited.

Output

For the most part, tablet-style PCs use the built-in screen for output. Since most tablet PCs have some sort of expansion capability via USB or other standard or proprietary expansion ports, however, it is conceivable

---

[6] See *www.lboro.ac.uk/research/husat/news/prog/jn_presentation.html.*

that a tablet-style PC could be made to use speech output (as well as input). Note, however, that one of the driving features of the tablet PC is its ability to act like a regular writing tablet—and thus interact in a primarily visual manner. Since most of a tablet PC's footprint comes from its built-in display, this form factor is probably suboptimal for people with visual impairment.

Most tablet PCs will use an LCD panel for visual output. Some of the early devices, like the ill-fated ePods device, only had a 256-color display.[7] This was quite a limiting factor, considering that most users are used to at least 24-bit video. Modern tablet PCs, however, ship with standard SVGA LCD displays.

THE LOGICAL LAYER

As with any electronic device, there is a war to see who will dominate the tablet-style PC operating system market. And Microsoft is betting that they will, primarily through their Windows CE operating system and other up-and-coming versions of the Windows OS. There aren't many other options for the tablet-style PC. One operating system that has been successfully used on a number of traditionally WinCE-dominated devices is GNU/Linux.[8] Unfortunately, however, few commodity devices ship with GNU/Linux, and the GNU/Linux system is just not ready yet for the "average" user. It is a system that has traditionally been geared toward power users, and if it is ever successfully adapted for use by the general public, it will lose a lot of its power. Apple's Mac OS X is probably the closest thing to a user-friendly UNIX now available.

With all that being said, most tablet PCs use the same operating system, which at least provides a modicum of consistency. Typically, versions of

---

[7] Actually, the device was capable of 16-bit color. See *www.geocities.com/epodsfiles/fun.html#Videolink* for instructions on how to hack your ePods to get 16-bit video.

[8] Most people simply condense this term down to "Linux"; "linux," however, refers only to the operating system kernel itself. At the time of writing, all distributions of the Linux kernel come bundled with a lot of software written by the GNU Foundation (*www.gnu.org*).

most full-featured programs will run under WinCE. Upcoming tablet PCs may obviate the need for a separate operating system for this sort of portable device; the same OS that will run on a laptop will run on next-generation tablets.

THE COGNITIVE LAYER

From a user's standpoint, using a tablet PC is very similar to using a laptop, with a couple of notable exceptions: most input is driven through a stylus, and tablet PCs are completely portable, just like a pad of paper. Arguably, tablet PCs are easier to take places than a laptop. The fact that they are usually designed to be balanced in a single hand means that most input will be carried out using a single hand. This is not significantly different from the way a PDA-style device would be used. However, there is a major difference between a PDA and a tablet PC: the display. Rather than being limited to the tiny 160-pixel-by-160-pixel display of a PDA, the user has an amount of workspace comparable to that of a laptop computer. This means that a lot of the design restrictions common to PDAs do not apply to tablet PCs.

Ken Hinckley et. al.[9] have proposed a series of features for portable computing devices, including tablet PCs, that are aimed at increasing the usability of such devices through the inclusion of sensors. The basic premise of their paper "Sensing Techniques for Mobile Interactions" is that wireless computing devices can be made more usable if they become "context aware"; that is, a device should function according to how the user interacts with it. For example, if a user picks up a tablet PC and holds it close to their face, the tablet PC could "know" to switch into voice memo mode or the screen could self-magnify. If the user turns the tablet from landscape to portrait mode, the video driver should know to turn the video to match the orientation. Tilting the tablet should allow for scrolling the display in the "correct" direction.

---

[9] See *http://research.microsoft.com/users/kenh/papers/PPC-Sensing_color.pdf.*

Troubleshooting content that is designed to be displayed on a tablet PC is not as complicated as troubleshooting on many other sorts of portable computing devices. This is primarily because the software that drives tablet PCs is usually widely known, and usability testing at the operating system level has already occurred. Additionally, many problems that occur with smaller devices do not occur with tablets, since their displays are often the same size and resolution as a laptop PC. The version of the browser that is used may be an issue, however, since some tablets run a "lite" operating system like Windows CE. Internet Explorer for Windows CE does not have as complete a feature set as the full version.

CHAPTER SUMMARY

Tablet PCs have been in the imagination of inventors and futurists for decades, but the technology that can produce such a creation is finally available today. Browsing Web content with a tablet PC is similar in experience to browsing with a "standard" desktop or laptop PC. However, significant differences exist in the means of interfacing with a tablet PC. Furthermore, the computation power and other resources available in this form factor are usually significantly less than those available in desktop and laptop PCs.

HANDS ON

1. Mock up a paper prototype of a tablet PC. What sorts of controls should be dedicated to buttons on the device, and which should be offered in software instead?

2. Discussion: Besides stylus input, what other mechanisms for tablet PCs could increase their usability?

3. Discussion: What sorts of environments and users could benefit the most from a tablet PC? Why? Where would table PCs be impractical? Why?

12

A CASE STUDY

It's one thing to theorize ad nauseam about any given topic, but it's quite another to actually do something about it. The account presented in this chapter is intended to illustrate how the information in this book might actually be implemented. The company, people, and actions described are all fictitious; however, all the components have been drawn from actual experience. The reader will note that in the example testing scenario described in this chapter, the fictional team has been given a goodly amount of fancy equipment. This was done partly to reflect the capital equipment outlay that many companies made during the Internet Boom. It should be stressed that the extra goodies mentioned in this chapter are not strictly necessary but should give you an idea of what you can accomplish with a reasonable budget.

Please note that detailed implementation for the test plan itself has not been provided in this chapter; but some of the information can be found in Appendix B: Usability Testing, as well as in the *Web Site Usability Handbook*. In Appendix C there is also a sample plan to use as a guide.

Let's begin by meeting the cast of this chapter. Our usability trials take place in the city of Springfield at a software company called Xolax Software. Xolax employs a small team of four full-time usability experts.

Traditionally, these experts have been assigned the task of making sure that the company's corporate Web site and intranet are usable by the respective user populations (customers and employees). Recently, however, they have been charged with the monumental task of making sure that their corporate intranet is usable and accessible via handheld wireless devices. Sales and marketing needs to be able to pull up information from the intranet on their Palm VIIs from any location inside the various Xolax campus buildings as well as outside company walls. Engineers need to be able to pull up bug reports on their tablet-style PCs from anywhere in the company. Finally, customers need to be able to access certain parts of the Xolax Web site via BlackBerry, specifically via the RIM 957 and 857 model interactive pagers. The usability team has been charged with making this process as intuitive and easy to use as the "regular" Web interface everyone is used to.

Heading up the usability team is Ruth, who came to usability via Web design. Ruth has logged countless hours in Web site production, design, management, and, most recently, usability testing. She typically functions as the test monitor and plays a substantial role in drafting usability test plans. She also interfaces with senior management to gather design requirements and feedback on the redesign process. She is responsible for relaying the findings of the usability group to the design groups— not always an enviable task.

Eduardo is a technically minded fellow whose background is in video and audio engineering. He initially came to Xolax as a contractor responsible for designing and setting up the new usability testing lab's video and audio equipment. Intrigued with the work that went on in the lab, he applied for a full-time position with Xolax and has since added much to his technical arsenal, including a great working knowledge of a variety of portable computing devices. He has contributed to the group in a variety of ways and is a sort of "jack of all trades."

Xia, who holds a master's degree in human-computer interaction from a well-known program at a famous university, came to Xolax as a seasoned

FIGURE 12.1 *Xia, the HCI/stats guru.*

UI guru (Figure 12.1). Her previous work focused on the user interfaces of many sorts of devices, ranging from small, integrated appliances to control consoles for computerized industrial machinery. She is a scientific person but also has a penchant for art, which makes her perfect for this position. Her ability to "think out of the box," abandoning the rational and taking up the improbable when needed, affords her the ability to problem-solve quite well.

Johan was originally on the marketing team at Xolax but made a major move to the usability team after being frustrated with his interactions with customers who weren't getting the type of experience from Xolax products they were expecting (Figure 12.2). He began to see how important the customer's experience with the software was to the bottom line of the company and independently came to the conclusion

FIGURE 12.2 *Johan, the group's marketing mind.*

that designing from the perspective of the user—not from a sales and marketing perspective—was the key to happy customers. When he found out that Xolax had a usability team, he signed on as both the liaison to major customer accounts and as an active participant in the execution of usability testing plans.

Xolax's fledgling Web usability division has gone from being a rag-tag bunch with little support from senior management to an integral part of the company's philosophy. This development owes largely to the huge progress the team has made in forging better customer relationships by providing better interfaces and Web content. The recent addition of a decent testing lab complete with video equipment heralded the significance of the group. Now all eyes are turned on them as they attempt to empirically improve the usability and accessibility of their various sites via a handful of assorted mobile computing devices.

INITIAL DESIGN

Long before the first page of content is created, the usability team will engage in groundwork that will help them fashion a more usable product from the start. It's important to remember that usability is not merely an afterthought applied only to broken systems. It is, instead, a comprehensive philosophy that permeates the entire design life cycle.

Xia and Ruth schedule a series of site visits to perform field studies of the sales/marketing and engineering groups at Xolax. They have a joint purpose of observing how these groups currently interact with existing systems and of developing a working dictionary of user terminology for tasks and related information. These site visits are relatively informal; Xia and Ruth really just want to hang out with the various groups and observe them doing what they normally do, while being as noninvasive and inconspicuous as possible. They will occasionally ask questions aimed at uncovering the meaning of certain interactions they are unfamiliar with. They realize how important it is for the team to get a good feel for the current work-flow system, since this knowledge will help them understand how to adapt the system to this new set of media. Moreover, building a dictionary of user terminology will enable the usability team to observe one of the most important laws of usability: speak the user's language. They are fully aware that many usability problems can result when designers use nomenclature that is incongruent with the user's familiar world. Leveraging the user's own language speeds up the learning process, since there will be fewer new words to learn—or old words to unlearn.

The team repeats this process for the client's participants. They perform the same site visits (after signing nondisclosure agreements from the client's legal department) and also create a dictionary of user terms. Additionally, they learn a lot about how their client operates. Many of the client's corporate culture quirks come out in the visit, which helps the team head off some potential conflicts and ambiguities. The hidden agenda behind the site visit is for the usability team to serve as a sort of ambassadorship from Xolax in order to spread a sense of goodwill to the client. Since Xolax is involving the customer in the design process, the hope is that this will instill a sense of confidence and appreciation in the customer. Few companies extend this sort of quality of service to clients, so Xolax's approach differentiates it from the masses.

Once Xia and Ruth have gathered information regarding how the groups currently operate, and once they have assembled a vocabulary of user terms, they are ready to begin thinking about the content designs from the ground up. The group has inherited existing intranet site designs that were originally created quickly, probably in response to some last-minute need. Although the designs are in woeful shape and in need of a complete overhaul, management is loath to authorize such an overhaul. But the team has a plan. They are going to measure the usability of all the intranet subsites, implement changes on their test Web server, then run the same set of tests again with different participants.[1] Based on their findings, they anticipate that whatever changes they implement will elicit a dramatic increase in usability. They then hope to use this data to fuel accord within management for a total site overhaul. The team realizes that they must always keep a running total of how much they believe the changes, if implemented, will impact the bottom line. Speaking the universal language of business—money—will help them communicate the importance of the usability trials to upper management. This modus operandi is what has enabled the group to grow and obtain additional funding: they are now seen as a significant cost-saving point in the organization. It will largely be up to Xia to show the return on investment for the trials.

Step One: The Plan

Over the course of a week, the group meets frequently to discuss the technical details, staging, and timeline for the upcoming usability trials. During this time, they craft and refine a comprehensive usability plan that covers all of the devices and all of the content—an ambitious goal,

---

[1] A quiz for those of you who've read the *Web Site Usability Handbook*: Why use a different set of participants? Shouldn't the team stay with the same group to make sure that they are measuring apples and apples?

but they are under extreme duress. Senior management has set deadlines for this project to be completed, so the group needs to meet them. In short, the plan consists of two branches: one that will focus on the intranet content and another that will focus on the regular Web site content for one of Xolax's major customers. In this branch of study, the team will measure the usability of some Xolax proprietary search technology they have designed for the customer to intelligently index their immense content. The search engine itself is housed on Xolax's premises, which connects to the client's computing infrastructure over a high-speed, private fiber-optic link.

The participants for the studies will come from two different sources. Participants in the study on external content for the customer will come from a random pool of employees at the customer's site. The human resources department at the customer's headquarters has agreed to help in this capacity. Participants for the intranet testing will come entirely from inside the company. Both of these selections make sense, since each sample is truly representative of the population being served. The team also briefly discussed bringing complete novice users in from outside recruiting firms in order to accurately measure the outlying data points. They expected to select participants randomly among the eligible candidates; that is, special care would have been taken to select a cross-section of men, women, people from different age groups, and so on. This random selection is necessary in order to reduce the possibility of confounding variables, or traits that are common to a group that can have the effect of skewing data unnaturally. Such confounding variables can poison an entire study.

Because of problems with nondisclosure agreements, however, this notion is quickly abandoned, and the group gets permission to allow nontechnical people from inside each respective organization to participate. These users, who have no previous experience with any of the devices or content and, in some cases, little to no experience with electronic devices or computers in general, are inelegantly called "least competent users" by some texts. The group uses the notation "ultra novice" as a slightly less disparaging label. The data points collected from these users are likely to represent the absolute bottom end in terms of successes at the prescribed usability tasks. The reason they are included in the study is to show that if they are able to get around at all, experienced users are likely to get on pretty well.

The team drafts up the final testing plan, which then becomes the blueprint for the remaining weeks of trials. It contains the operationalization of all the steps in the process, which helps keep all the members "on the same page" with regard to timelines, expectations, and responsibilities. The plan is used to describe all the needed resources, deliverables, and schedules for usability testing. At the end of the trials, the results will be tabulated, data will be transformed into meaningful pointers, and recommendations for change will be made to the development teams. Then the whole process will begin again. The second round, however, (as well as a third round, if needed for this release cycle) should, at least in theory, be much shorter than the first, since most of the serious usability issues will have been weeded out in the first round. Of course, electronic content is never "done," but may just be at a stage that is fit for customer consumption.

This test plan is going to be unlike any previous one, since most of the task scenarios are going to be real-world—they will be conducted in the myriad places around the Xolax campus where users wander, and, in the case of the external Web content, the participants will be in a variety of places outside the company walls. The team calls the various routes "obstacle courses," since each location on the route has been selected because it reflects some real-world barrier, like high ambient noise or poor signal strength.[2] This has several implications for the test design. First, the test monitor will have to accompany each participant along the course in order to accurately record information, like the time to com-

---

[2] Strictly speaking, this is a nonscientific study design. By not holding all other variables constant (called "experimental control"), the team is making it harder to determine whether the environment or the task influenced the outcome. However, through debriefing, the team can do a fair job of figuring out what happened, and the rapid time required to implement does not allow for more thorough design. Xian has explained this to the team, and they understand the implications before they break the rules.

plete each task. A large amount of data, however, will have to be self-reported. Because of this fact, the test plan needs to have validation built in to assess whether a participant might be "stretching the truth." Finally, there will need to be plenty of time for debriefing the participants and gathering as much qualitative data as possible, since some traditional quantitative data will be unavailable.

The test plan itself is put through the process of approval by senior level management, which the team has been able to minimize by interacting with one key officer who understands the point of usability. Since Xolax is very concerned with liability, the team must also gain the approval of an outside consulting firm that reviews the test plan for any ethical problems. Fortunately, the team has observed the code of ethical behavior in their test plan, and everything checks out fine. It's time to move on to step two of the process.

The plan goes through a dry run with others who are involved with the team; that is, several outsiders read the test questions to see if they make sense. This helps weed out the unpleasant surprise of being at the actual tests and discovering that a question makes no sense as it is worded—or even worse, that a question does not have a solution. Heading off problems like these early in the process helps ensure that things will go smoothly during the actual testing.

Step Two: Equipping for Testing

Although the group has a decent amount of equipment at their disposal, no one in the group currently has any of the various devices that are going to be targeted for usability studies. Furthermore, after quite a bit of discussion, the team realizes that they don't have an effective way of presenting findings to senior staff or the development teams. They aren't aware of a way to take screen shots of any of the devices except the tablet PCs, which have a native screen shot function in the Windows CE operating system. Finally, they'll need to establish service for each of the device types and purchase any sort of software needed to run the wireless device content service. Eduardo volunteers to head up the first phase of acquiring the necessary resources.

Initially, Eduardo calls a handful of vendors to see if they have loaner programs for people involved in usability studies of their product; to his dismay, it appears as if no one is foresighted enough to understand how immensely this could benefit their company, as no one has such a program. Even though Eduardo offers to rent the devices for the duration of the trials—since it is easier to get an internal requisition for a rental of equipment than it is to get a requisition for capital equipment outlay—he still has no luck. Nobody has rental programs for their devices, either. Eduardo shares his findings with the rest of the group, and they decide to push through the request to purchase the equipment outright, justifying the expense by amortizing it over the next year and a half. Since these devices represent supported platforms, it makes sense for the group to have some on hand.

Eduardo calls up the director of engineering to ask about the types of devices engineering is using and finds out that they are using Fujitsu tablet PCs. Eduardo communicates with the assistant in charge of placing the orders and puts in a request for two tablets on the next order. Next on the list are the RIM interactive pagers, which he orders from a nationwide service provider, who also activates the devices with wireless Web service. Eduardo discovers that the company provides special pricing for developers for sixty days[3] and takes advantage of this break to lower the operating cost for the trials. He orders two each of the RIM pager models 957 and 857. The 957 has a large display that rivals the display of the Palm—160 pixels by 160 pixels, but monochrome. The 857 is smaller, more like a traditional pager. Both feature a QWERTY keyboard and a trackwheel that serves as a mouse-like device.

The group decides that they are going to want to use screen shots for most of the devices in action in their reports, mainly to help the developers and senior staff visually understand the various problems they find. But since not all of them support some internal method for capturing the screen, they settle on a workaround: using a special document

---

[3] As of this writing, this is absolutely true of RIM. Your time may vary; check with the company to see if they still honor this.

camera to capture the screen on "real live" devices, and using software emulators on Ruth's laptop for some screen shots. Eduardo orders the document camera and integrates it into the testing lab's A/V setup.

The last thing that Eduardo decides to add to the list of equipment is a portable DAT recorder for the purpose of recording participant chatter during the usability trial. Since it will be too burdensome to videotape the trials, the team has decided that, at the bare minimum, they would like a high-quality audio recording of each session. After quite a bit of shopping around, Eduardo settles on a portable DAT recorder because standard analog audiocassette recorders are simply too noisy. The DAT player can accept a high-quality microphone as an input source, and the output is much better than the cassette alternative. Additionally, the digital audio output will work with the existing A/V setup, and Eduardo plans on extracting key bits of the participants' self-talk, saving it as an MP3, and integrating it into the slide show presentation the team will assemble at the end of the trials. The participants will be notified that they are being audiotaped, and any participant who requests it can have their voice put through a digital voice changer to preserve their identity.

Step Three: Preparing for Testing

After a great deal of coordinating with the human resources departments at Xolax and the customer's site, the usability team is able to schedule a total of twenty-five participants over the course of a week for the intranet study, and twenty participants over a second week for the external customer content. The participants will overlap somewhat, since there are not enough devices to go around for multiple sessions to run concurrently. The internal testing participants (called Group 1) will be using the Palm VIIs and Fujitsu tablet PCs, while the external testing participants (Group 2) will use the two models of the RIM interactive pagers. No single session is scheduled to last more than an hour, which is just about the right amount of time for both the participant and the test monitor. No more than five participants are scheduled each day, since scheduling more than this number can cause excessive strain and fatigue for the test monitor. The group decides that in order to maintain this aggressive schedule, both Ruth and Xia will act as test monitors. Although Xia typically does not fill this role, she has seen Ruth enact it many times, and she has sufficient interpersonal communication skills to competently perform the job. The group knows how important the test monitor can be in ensuring a successful round of trials.

The team reserves a room in the main campus that will serve as a check-in point for Group 1 during the first week of trials. The room is easy to find, but the other workers in the area are notified that the usability trials will be going on so that they will be prepared to direct any partici-pant experiencing trouble finding the location—thereby helping to min-imize that participant's stress. The team also arranges for a variety of refreshments to be brought in throughout the day for participants. Caf-feinated beverages are avoided, since excessive consumption of caffeine can cause participants to become even more nervous and agitated than they already are; this can affect performance and add a confounding variable into the mix.

Participant compensation is always an important part of usability test-ing, so the team obtains permission from Xolax headquarters to com-pensate each participant with a free vacation day as well as a chance to win a brand-new PDA. These attractive incentives ensure that they have plenty of willing participants.

At the monthly company meeting, the usability team presents a short slide show about the upcoming usability trials and explains the proce-dure, desired outcome, and impact that usability has on the bottom line. These monthly meetings provide the team with a venue for educating the whole company about the value of usability, which in turn makes it easier for the team to gain access to much-needed resources.

Johan schedules a meeting with their client and delivers a similar presen-tation; however, the direction of the presentation is different. This client has never seen usability testing in action before and does not know the value of it. Johan therefore makes a point of carefully explaining how Xolax is committed to creating the most user-friendly interfaces for their clients, and he explains how usability testing helps ensure that goal is met. The whole process is explained so that the client understands what to expect. Everyone at the client site is made aware of the fact that usability testing does not test the user, but rather the content. This helps alleviate any anxiety potential participants might feel. This premise is repeated on the actual day of testing during orientation.

The team has assembled a database of potential participants that they import into FileMaker Pro, although virtually any database program would work. Xia writes a quick script that randomly selects entries from the database—a total of thirty-five for the internal trials and thirty for the external trials—in order to allow for some of those people to opt not to participate while ensuring that the study retains the requisite number of participants. Once the participants are chosen randomly, they are each contacted by one of the team members and given a brief phone screening. The screening is designed to make sure that potential participants don't fall into one of the ineligible categories (the team decides that participants shouldn't have any substantial Web design or usability experience) and to confirm the participants' self-reported data about their relative experience levels. The team knows first-hand that sometimes a participant will self-rate a category like computer use experience much higher or lower than actually is the case. They realize how important it is to be able to properly profile participants when assembling final result data.

The team also decides ahead of time how they will handle participants who don't show up, who show up late, or who don't finish all the assigned tasks. The team has clearance from management to withhold any compensation from participants if they fail to show up on time and perform all tasks to the best of their ability. The participants are made aware of these restrictions during the phone screening and reminded of them during their orientation. That way, expectations are set appropriately and communicated properly.

Step Four: The Actual Testing

When the first day of the actual trials arrives, the team simply follows the testing plan. Although there are two discrete groups of participants and two discrete test plans, the same check-in point is used. Johan is stationed at the meeting point lounge, where he meets each participant upon arrival. Johan checks the participant in, notes the arrival time, and checks to see whether Ruth or Xia will be the participant's test moderator. Johan leads each participant through orientation, which consists of a set of questions, background information, and tasks that prepare the participant for the trials. He asks each participant to take the pretest questionnaire and to answer each question completely. The questionnaire is relatively short, since it has been designed to be completed in under five minutes; the team knows that few people show up on time and even fewer arrive early.

Although the questionnaire contains a minor internal validity check (to make sure the participants aren't fibbing on the self-reports), a handful of other quick tasks that the participants are asked to complete after the main trials and before they leave the testing lab are designed to weed out those who simply don't have a grasp of the way things work or who may have stretched the truth on the self-reports. Participants may misrepresent themselves on the self-reports for a number of reasons: some may not be able to accurately gauge their own standing with regard to some scales; others might inflate scores for egoistic reasons. Whatever the case, the team knows that self-reported data is really just a starting point and should never be taken as 100 percent accurate.

The usability team makes it absolutely clear to each participant that their individual results are not going to be reviewed by anyone outside of the usability team, and that their individual data will never be correlated to their real name, employee ID, or any other distinguishing information. This is done to allay any participant fears that their superiors might use the data acquired during the testing as justification to lay off or fire those who "don't do well." Each participant is made aware of the complete anonymity of the results and is told that participation in the trials is completely voluntary and that anyone who feels uncomfortable should communicate this immediately to the test moderator.

Johan explains that parts of the session will be audiotaped and that parts of the debriefing will be videotaped. He then obtains written permission from each participant to do so. Johan tells the participants that the videos will be destroyed after the team has had a chance to review them for accuracy and to double-check phrases and actions against the transcription of the session. Audio will be altered using a voice-changer so that individuals cannot be identified by voice. All of these safeguards are communicated as being ways that the team helps protect the anonymity of the participants. Johan stresses that it is important for each participant to avoid discussing the results of the trial with anyone outside the group, since this could allow identification of a particular participant through the process of elimination.[4]

Finally, the participants are asked if they have any questions about the whole process that is about to take place, and Johan makes it clear that from this point on, the team cannot answer any questions except to clarify the meaning of a poorly worded question. (Of course, this sort of problem will hopefully have been headed off early on by the team.) If the participants have no questions, Johan summons the appropriate test monitor to the lounge.

The monitor greets each participant,[5] hands them the appropriate wireless device, and proceeds to the first point on the "obstacle course." From there, the monitor simply follows the test plan and guides the participant from location to location. Each section of the test plan has carefully crafted scripts, precise instructions that the test monitor must give the participant for each task. The test monitor may find it necessary to periodically reassure participants who find the trials frustrating. The test monitor records as much information as possible, which will be transcribed onto a form once the session is complete.

---

[4] If this sounds paranoid, it is. Just imagine how you would feel if one of your participants got fired because of your work—even if you did everything you could to preserve anonymity. This can be a career-ending move for you and the participant.
[5] Generally, most parts of the test monitor's side of the participant-monitor dialogue should be scripted, but leading off with a corny, canned greeting can flatten the experience for the participant and result in a lot of discomfort.

Step Five: The Debriefing

Although the debriefing is technically a part of the test plan proper, it's important to mention it here as well. During debriefing, participants are given the opportunity to ask any questions or express concerns about anything that felt uncomfortable during the trial. This is also a time for the test monitor to gather as much qualitative information from the participant as possible by asking probing questions about particular tasks. If the test monitor observes that a particular task presented an abnormally strong challenge to the participant, the monitor will ask the participant what they thought was hard about the task. Usually, the best possible information comes out during this debriefing period; all feedback is audiorecorded for detailed analysis after the session is over (see Figure 12.3).

FIGURE 12.3 *Xia and a participant chat during the debriefing. Xia has to remember to listen closely for any important information the participant has to offer.*

One of the most important parts of the debriefing process is when the participant is asked to share any thoughts or feelings about the trials, particularly about any tasks that seemed really difficult or impossible to accomplish. Since this part of the session is unstructured, virtually anything can happen, and the test monitor has to be efficient at capturing the participant's thoughts. For this reason, many test monitors videotape or audiotape the participant's commentary. Before making a video- or audiotape, of course, the test monitor must get written permission from the participant to do so during orientation.

Step Six: Assembling the Data

Once all the test trials are over, the usability team will need to assemble the data into some sort of coherent picture. Some of the important data points collected will include the number of participants who "failed" or "passed" each task on the test plan. If the team sees a trend for a task—like a high number of failures—they know that they need to drill down into the nature of those failures. Usually, the test monitor will hear about particularly difficult tasks from participants during the debriefing session. Often, this will provide all the details necessary to make a recommendation for change.

The team will seek to answer the primary questions asked by the test plan, and they will also attempt to delve further into specific areas that need more work. The final output of the report should be a succinct analysis on the usability health of the system as it stands, as well as what changes need to be implemented in order to effect the highest possible level of usability. Once Ruth has made this report to senior management, management make decisions about the next steps the company will take based on the team's work. Ruth and the team convince management to implement changes based upon their usability study. Once the new changes have been implemented, the team repeats the usability test on the new, improved site. Since they have a baseline of usability from the previous site, they can show progress against the earlier benchmarks. But that, of course, is another story!

THE ITERATIVE REDESIGN PROCESS

So the team is done and can all go home now, right? Fortunately, no. As you probably know, a Web site, whether it's designed for traditional Web browsing or for wireless Web access, is always a work in progress. New iterations of the content are introduced all the time; new features are added and old, obsolete features are removed. Each phase of new design has to be tested to ensure the highest level of usability.

Since it isn't practical to run a complete comprehensive usability test for each minor change made on the Web sites, the team proposes to management that they follow a schedule for testing. A comprehensive usability test plan will be executed twice a year at the minimum, and each time a major modification is made to the sites the team will stage a series of trials that focus solely on the new modifications and their integration into the rest of the site. This way, few usability problems will slip through the cracks, but the team won't get buried under work.

PUBLISHING THE FINDINGS

Many companies have very strict policies regarding the control of research conducted within company walls, and Xolax is no different. If a competitor were to gain access to an uncensored usability test plan and its results, it could mean that the competitor could gain material inside knowledge of Xolax's workings and projects. So, like most companies, Xolax upholds a very high level of secrecy for all usability test results.

Xolax, however, is also seen as an industry leader in the area of wireless usability, which is beneficial to the company in many ways. The trends they establish become de facto industry standards, which then put them in a position of power. The company's visibility in the usability arena also inspires customer confidence, which translates quickly into the bottom line. Since Xolax management recognizes the benefit that this visibility buys the company, they encourage the team to participate in usability conferences, seminars, working groups, and other usability/accessibility efforts outside the company.

This officially "blessed" participation also allows the team to publish carefully crafted versions of their usability findings. These reports are designed in such a way as not to give away the names of their clients (nor allow for guessing of the client's name). The reports do, however, describe usability barriers that are discovered and what the team has done to overcome them through redesign and adaptation. Screen shots are supplied to illustrate points in the reports; however, the shots are crafted so as to illustrate the point without revealing inside information to the reader. Privacy is a major concern with this sort of endeavor, and so a panel of volunteers at Xolax agrees to review all proposals for publication to ensure that they are "safe" for both Xolax and customers alike.

Publication of findings helps everyone in the usability business, although at the time of this writing, there is virtually no literature available via the Web regarding wireless device usability other than anecdotal blurbs. Visibility of usability documentation also helps the people in the field of usability, since it provides them with leverage to justify recommendations for change.

13

The Future of Pervasive Computing

Although this book is nearly at an end, it has only scratched the surface of the vast topic of creating usable systems for pervasive computing devices. It should, however, provide you with a framework that will allow you to assess the usability of virtually any system—even those that may not have existed at the time of writing—the breakneck speed at which new types of technologies, manufacturing techniques, and ways to implement devices change will undoubtedly give rise to challenges we can only guess at. Many developments currently in the works will have a profound impact on the way mobile computing devices are made and used, and as these things change, you, as a usability expert, must draw upon the material given to create up-to-date techniques for your usability metrics. Remember that even if the heuristics themselves change, most of the basic tools of usability—the heuristic evaluation, classical usability testing, the interview, field studies, and so on—will remain constant. This final chapter focuses on some up-and-coming technologies that will have an impact on computing devices and on how these technologies might impact usability and accessibility. It will also focus briefly on a handful of sociological, philosophical, and technological issues that will probably impact wireless computing.

OLED DISPLAYS

As mentioned earlier, OLEDs (organic light-emitting diodes) are a relatively new invention that could eventually replace computer LCDs. OLEDs, which are already being used in many consumer electronics, like stereo systems and cellular telephones, offer a wealth of advantages over their nonorganic counterparts. OLEDs use organic polymers as their light-generating source; unlike conventional LCDs, which require backlighting as well as color-generating cells, OLEDs actually generate light in addition to creating color. This characteristic, along with other physical properties, allows OLEDs to generate an equivalent amount of light at a significantly lower amount of energy consumption. This translates into extended battery life, as well as a more cost-effective device.

OLEDs can also be manufactured in such a way that they can be used in a flexible substrate, meaning that a display can be folded, twisted, reshaped, and generally fit to a particular space requirement. A future in which your house could be wallpapered in flexible OLED display sheeting that could be changed as easily as a screensaver by your central home computer may not be too far off!

MICRODISPLAYS

Those cute little heads-up displays worn by the Borg on Star Trek aren't just fiction any more. Several companies have now produced head-worn display systems that project a computer screen image onto a tiny microdisplay that floats just in front of the eyes. The end result is that the user "sees" a virtual PC screen that appears to be floating in front of them—at a size of about 75". This sort of head-worn display can take on many shapes and forms, ranging from goggles (reminiscent of those worn while playing virtual reality games) to little flip-down eyepieces to displays that actually project directly onto the viewer's retina. A surgeon might wear a heads-up microdisplay that superimposes imaging data obtained through an MRI (magnetic resonance imaging) scan onto the patient during a procedure, thus becoming privy to a sort of x-ray vision. In a much less life-or-death scenario, a heads-up display might be used to give video games a new level of realism.

This sort of display technology clearly is interesting to organizations like the military, but it can also be applied in a myriad other settings. The implication for usability is that a new mode of interaction will come to be as soon as this technology is mature. Specifically, usability specialists will need to look at the interactions users have between the computer "foreground" and the real-world "background."

ENHANCED BATTERY TECHNOLOGY

Although batteries aren't exactly the most interesting part of any kind of portable device, they are often a limiting factor in many ways. Batteries can be heavy, bulky, expensive, and restrictive. The inefficiency of conventional battery technology has limited the growth of portable technology in many ways. Admittedly, we've come a long way even from the giant lead-acid-gel battery in the Macintosh Portable to the slim, rechargeable batteries found in many sleek, ultra-thin laptops. Nevertheless, advances in battery technology have not come close to keeping up with advances in other technological areas. New innovations in battery design may overcome this limitation in the near future, however.

One such innovation is the project recently undertaken by Motorola and the Los Alamos National Laboratory, which seeks to make use of miniature fuel cells as a replacement for conventional batteries. In general, a fuel cell converts chemical energy directly into electrical energy. Typically, hydrogen is used as the fuel source in the cells, but researchers in this joint project have been able to use inexpensive and relatively safe liquid methanol (wood alcohol). The cells "breathe" in order to combine air and the fuel source, which in turn generates the electrical energy.

One problem with fuel cells is that they generally produce voltage levels that are too low for use without stacking them deep enough that the benefit of their small size is undone. Unique circuitry produced by Motorola, however, has enabled the fuel cells to efficiently get "pumped up" to usable voltage levels. The life span of such fuel cells is much greater than that of an average rechargeable battery; a typical cell phone, for example, could be powered for a month on a single cell.[1] As advances in this area step up, it could be possible within the decade to see fuel cell technology become the de facto replacement for conventional batteries. The major challenges that remain for fuel cell technology are cost and size: it has to be cheaper to manufacture and use fuel cells than batteries, and they have to be smaller and lighter than existing batteries to gain widespread acceptance.

QUANTUM COMPUTING

There are many physical laws of the universe that put a hard cap on the limits of computing, assuming we continue with computing architectures that use silicon and electricity. Scientists, however, see a new, phenomenal brand of computing on the horizon: quantum computing, which uses photons or other tiny particles as bits. Such quantum bits are known as "qubits." Although the large-scale implementation of quantum computers is not quite at hand, the principles of quantum computing are fairly well understood. In traditional computers, a bit is truly binary: it can only be in one state or another at any given time. In contrast, a qubit can be in more than one state at a time—a concept that is admittedly difficult to grasp, even for world-renowned physicists— which makes the number of computations that a qubit can participate in dramatically larger than its binary cousin. To put it in perspective, a quantum computer that consists only of around 500 qubits would be able to simultaneously compute the results of 2^{500} "states"—that is, combinations of binary 1s and 0s—simultaneously. The number 2^{500} represents a 1 followed by 150 zeroes, which is larger than the number of atoms in the universe. This means that a quantum computer can compute things that were previously utterly unimaginable—so much so that humankind can only grasp at the most elementary uses of such a vast power. Quantum computing is certainly going to be a part of the

---

[1] See *www.dpreview.com/news/0001/00012004motorolabatt.asp.*

next generation of computing, and it will also underscore the vast gap between humankind's technology and humankind's maturity as a race.

WIRELESS ACCESS

As of this writing, the wireless network infrastructure in most parts of the world is in its infancy. Different devices gain access to the Internet wirelessly through a variety of means, such as cellular telephone bands, packet radio, and satellites. However, no single wireless standard is as pervasive and consistent throughout the entire planet as Ethernet has become for wired net access. Wireless access is also less available than its wired counterpart: typically, only major metropolitan areas[2] feature any sort of wireless access that is not borne over the cellular telephone network. For example, Ricochet radio modem service, which features a top speed of 128 kilobits per second, is available in a very small number of cities in the United States. Of the handful of areas that do feature this service, even fewer have the high-speed 128 kbit service. It is very likely that over the next few years, wireless network availability will increase.

WIDESPREAD STANDARDS

As more and more service providers enable wireless Web activity through high-speed wireless data networks, it will be absolutely critical for vendors to adopt standards for data transmission, content format, and most other aspects of end-to-end delivery of data. Additionally, some degree of standardization will have to be attained by vendors in the way of operating systems, feature sets, and nomenclature for their devices. It is not being suggested that everyone should run WinCE, but the general public's interest is not necessarily being served by every PDA, pager, tablet, and cell phone vendor running proprietary and generally very different operating systems and application software.

The hallmark of next-generation wireless information devices will be their ability to be pervasive: that is, their ability to go anywhere and be

---

[2] At least in the United States this is the case.

part of anything. Thermostats will communicate wirelessly with a home automation controller. Bluetooth-enabled devices and applications will cooperate with each other across short distances. Field workers will interact with each other across great distances.

SECURITY AND PRIVACY ISSUES

Increasingly, information is one of the most highly valued resources that the "civilized" world has. Data security has become a topic of extreme import over the past decade. In many cases it has become effortless to obtain vast amounts of data that would have been nearly inaccessible to all but an elite few prior to electronic data storage and the widespread availability of Internet access. Added to this mixture the fact that much of this private data is unencrypted and possible to record with only commodity electronics and a small amount of modifications and know-how. According to Forbes.com, for example, two system crackers[3] used a makeshift getup to eavesdrop on Sun Microsystem's wireless network while sitting in the company's parking lot.[4]

Recent studies of attacks on the most commonly used encryption in wireless networks, called WEP (Wired Equivalent Privacy), moreover, have shown the standard to be seriously flawed, allowing off-the-shelf hardware to be used to decrypt traffic through unauthorized means.[5] This is very serious indeed, since, unfortunately, technologies like encryption often falsely lull users into a sense of safety, which in turn usually elicits a loosening of other common-sense security measures. The net result is a very weak spot in the chain of defense against information thieves. In the 1980s every computer neophyte who saw the

---

[3] The term "hacker" has been consciously avoided here. Originally it denoted a highly skilled programmer or just someone who loved taking things apart and learning how they worked. The media has perverted the term, however, through repeatedly using it to refer to someone who hacks, often without much skill, for personal gain.

[4] See *www.forbes.com/2001/05/22/0522wireless.html.*

[5] See *www.pcworld.com/news/article/0,aid,40442,00.asp;* for more information about the specific vulnerabilities in the WEP protocol, see *www.isaac.cs.berkeley.edu/isaac/wep-faq.html.*

movie *War Games* came to understand how to discover phone lines that responded with a modem carrier tone by programmatically dialing every number within a given area code and exchange. Once these "war dialers" found a few modem lines, it was only a matter of time before social engineering, cunning, and brute force allowed them to gain access to valuable information.

War dialing isn't quite as popular as it used to be, primarily because poorly defended systems are now available to the Internet at large, not just those with the proper software and time to kill. A new variation on this pastime has emerged recently, however: war driving. As the number of personal and corporate wireless networks grows, the number of poorly configured and easily penetrable systems available for cracking via radio frequency also grows. Crackers with a modicum of equipment can drive around areas likely to host wireless networks and see what they can get into. Many wireless networks are easy to gain access to—just stand reasonably close to the suspected location of the base station, plug in a wireless Ethernet card, and tune in. Some software packages include wireless Ethernet "sniffers" that allow an attacker to analyze traffic on a wireless network (including clear-text POP3 passwords, telnet passwords, or any other unencrypted data), often with bountiful rewards.

Securing wireless data transmission is vital to the longevity and success of wireless data communication. Without robust, widely implemented encryption, wireless data transactions will become as publicly accessible as ham radio conversations. Traditional wired networks impose at least a tiny amount of a deterrent to would-be snoopers, in that access to the wired network is needed to get at the coveted bits. On the other hand, anyone with a modified receiver, a laptop, and some software can intercept your phone calls—voice or data—and steal your information, without your ever knowing anything about it. Over-the-air communication has suffered this flaw since the invention of long-distance communication, and the race has been on ever since: code makers trying to outwit code breakers, and vice versa.

Suffice it to say that securing the wireless Internet is a major obstacle to both the longevity and short-term acceptance of mobile computing solutions as mainstream technology. Data encryption is outside the scope of this book, but nonetheless remains an important issue to keep in mind. The usability of a system can be affected adversely if the users of the system inherently distrust its capability for security. Would you conduct a banking transaction over a wireless computing device if you suspected that someone nearby was sniffing your wireless traffic? Probably not, if your transaction were completely in plain-text (unencrypted). If the transmission itself were encrypted up to the point of the base station (wireless receiver) but was then in plain-text for the rest of the transmission, how confident would you feel about that transaction? It's likely that a winning combination of encryption will involve encryption on both the transmission protocol—whatever wireless communication method is used—and at the application level as well.

The widespread use of mobile computing has enormous implications in the area of personal privacy. If transmitted data is unsecured, then personal data and identity theft will become even more rampant than it is slated to become in the near future. Wireless devices can become a weak link in the chain mesh that keeps thieves out of our personal identity space. So what do thieves do with a person's identity once they have stolen it? According to a study conducted by the U.S. government, stolen data is primarily used to accomplish goals in one of the following four areas:[6]

- **Credit card fraud:** Approximately 54% of consumers reported credit card fraud; i.e., a credit card account opened in their name or a "takeover" of their existing credit card account.

- **Communications services fraud:** Approximately 26% reported that the identity thief opened up telephone, cellular, or other utility service in their name.

- **Bank fraud:** Approximately 16% reported that a checking or savings account had been opened in their name and/or that fraudulent checks had been written.

---

[6] See *www.ftc.gov/os/2000/07/idtheft.htm.*

- **Fraudulent loans:** Approximately 11% reported that the identity thief obtained a loan, such as a car loan, in their name.

Making the user feel at ease about using your content is part of the total usability picture. Ensuring privacy in an age of increasing information availability is a juggling act that you must perform. In this litigation-fraught time, you cannot afford to be the target of a lawsuit brought about because of under-engineered security in your content.

SPEECH INPUT/OUTPUT

Although many applications currently feature at least some aspect of speech recognition or speech output, we are still a very long way off from having operating systems, or even applications, that are entirely speech driven. At the time of writing, no existing Web site appears to use speech in this fashion. Speech recognition can take up a very large amount of resources, which is usually a reason why it does not become a standard part of small portable devices. You might assume that speech recognition would be the input/output panacea, but in reality it isn't that simple. Many obstacles have to be overcome that can only be understood through detailed study of the human psychoacoustic process. For example, a human being can pick out a single conversation out of a crowd of thousands and follow most, if not all, of that conversation's meaning. A computer, on the other hand, will have to struggle with all of the background noise that all sounds very similar to the user's voice. The way humans are able to perform the feat of selective hearing isn't yet completely understood, and modeling this behavior in software might prove to be too difficult for human programmers to accomplish.

Speech synthesis, or speech output, has not evolved terribly far from the days of the robotic-sounding, froglike speech of the old DEC speech synthesizers. Next-generation devices may consist of simple portable "dumb terminals" that feature cellular telephony and a Palm-like form factor and functionality. The device will be optimized for delivering human speech and data simultaneously over the cellular network to large computing clusters on the back end and to the user's ISP, which will perform speech recognition and natural language processing.

Results of user queries will be sent back along the cellular pathway to the handheld display or via speech output.

ENABLING HUMANITY

The not-so-subtle underlying message throughout this book has been simple: technology does not necessarily make the planet a better place to live, nor does it automatically address human needs that existed prior to the advent of electronic technology. Inventions like fire, the wheel, shelter, and medicine address problems that directly relate to the survival of the species. Often, the only purpose served by inventions of an electronic nature is to drive sales of more and more electronic devices, which in turn oils the wheels of production, which in turn cranks out more … and so on. Very few organizations consider whether they are contributing to the success of the species or just enabling human beings' fixation with electronics.

The truth is, systems that do not address a real need—systems that put the technological solution "cart" before the "horse" of need—fail. Many failures of products, devices, and ideas can be traced to the violation of this essential concept. You must start with a need and craft a solution to that need. A great many companies put together a "solution" before knowing if there is, in fact, a need for that solution, and they end up having to retrofit a "need"—potentially, an artificially created one—to the solution. On the other hand, development of these products is also a valuable part of researching what can actually be done. Many scientists are given the task to discover, invent, and explore. Many great ideas have come from this research and will continue to be a major part in moving technology forward.

One area that could use more attention, however, is the development of products to help people address human problems. Many of the current technologies will go through various modifications and improvement cycles, before they will be geared to helping those with disabilities or providing solutions to the greater problems of society. But as a usability specialists you are contributing to the collective experience of the human race with every move you make, so keep in mind one basic question as you work: How does this address humankind's needs?

CHAPTER SUMMARY

Technological innovations have been increasing in level of sophistication and time to market, and will probably continue to do so. Technology shapes the world we live in, and redefines the way we interact with each other. Technology designers should be mindful of these facts when adding to the collective pool of information and innovations, with the goal of enabling humanity being a key priority.

HANDS ON

1. Discussion: What are the sociological implications of a completely "connected" (in the electronic sense) society?

2. Write down a list of ten information devices—they can be new, old, or non-existent (like devices from sci-fi that may not exist yet, but might one day). What basic human needs/problems do each address?

3. Discussion: If you were to invent the next generation mobile computing device, what would it be? What features would it have? Who would use it?

INTRODUCTION TO USABILITY

ACHTUNG!!!

Das machine is nicht fur gefingerpoken und mittengrabben. Ist easy schnappen der springenwerk, blowenfusen, und corkenpoppen mit spitzensparken. Ist nicht fur gewerken by das dummkopfen. Das rubbernecken sightseeren keepen hands in das pockets. Relaxen und vatch das blinkenlights!!!

WHAT IS USABILITY?

According to Greek legend, near Eleusis, in Attica, there lived an unusual fellow named Damastes, who eventually acquired the nickname Procrustes, or "The Stretcher." His claim to fame—or infamy—was that he had an iron bed on which he forced travelers who came through his neck of the woods to spend the night.

His modus operandi was to stretch his unwitting guests that were to small to fill the bed until they "fit." If the guest was too large to fit the bed, well, Procrustes simply cut off any part that hung over the sides. Of course, there was never a guest who came into the unfortunate inn with just the "right" proportions, and no guest ever left the inn alive.

Originally published in the *Web Site Usability Handbook*.

Since that time, any action that requires the doer to "stretch" unnaturally to accommodate an action or a thing—often as a result of bad design—is referred to as "Procrustean." Therefore, design that requires the user to adapt, to accommodate, to memorize, and to suffer—the bane of this book—is called *Procrustean design*.

The Gold Rush of the 1990s

In a mad rush to race Web documents to "go live," many Web sites have been poorly designed and lack the essential features necessary to make them do what they were originally designed to do: work. The fact of the matter is, Web sites are very much a type of user interface, and increasingly, more people rely on the Web to do business, correspond, collaborate, do research, and much more. The Web site that is poorly designed is both frustrating to the end user and a blemish on the company that produced it or for which it provides a "storefront."

Our duty as usability specialists is to seek out the problems in Web sites that cause them to be frustrating, confusing, and generally useless. To accomplish this goal, we use a series of tools, techniques, and tips throughout this text. The thing that sets usability specialists apart from general nitpickers is that we attain our goal through a scientific method; furthermore, we seek to turn our findings into recommendations for change.

The First Continuum: Form vs. Function

In the grand scheme of things, usability specialists find themselves on one end of the continuum of Web site goals: form versus function. We often find ourselves playing devil's advocate to the aspiring designer in ourselves, or, most often, other members of our Web design team. In reality, the need for beauty and the need for usability can be balanced, much like the yin and the yang of Zen. The truly great Web sites combine both aspects to make a Web site that is both aesthetically pleasing and truly usable.

Although usability principles, taken to the extreme, can result in unsightly and aesthetically unpleasant Web sites, such extremes are rarely needed. The purpose of this book is not to turn you into a militant usability guerrilla. Rather, the hope is that you will walk away from this book with a sense of moderation, because anything in extreme quantities is bad.

The First Continuum discussed in this book is that of form versus Function—that is to say, how pleasing the site looks (and, perhaps, sounds) as opposed to how serviceable it is for the purpose for which it was designed. Somewhere between the two extremes lies the happy medium: the place where it all comes together. Arriving at this place can be done only through compromise and cooperation on the behalf of the designers and the usability specialists. It may be that both of these parties are you, struggling within yourself!

The area of Web site usability is currently considered a specialty area, much like that of a Web server administrator, a content developer, or a Web programmer. Unlike these other well-established Web technology roles, the role of the usability specialist is one with which, unfortunately, far too few company decision makers are familiar.

Misinformed Decisions = Unhappy Users

As of the writing of this edition of the book, most decision makers have not caught on to the fact that the state of usability of their Web sites plays a far greater role in the success of that component of the business than any flashy, last-minute display of state-of-the-art technology ever can.

In the current generation of Web site design, people who are not experts in usable systems are making lots of decisions. They are management types and marketing types who hear buzzwords and insist blindly that the company Web site needs "more Java and more flash!" They don't take into consideration that adding features does not automatically make the end user's world better; in fact, it often makes the user's world much worse![1] Such ventures are usually doomed from the start because a Web site that is not usable is useless.

---

[1] Take, for example, the major change that Microsoft made to the Macintosh version of Word during the upgrade from version 5.1 to 6.0. Many who bought the upgrade ended up reinstalling the old version and were outraged at the way the program had been changed.

The purpose of this book is to familiarize you with the principles of user-centered design (UCD) and usability concepts to enable you to educate your organization about the need for usability. A great part of your job in this new era is to educate people about usability to the point that it is ubiquitous as the word processor, the fax, and the coffee machine.

Start with a Purpose

In our journey to attain Web site usability, we must start at the beginning: we must determine the purpose of our Web site. In your career, you have probably experienced executive decision making along the lines of, "We need a Web site and we need it now." Such decisions are often devoid of calculated thought, which leaves Web site usability in the trash can. The fact of the matter is, without a carefully laid plan for what your Web site will provide, it simply cannot do anything well—except annoy your users.

The subject of determining the purpose of your Web site is outside the scope of this text. However, it is a critical concept that you must understand before you can proceed. In a nutshell, the first step toward Web site usability is to figure out the main goals of your Web site. For labeling purposes, we will call these *goals of the purpose*.

For example, if your company sells a particular product—let's say the Wonder Widget 2000—your CEO may decide that the corporate Web site should feature an online store. This online store would feature the Wonder Widget 2000 as well as all its additional accessories, in a convenient format that makes it easy to purchase products. Additionally, your company may decide to offer technical support for these products on its Web site in an effort to reduce technical support expenses.

You can summarize these two main points in two sentences:

- Provide a sales channel for the Wonder Widget series of products.

- Provide a technical support forum for existing Wonder Widget customers.

Although these points may seem like common sense, you will quickly find out that there is no such thing as common sense; common sense is quite uncommon. Focusing so clearly on the purpose of your Web site allows you to construct the remainder of your Web site usability plan.

Although this book is mainly concerned with Web site usability, a term we'll define in a moment, it is important to understand that the general concept of usability engineering, usability testing, and UCD are by no means new.

The material in this book explains the philosophy and process of applying usability principles to Web site design as opposed to avionics, platform-dependent software graphical user interfaces (GUIs), or automobile control consoles. The techniques presented are deeply rooted in the general science of human factors and usability testing. However, we approach the task of designing—or redesigning—a Web site, taking into account the toolbox of usability that we have at our disposal to make sure that the resulting site is truly usable.

For example, if we are designing a commercial Web site for a software company, we may know that one of our principal design goals is to make it easy for clients to order software over the Web via this site. In the process of accomplishing this goal, we go through many steps to ensure that when we are done, each and every end user has the easiest and most problem-free time achieving his or her goal: to order the latest software package.

As usability specialists, we have an array of tools at our disposal to ensure our goals are met. The purpose of this book is to introduce you to the *usability toolbox* and to give you a methodology for implementing the individual tools therein in a consistent way.

Depending on the corporate philosophy of our company, we may also have, as a principal design goal, making customer support easily available in order to strengthen customer loyalty and reduce the total number of dollars spent in technical support-line costs. (To the best of your estimation, how many companies clearly embrace this philosophy? Name two.)

Surfing, Known-Item Searching, and Task-Oriented Interaction

For many reasons, people will come to your Web site. They could be on their lunch break or, for shame, Web surfing on the company clock and just looking for amusement. They might have typed a keyword into a search engine that landed them on your site; they might be looking for a product or service that you offer. Or they might be on your site to get work done.

If we are designing a site principally for the purpose of getting users to surf and hang out on the site, we might not want to make things particularly efficacious for them. After all, if our users can quickly find what they are looking for, they may leave the site after finding it! This sort of reasoning has actually led some companies to produce sites that are purposefully difficult to use, just to keep users groping around the site a bit longer.

I don't advise that you take this approach; my point is that different styles of Web sites should have different approaches to user interaction. If you want your users to stay on your site longer, you need to cook up some clever magnet content that your users will want to hang around for. That, too, is outside the scope of this book, however.

Instead, we're primarily interested in the other two types of utilization: *known-item searching* and *task-oriented interaction*. Our goal is to actually speed our users through the successful completion of their errands so that they can get back to idle surfing and having fun.

The Web has brought an odd element to user interface principles. You can use the Web for both fun and business. You can do your banking via the Web. You can also watch stupid but oh-so-hilarious cartoons about a deranged donkey and his psychotic buddy (a Don Quixote for the Prozac Generation).

WHAT ISN'T USABILITY?

Usability Is Not Accessibility

Two buzzwords in the field of Web design are often wrongly equivocated: *accessibility* and *usability*. Note that these are not the same thing.

However, accessibility *is* a component of usability, and therefore I have devoted a chapter to this topic.

In a nutshell, the generally cited concern of accessibility involves making Web site content available to and usable by people with disabilities. For example, if a Web site is designed so that it is 100 percent graphic images (to make the site more visually appealing by forcing exact layout and control over font appearance), it considered not accessible to the visually impaired. If a visually impaired user encounters such a page, he or she will be clueless as to the content and unable to navigate or use the content of the site.

This outlook—that accessibility is needed only to accommodate users with disabilities—is myopic, however, because when a Web site is designed with accessibility in mind, people with disabilities represent only one group of beneficiaries. For example, Web sites that rely less on images to communicate are more accessible to automated search engines, are easier to index, and are more available to other browsing platforms, such as the stripped-down Web browsers embedded in personal digital assistant (PDA) devices and personal communication service (PCS) phones. This is only one nontrivial example of how designing with accessibility in mind benefits everyone, not just people with disabilities.

Usability Is Not Marketing Research

Usability science is also different from marketing analysis or Web server log analysis. The goal of usability science is not to increase awareness of a product, to entertain, or to make sure that the "user experience" guides a consumer through a carefully laid "entry tunnel." None of these areas qualifies as usability science, although arguably they are all important to the success of a Web site.

It is critical to note that usability is geared toward improving how easily users can use a Web site to accomplish specific tasks. This is completely different from the goal of entertainment or even "infotainment." Web sites that are intended to entertain have a very different philosophy than Web sites that are designed to get work done. Sometimes, a successful

Web site will be a synthesis of both goals: to entertain and to accomplish a goal. Think of Amazon.com. As Jared Spool pointed out in his book, *Web Site Usability: A Designer's Guide*, likability—the degree to which a user likes a Web site—does not necessarily correlate with usability. In his book, Spool does a usability audit of several Web sites and finds that the most entertaining and fun (and most likable) site of the bunch—Disney.com—was considered to be one of the least usable.

Note, however, that people concerned with marketing are also necessarily concerned with usability of the Web site because ultimately, no matter how well conceived the marketing ideas, an unusable Web site can shoot the marketers right out of the water.

Usability Is Not About "Crafting the User Experience"

Before you protest, read to the end of this paragraph! Clearly, the state of usability of a Web site determines whether the user will have a good or bad experience with your Web site. There is no denying this fact. However, a number of authors and well-known Web designers have spent much time trying to convince other Web site designers that they need to be concerned with channeling a Web site user's visit to their site into a type of orchestrated, electronic performance.

This kind of design works fine if what you're trying to do is create a piece of performance art, the access to which you can completely control. Furthermore, you should also be able to ensure that no one will gain entrance to your site through any page or search engine other than your carefully crafted entry portal. In the real world, however, we all know that there is no way of predicting how users will enter your Web site; it could be through bookmarks, search engines, or hyperlinks from other Web sites. In my humble opinion, this is an exercise in OCD[2] rather than UCD!

---

[2] Obsessive-compulsive disorder.

Usability does not concern itself with arbitrary coercion of the users' path through your Web site. It ensures that regardless of how, when, or where your users enter your Web site, they will be able to use it.

A BIT OF HISTORY

Not so very many years ago, a man named Tim Berners-Lee came up with a way for researchers all over the world to share scientific documents with their peers. The rest is history. The tool that Tim created would soon turn into the fastest-growing technology in the history of humankind: the World Wide Web.

The first generation of Web pages was primarily made of very Spartan-looking documents, authored by scientific types. Most documents were almost entirely text, with an occasional splash of color here and there and the occasional image to illustrate a point. This type of document was really just that: a document, and of the static kind, at that. There was little to no "interfacing" that the end user had to do besides read it.

The second generation of Web documents saw a shift from simple text to a little more, when images became popular on the steadily growing World Wide Web. One major milestone in the growth of the Web happened somewhere in this era: people outside the realm of the slide rule and the atom smasher began to noodle with the Web. Ordinary people were starting to catch on to what the Web had to offer, and the boom that is still happening began. The use of enormous image files and the long download times associated with them caused the Web to become known as the "World Wide Wait."

The third age of the Web, which some could argue we are in now, saw the advent of Web sites not as mere curiosities but as tools for conducting business across great distances. Now a Web page is more than just something to look at; it is a means to an end. A Web page can be the thing that allows you, the busy technologist, to avoid going to the crowded grocery store after working a long day. A Web page could allow you to book that flight to Sydney for a lot cheaper than your old travel agent was willing to go. And of course, a Web site could allow you to make a small fortune in day trading. What a marvel of technology, this Web thing.

With all the excitement of a new technology comes the inevitable rush of pioneers who are willing to forsake common sense and good manners to attain precious gold. In the wake of the World Wide Web extravaganza, we are left with thousands—even millions—of poorly designed Web sites and Web pages that don't serve any purpose well, except perhaps to annoy and baffle those who try to use them.

Many Web sites have been designed from the beginning with no real purpose, no guiding principle. The result? Unusable information that adds to the ocean of ubiquitous World Wide Noise.

One of the driving goals of Web site usability specialists is to increase the signal-to-noise ratio for our users. In other words, we should, through many different types of techniques, make it as easy as is technologically feasible for users to find the golden islands of information in the tumultuous seas of information noise.

At the current exponential rate of expansion of the Web, without intervention, the result will be a totally unmanageable mass within a few years. End users are frustrated enough at the inconsistency of transactional sites today; what will happen when things are *really* out of control?

A BIT OF JARGON

You might have seen the terms *usability, usability testing, human factors, HCI, CHI, UCD,* and so on, and wondered how they all fit together. As if all this complexity weren't enough, the authors of a recent Web site usability publication have coined the new term, *user-centered design (UCD).* This book attempts to sort all these terms out bit by bit, but for now let's define the term *usability* thus:

> *Usability is the broad discipline of applying sound scientific observation, measurement, and design principles to the creation and maintenance of Web sites in order to bring about the greatest*

ease of use, ease of learnability, amount of usefulness, and least amount of discomfort for the humans who have to use the system.

This broad umbrella encompasses the use of testing methods, casual observation, expert evaluations, and many other tools that are all useful in reaching the goal of a usable Web site.

Let's take a brief stroll through some of the terms and acronyms mentioned above, partly to define them but also to give a frame of reference to see where our field comes from in the first place.

HUMAN FACTORS

The field of human factors has its roots in the field of psychology, and in fact, many of the first specialists in this area were military researchers performing studies on how U.S. soldiers performed under varying types of stress and in varying environments. Since those early days, human factors psychologists have become part of many industries, including the automobile industry, the telecommunications industry, and many other fields that require humans to interact with an essentially nonhuman interface of some sort.

An example of the type of issues that human factors attempts to study is that of human vision, its limitations, and ways to leverage its strong points to enable humans to make better use of systems. As a Web usability specialist, you might find it very useful to know that selecting the color blue for text on your Web site will render many elderly users of your site unable to read it, due to certain types of degradation that occur in the human eye with age.

Some other examples of human factors at work involve studies on the nature of human memory, learning, and forgetting. Having an understanding of these areas enables us to design sites that leverage our users' abilities to use Web sites as well as be able to remember how to use sites over the long haul.

If, for example, we know that the principle called *interference* causes users to become confused on our Web site when part of our interface looks similar to another interface that they've used before but that works differently, we are more able to competently troubleshoot the problem and resolve the issue.

Although it is not entirely necessary to have a degree in psychology to become a Web site usability specialist, it certainly does not hurt; in fact, if you have a background in psychology, you will find the field a very natural fit for you.

Human/Computer Interaction

Human/computer interaction (HCI), which is sometimes also written *CHI,* is the field that seeks to apply the study of human factors specifically to the way humans interact with computer systems. HCI concerns itself with issues such as GUIs, the logic and functionality of the features the software provides, and the way that humans interact with the input and output devices. Another area of HCI, *ergonomics,* concerns the particular hazards that these devices can pose to humans and how we can avoid those hazards.

Much research has been done in the area of HCI. In fact, there is a Special Interest Group (SIG) of the Association for Computing Machinery (ACM) called Computer/Human Interaction (CHI). This SIG focuses entirely on the area of computer/human interface, and much of the literature in this area has been published in the journals of this group. If you have a budget for professional association membership fees, it would be wise for you to join the ACM and, in particular, the CHI SIG.

If this area of usability is of particular interest to you, you might also want to peruse the University of Maryland's HCI Web site *(www.cs.umd.edu/hcil/)*, which has many online publications and other resources of interest. Also check out *comp.human-factors* on Usenet.

By the time you are finished reading this book, you might take issue with the small semantic distinction between the wording of HCI and CHI. In the acronym CHI, the computer is put before the machine. This goes against the philosophy of UCD, as discussed in more detail in the next section.

Whatever you call it, HCI is a fairly scientific, empirical field that is usually left to the domain of the scholarly researcher with a lab, graduate student helpers, and funding to do the work. Nonetheless, we can certainly use HCI findings in our everyday, hectic schedule of Web site development.

User-Centered Design

UCD is both a philosophy and a methodology of product development that to be done properly, must necessarily permeate the entire infrastructure of an organization or a business. The simple idea is that no product, Web site, or software system matters—at all—unless there are users to use it.

Products and services that fail often do so for the simple fact that their designers never thought to ask the people who would be using the product what they thought they needed or how they currently performed their jobs with existing products. It's not quite the technical embodiment of "the customer is always right," because in reality this isn't always the case.

To provide a point of contrast, let's go back to the days before computers were mainstream, when they were still the mainstays of thick-glassed, pocket-protector-wearing types who loved to hack away at electronic and other gizmos. Many of the original minicomputers were designed to be programmed by flipping little switches up or down, depending on whether the bit you wanted to create was a 1 or a 0. This was not a very user-friendly interface!

I used to have one of these minicomputers in my office at the lab; to boot the operating system required flipping the levers in a mystical pattern that few people knew. If I had taken the computer to an average person's home and asked him or her to use it, he or she would probably have called the police! Clearly, the designers of the computer (in this case, a Digital PDP-11) were one and the same as the end users.

As computers became more and more mainstream, the user population began to change dramatically. Regular, nontechnical people began to use computers; accountants had to learn how to use one of the fancy new programs such as VisiCalc or become extinct. Today, the personal computer is ubiquitous; when Apple released the iMac not too long ago, even grandmothers bought them because they wanted to get recipes and stock tips over the 'Net.

Clearly, times have changed since the days of the minicomputer. But one thing hasn't changed much: the people who design microchips and computer systems are still just as technically oriented as they were 30 years ago. The beginning of failure is to let these engineers and programmers wholly design a product that is meant for use by the masses. Anyone who has ever been frustrated by a VCR has felt the bite of designer-centered design: products designed without thinking about the user lead to failed products, bruised reputations, and often, bankruptcy.

We'll talk a lot more about UCD as we go along, because it is the underlying principle that guides us, as usability specialists, toward our goals.

WHY USABILITY?

If you have ever been involved with the development of a software product, you know that a smart company spends a lot of time and money making sure that its software is easy and intuitive to use. You also know that smart companies make sure that in general the users of the software won't tend to make critical mistakes because of some poor design element. Usability testing and other usability tools are an integral part of the product development life cycle.

Why? Because, as mentioned, systems that do not perform up to users' needs and expectations usually fail. Take, for example, the Coleco company, which lost $6 million in 1983 on its failed Adam home computer product. I still have an Adam, and I still marvel at how good it actually was for the time. It was a home computer system, complete with printer, all of which sold for $600 retail. It had an innovative technology that provided secondary storage on a high-speed magnetic tape instead of a floppy disk drive. Floppy drives were very costly then, and tape cassette transports and media were relatively inexpensive.

The whole outfit should have done very well on the market, but the package had one fatal flaw: poor documentation that was too complex for the home users who bought the Adam. As a result, high returns from unhappy customers resulted in a failed product. Maybe, if the company spent more money in user-centered testing of the documentation, it could have averted disaster, and perhaps we'd all be using Coleco computers on our desktops today!

Take another example. In the mid-1960s, Honeywell created a very futuristic product: the H316 General Purpose Digital Computer, a.k.a. the Kitchen Computer—a computer for the kitchen. It was a $7,000 monster that had a built-in cutting board, looked like something right out of *The Jetsons,* and required the user to program the thing himself or herself in a language called BACK. Honeywell didn't sell very many of these, and it's likely that the project had never been market tested or designed with the user in mind. Who wants to write a program when they are sautéing peppers?

How Things End Up Unusable

It is one thing to simply complain that a system is unusable; it is quite another to understand how systems can go wrong in the first place. The following list of reasons is by no means an exhaustive one. However, it will give you the general idea:

- **Reason 1.** All too often, the developers of a Web site focus on the site's features or its technical implementation while never paying any attention to the end user. This defies the first law of UCD: Know your user.

- **Reason 2.** The designers of Web sites are often highly technical people who possess skills in programming and other analytical areas. Unfortunately, the way these people think and act is usually totally different from the way the end user does. Assumptions these designers make simply do not generalize to the people who will actually be using the site.

- **Reason 3.** People who are in charge of the development of Web sites often give in to trends, assuming that incorporating the latest and greatest technology will give them the edge over their competition. In fact, this type of behavior usually works exactly the opposite: it reduces the actual usability of the Web site, giving less state-of-the-art competition the edge. Remember, just because a feature exists does not mean that you are obligated to use it.

- **Reason 4.** Most people merely assume that good usability results from common-sense reasoning. Most people don't even think of usability as a discipline. In reality, you'll find that common sense is really quite uncommon. Highly usable Web sites do not happen accidentally; they're the results of iterative redesign and exhaustive testing.

- **Reason 5.** Unfortunately, people with little or no user interface design experience are making critical decisions about the look, feel, and logical model of Web sites.

Not Just a Gratuitous Moral . . .

Take, for example, the story of browser incompatibility and how two of my students created a Web site that caused a catastrophe. These two students worked for a division of the U.S. government. They were commissioned to create a brand new Web site for their department. Despite the fact that these two students were taking a HyperText Markup Language (HTML) course, where the dangers of using What You See Is What You Get (WYSIWYG) HTML editing programs is discussed, they used a very well-known, popular HTML editor to produce their entire site.

Unfortunately, this very popular HTML editor leverages several known bugs of a competitor's Web browser as well as several illegal HTML constructs to render its output unusable by the competitor's browser. The students assumed that this would never be a problem because their internal IT department allowed only the use of the "compatible" Web browser and, after all, they were designing the Web site for internal use within the department.

The students never bothered to check their Web site as viewed by the competitor's browser. After considerable taxpayer dollars had been sunk into the site, the deployment date was at hand. It was only then that the two found out that 50 percent of their users were, in fact, using the competitors' browser. Furthermore, these users were unable to use the browser for which the site was designed, because they lacked the staff to implement the new browser and support it.

We'll never know exactly how much pain these two students went through when they had to uncover all the proprietary, deliberate breakage in their code and fix it.

The moral of this story is that whether you are the designer or the usability expert, you absolutely *must* preview all your Web pages using all available browsers. That includes outdated browsers that you assume no one uses anymore. Read your Web server logs that record visitors to your site; you'll be amazed. If you fail to observe this simple rule of design, you will lose. Had these students done an initial on-site visit to get information from the users' perspective, they could have circumvented the entire calamity.

In addition to these five broad areas, there are hundreds of other, smaller ways that usability problems can creep into your Web site design. One concept to take away with you after reading this book is the idea that virtually every usability problem can be traced back to the violation of one or more well-known principles of UCD.

WHAT YOU NEED TO GET STARTED IN WEB SITE USABILITY

So far, so good. You've got this book, which is a start toward understanding usability. A common myth about usability is that you need a Ph.D. in psychology in order to be able to conduct usability testing, or any other sort of usability, for that matter. This is untrue, as is the myth that you need lots of money and a fancy laboratory. The fact is, all you really need is one or more people who are interested in making usable Web sites and a small area in which to do testing (this can be your office, a conference room, or even a janitor's closet[3]). You'll also need a decent stopwatch and of course at least one potted plant to improve the ambience. Because you will be testing the design of a Web site, you'll need at least one computer running an operating system comparable to the one your end users are using.

What you will find as you go along is that usability science can require very little material and fiscal resources, but you can also do much more sophisticated work if the budget allows. My guess is that your particular company might not be aware that such a thing as usability science exists, nor of the hidden costs of not integrating UCD into the core philosophy of your corporate Web site. Part of your duty as a usability specialist is to educate and inform; hopefully, by the time you finish reading this book, you will be able to make a case for integrating usability as part of your corporate philosophy.

Checklist for Getting Started

Here are the basics you need to get started in Web site usability:

- Digital stopwatch
- Computer workstation (similar to the type your users are using)

---

[3] The Chandra x-ray telescope, which was sent into space at 7:47 a.m. EDT on July 23, 1999, was operated from the Chandra Operations Control Center in Cambridge, Massachusetts. Most of the impressive hardware and control components for the center were housed in a janitor's closet.

- Clipboard
- Web browser that your users are likely to use, plus any other browsers likely to be used to view your site
- Comparable operating system to what your users will be using
- Comparable Internet connection to what your users will be using
- Small, quiet room with minimal distractions
- Two comfortable chairs

The first item, the digital stopwatch, is a critical piece of equipment, even if it does seem a little archaic. You need this piece of equipment when you are performing usability testing, which is one of the tools in the toolbox.

You need a digital stopwatch that is capable of displaying milliseconds, because in many cases, tasks that you will ask users to perform will take only seconds to complete. You'll also want a stopwatch that makes as little noise as possible; noise can be distracting to your participants and make them more aware of the time constraints of testing. Make sure that your watch is easy to reset and that the display is large and easy to read.

How do you know what kind of computer workstation your users are using? Hopefully, by the time you are doing testing, you will have amassed some statistics about your users by way of questionnaires or screening phone calls. Asking questions related to your participants' home and business computers is a pretty normal part of the process. This will help you get a general idea for how fast or powerful your testing workstation should be. Obviously, you don't want a computer that is so ancient that it can barely run a Web browser; on the other hand, you don't want to have the absolutely latest and greatest machine on the planet, unless all of your users have them as well.

As of this writing, the lion's share of the PC market belongs to the Wintel[4] platform. Therefore, you can assume that you need to perform usability tests on only that platform.

---

[4] Windows and Intel—the two-headed colossus of 1990s computing.

Careful—this line of thinking will get you into hot water! You can choose to believe otherwise, but there actually *are* other platforms that are widely used. The day is coming very soon that the notion of "platform" will change dramatically. Web browsers now include many types of devices, including telephones, Web TV, Palm Pilots, and other non-Microsoft operating systems, like Mac, UNIX or Linux.

Therefore, you should remain open to the notion of testing your site designs on many different platforms and devices. In the rapidly approaching future, keeping up with all the new innovations in alternative Web browsing devices will be a full-time job and will become a much more critical role of the usability specialist.

You probably have noticed that the computer workstation, Internet connectivity, Web browser, and the operating system of your test machine should all be similar to what your actual users will be using in their real environments. It's critical that you match the lab setup as closely with the real-world environment as possible.

But You Can't Completely Replicate the User's Environment

So, you may wonder, is it necessary to replicate the entire environment of the user? If a user has a toy on the monitor, do you need to have a fuzzy toy on the test computer's monitor? The answer is no. Although the objective of a laboratory environment is to account for as many variables as possible that might affect user performance, you can't possibly replicate each user's unique environment. It isn't feasible.

What you do want to guarantee, however, is that during testing, each and every test participant gets the same, homogenous test environment. This at least ensures that the environment will equally affect the overall performance of participants. It also means that you don't have to take environmental fluctuations into account to explain variations in performance.

This approach has been criticized many times because a sterile lab environment does not necessarily duplicate the user's real environment. Nonetheless, it is important to control the environment in order to make sure that some random force isn't influencing users' performance. This way, if the lab environment itself has an effect on users' performance, we know that it should be approximately equal for all participants, therefore canceling out any random differences.

The rule of thumb is, the fewer things that go on in the test environment that you can't control (such as loud noises coming from a construction project outside your window or cold temperature one day and hot temperature the next), the more confident you can be in your findings. We look at experimental control in more detail in Chapter 7, "Usability Lab Setup."

A Word on the Scientific Method

This book is almost wholly adopted from a college course that I designed and teach. In the early days of the course, it included a vast amount of research design technique and even an entire module on statistics. I was determined to make my students observe traditional experimental research conditions and exercise the utmost in experimental control over confounding variables.

What I began to see was students' eyes glazed over during this part of the lecture and that the work they produced exemplified few to none of the carefully orchestrated research design methods that I learned in college. But one thing bothered me even more than the absence of control: the fact was, students still managed to uncover a wealth of usability problems, and after implementing changes, the end users were very happy. The end result was an absolute success.

At this point, I had to modify my concept of doing "good" usability work. A little usability is better than none.[5] In fact, I began to develop the notion of a continuum, on one side of which is the need for usability that adheres to classical experimental conditions and on the other side of which is the need for speed and thrift.

---

[5] See Nielsen's article, *Guerrilla HCI: Using Discount Usability Engineering to Penetrate the Intimidation Barrier* at *www.useit.com/papers/guerrilla_hci.html*.

Let's look at a contrived example to illustrate the difference between the two ends of the continuum. Imagine that in the not-too-distant future, a Web site is created to manage the critical day-to-day functioning of a nuclear reactor. The Web site would be an application that the control operator would use to manage practically every facet of the reactor. Because, as we know, it is generally a really bad thing for a nuclear reactor to fail, the Web interface would have to be rigorously tested under every conceivable condition, all under absolutely precise experimental control.

The way test data would be accumulated and interpreted would have to comply with all known statistical measures used to ensure data integrity, reliability, and validity. Many millions of dollars would go into this project to ensure the safety of thousands of lives.

On the other end of the spectrum, we have a company that sells glow-in-the-dark yo-yos. The company has an annual revenue of $250,000. It is looking to do usability testing on its online store to make sure it works. For this company, a simple heuristic evaluation will suffice. The data collected can be distilled into simple percentages.[6] The vast majority of usability problems can be caught in a single day, and the budget for such an endeavor will be minimal.

In the real world, you will always be somewhere on this continuum. Your project might call for exacting measures because you'll need to replicate the test in many worldwide locations, or you might need to focus tightly on the effect of the presence of a new technology that has

---

[6] In general, presenting data in terms of raw percentages has little use. A plain percentage is a very misleading figure because it cannot account for the element of chance. For example, if 50 percent of your test subjects cannot find a particular piece of information on your Web site, how much of that 50 percent is attributable to your design, and how much is due to random chance? Even a nearly perfect site design still presents problems to some percentage of users. These problems are due to chance, factors for which you cannot control. Statistical analysis allows you to figure out how much of the result is due to chance. This type of interpretation is not accepted by everyone, but keep reading.

been recently incorporated into the site. Or you might simply need to repair a badly designed site as quickly as possible.

EDUCATING OTHERS ABOUT USABILITY

As of this writing, the number of people involved in Web site usability is relatively small—much smaller than the number of people who know how to crank out a shaded sphere in Photoshop or the number of HTML gurus; even smaller than the number of people making the critical decisions that forge the Web sites of the world.

Therefore, one of your responsibilities as a usability specialist will be to teach others in your organizations about the need for good usability. Because the whole idea of UCD and usability testing is philosophical in nature, people in your companies and organizations must understand the importance and embrace usability as not just some strange voodoo, but as a way of life.

Because the effects of good usability often are not directly observable—the way a flashy graphic or new look and feel might be—the results can be indirectly observed and usually translated into a language that the "higher-ups" can understand. You may opt to translate the results of good usability into a dollars-and-cents summary, as in "We estimate that last year we lost $125,000 in revenue from partially completed sales transactions on our difficult-to-use Web store interface."

Alternately, you may need to translate the absence of good usability into the accompanying negative consumer opinion of the business—for example, "In our survey, 85 percent of our respondents said that they thought our company was unprofessional because of our clumsy Web site."

You can also take a more optimistic approach and show the good results of the limited usability improvements that you can make with little initial investment, in the hope that doing so will propel the decision makers into funding more study. For example, "After performing a heuristic evaluation of the site, we were able to uncover 15 serious usability problems. Since we have located these problems and fixed them, our Web user satisfaction has risen 40 percent."

The approach that you must take to educate the decision makers in your own organization varies. The objective is the same, however: to help them understand the need for usability and how usability fits into the grand scheme of things. You must also make it understood that occasionally you must make decisions about usability that are contrary to what seems "cool"; decisions like these are always more compelling when they are backed up with solid data that you have acquired during usability testing. Otherwise, it's your opinion against another person's, and without backup, you will probably find that you'll lose in the end.

Approaches to Education

Whenever a Web design team from a major company approaches me to come on as a usability consultant, there is one step that I always take. I make a brief presentation to the decision makers to explain what usability is all about, how it is done, and what the return on investment (ROI) will be to the company, should it decide to implement it. If you are an independent contractor, you would be wise to develop just such a presentation for yourself.

Preaching to the Converted

Unfortunately, the people who are interested in doing the usability study are often not the people who have the authority to actually implement the changes you recommend in your final report. You'll need to overcome this hurdle by way of early education, before you expend any time and effort in developing a usability plan and executing it. Be sure to determine early on who is actually in charge; otherwise, you may be working hard to sell your ideas to people who can't actually do anything about them.

One of the worst feelings in the world is to design and run the perfect usability plan, only to have the client say "OK, great, now we've done usability stuff" and throw the results away. When this happens you can be fairly certain that no one really bought into the idea in the first place. This is not only a letdown—it also reduces the chance for an ongoing relationship with the client.

Prepare Your Material

To attain the goal of educating your clients (or your employer) about Web site usability, you can do several things to make things easier on yourself. The first action is to develop a presentation that explains what usability is all about: the philosophy behind it and how it ultimately affects an organization's bottom line. The CD-ROM that accompanies this book includes a PowerPoint presentation that is covered under the GNU public license. You can use the presentation free of charge. You can modify it, and you can even distribute it as long as you distribute it in its entirety (including any modifications that you make) and include the same GNU public license conditions that I have. Please refer to the CD-ROM "README" file for more information.

Case Studies

Another great tool to use is the case study. As you develop a portfolio of clients, you can obtain permission from them to use their results as part of a case study. When you present your client or employer with concrete facts about other, similar businesses that have had good success in implementing usability studies, it becomes easier to sell the idea. It also helps crystallize just what it is they can expect of you and the service you will provide.

Public and Private Seminars

If you are a consultant, it's a great idea to offer public seminars on usability (at a local hotel or conference center) and invite local companies to attend for free or for a minimal charge. This way, you get to educate your potential client base while you do some self-promotion.

Depending on your goal, you could place ads in local computer circulars, post the conference details on Usenet, or use any of a variety of other techniques to get the word out. For a minimal investment, you will be spreading the word about usability and developing a network of potential clients at the same time.

SUMMARY

- The point of Web site usability is to make Web sites perform the function for which they were designed, with the minimal amount of user frustration, time, and effort.

- Web sites that exist primarily to entertain are very different from sites that exist to fulfill specific user needs. In this book, we are concerned with the latter, not the former.

- One of our primary responsibilities as Web usability specialists is to educate others about the need for Web site usability.

- It is critical to understand the purpose of a Web site, since no other usability study can happen until it is determined.

- User-centered design (UCD) is a keystone of good Web site usability.

- Human factors psychology is in many ways the roots of how we study usability.

- Designs that are not based on user input are doomed to fail.

- It's important to be as scientific as your circumstances will allow, but in reality, the nature of our field restricts how sterile we can be.

- Some usability is better than none.

- You don't need much to get started in usability.

HANDS-ON EXERCISES

Take a look at the slide presentation included on the CD-ROM. Begin to think about how you will customize it for your own use.

1. What is the purpose of your Web site? Talk to the people involved with the Web site in your organization, and write down the important goals for the site. Then write a paragraph or two that captures

the essence of the site's *raison d'être*. This material will become the foundation for your usability plan.

2. Do you have a record of user feedback on your site, such as e-mail to the Webmaster? Amass all the input you can, for starters. What trends do you discern in the feedback?

DISCUSSION TOPICS

1. What were your preconceptions about Web site usability? Do you think differently now that you have read the chapter?

2. What are the 10 things you hate the most about the Web?

3. What are the 5 things you love about the Web?

4. What are your favorite products out of those you have used, and why were they your favorites?

5. If you had to make the decision to perform a comprehensive usability plan on the Coca-Cola Web site or the Microsoft Web site, which one would you choose? Why?

B

USABILITY TESTING

NOT JUST ANOTHER TOOL IN THE TOOLBOX

Web site usability testing is the most complex tool of our toolbox. It requires the most planning, the most training, and the most resources of all the tools. It is also the most productive of the tools, in that the data that you can gain from testing will be the most detailed and closest to the actual user that you can get.

Remember that the cornerstone of your entire effort at usability is a *comprehensive usability plan*. A usability plan includes details on all aspects of everything that you will do to enhance usability, at every phase of the redesign cycle. This plan is different from the *usability test plan*, which is just one part of your all-encompassing comprehensive plan. The usability test plan is the blueprint and instructions for one particular kind of test—the classical usability test, which is the subject of this chapter.

Every comprehensive usability plan probably includes at least some actual usability testing. The degree to which you use this tool will depend on where your needs fall on the continuum of correctness.

Originally published in the *Web Site Usability Handbook*.

Because this tool is by far the most expensive one to implement, the degree to which you can use it is governed partially by your budget. If you are designing a site that runs a nuclear facility, you will do an awful lot of user testing. (We hope!)

CLASSICAL EXPERIMENTAL RESEARCH DESIGN

If you have done any research , perhaps as a student or in your professional life, you will note that the design of our usability tests don't quite follow the rules of traditional experimental research design. This is, in fact, the case, and there are several reasons this is true.

The primary reason is that it is simply not feasible to observe classical experimental conditions in the workaday world, where deadlines overrule science. Most of the projects that you will work on will require such short turnaround that you won't always be able to do "real" experimentation. Normally, you want to maintain perfect control over all factors in your study; you would perform a pretest on the unmodified (original) site, make changes, and then retest, at the very least. Therefore, what we are talking about here isn't real science; it's more like art. Regardless, what we desire are results, and if an unscientific approach will get us there, why not?

Establishing Benchmarks

As your site matures and you perform more and more testing on it, you will certainly want to keep an archive of test results that you can use to compile company standard benchmarks of performance. For example, when you run your first usability test, you'll more or less have to make a best guess at how long each task should take to complete.

However, as you begin your second and subsequent rounds of testing, you will have established a maximum time to complete each task; simply calculate the mean (average) of the successful completion times from your previous rounds of testing. These times will become the milestone by which you can measure future performance. If the figures go up, you know that whatever changes you made were bad, or at least they took you in the opposite direction from where you wanted to be!

Start with a Plan

To get started with user testing, you need the materials mentioned in Appendix A. Let's refresh your memory—here are the basics you need to get started in Web site usability:

- Digital stopwatch
- Computer workstation (similar to the type your users are using)
- Clipboard
- Web browser that your users are likely to use, plus any other browsers likely to be used to view your site
- Comparable operating system to what your users will be using
- Comparable Internet connection to what your users will be using
- Small, quiet room with minimal distractions
- Two comfortable chairs

Besides these items, you need to develop a test plan for your site. This test plan will serve as the blueprint for everything that you do as part of your user testing.

Your test plan should be usable as a means of replicating your study. For example, if you develop your test plan for the Chicago branch of your company, a colleague should be able to look at your plan and have no trouble replicating the study at the Sydney branch of the company and get similar results.

Therefore, it is critical that your test plan be written in such a way that you are not the only one who can understand it; it needs to be shared with your colleagues, your clients, and potentially others. Always write your usability plans and reports in a clear and consistent fashion, and never assume that the reader has any *a priori* knowledge of the topic or how to perform usability testing. Particularly, you should make an effort to be clear in the methodology section of your test plan, since this is the section of the plan that communicates the "how-to" to potential colleagues who might try to rerun your study.

The test plan is divided into several logical sections, which are detailed here. It is important to note that initially, you will not have a section for results and discussion of the results; those come later. However, the essential skeleton of the plan will remain the same over various revisions.

For your convenience, this book includes a sample usability test plan in Appendix A that you can reference whenever a topic or point in this discussion is unclear. Feel free to use this sample plan as the basis for your own plan template. The plan is also included on the CD-ROM that came with this book. It is in Microsoft Word format so that you can easily modify it to your liking.

Section 1: Purpose

In this section of the plan, you need to describe the function of the Web site you are testing. What does the site do? Whom does it serve? What is the vision for the site over the long haul? Finally, what is the reason for doing this testing? It is really important to make concrete the site's goals because, without this critical information, how can you tell how to measure the effectiveness of the site?

It is also critical to understand the expectations of the client (or your employer) with regard to this testing. What is expected to result from the testing? Does the client know what usability testing is all about? Is it understood that usability testing is not the same thing as marketing research? You must make sure that you and your client are "on the same sheet of paper," or the potential for chaos and mass miscommunication will be great. (See Figure B.1.)

The purpose section of the test plan steers the rest of the plan, so if you rush through this part, the rest of your plan will be haphazard, too. Think about this section a great deal before you dive in.

FIGURE B.1 *If you had to deduce the purpose of the site shown here from just screen shot alone, what would it be? Is the corporate philosophy clear from page 1, or is the purpose of the site a mystery—perhaps even to the people who designed it? © 2000 Pepsico.*

Section 2: Problem Statements

Your *problem statements* should be short, one-sentence summations of the kinds of questions you are looking to answer by doing this testing. For example, if you are redesigning your site to include a new Web-based storefront, you might be interested in knowing how well customers can use the new features to conduct business. The act of "conducting business" can be broken down into several parts, at least in the case of your site. They might be as follows:

- Can our users easily locate product information they need in order to choose the right products?

- Can our users successfully register for a shopping account?
- Can our users place items in their shopping carts and check out efficiently?

Note the order of things here. The purpose of the site (section 1) is pretty abstract, with only general concepts mentioned. Section 2, problem statements, requires you to be a bit more concrete, to start examining the subtasks that are required to fulfill the purpose of the site. In a bit, you'll need to fully operationalize the problem statements by generating individual usability tasks to answer each problem statement. We'll discuss how to do this shortly.

Section 3: User Profiles

Whenever you do user testing, you test a slice of your entire user population. This slice is called the *sample*. One of the things you want to do is test a sample that is representative of your population.

In other words, if you are hoping to generalize to female users aged 18–35, and your sample consists entirely of males over 50, you aren't going to be able to use your results for your originally stated purpose. You can't generalize to your target audience when you have the wrong sample. It's critical that you identify your target audience in this section of the report, explaining the various user profiles in your study.

Once you have acquired your participants and performed the testing, you will be able to show the "actual" sample that you ended up with (data to be taken from the questionnaires sent to the participants). This way, if you have ended up with a less than representative sample, it will be easy to see that fact.

So the user profiles section will undergo two revisions. Initially, you need to say for what group you are aiming in terms of a target audience. Then, after the testing is finished, you can tabulate your participants' demographic and personal information to characterize the group you ended up testing.

Section 4: Methodology

The *methodology* section is critical to the test's ability to be replicated by others. The methodology section is a step-by-step explanation of the things you will do in your test sessions. Note, however, that the methodology section does not include a task-by-task description of each usability activity.

For example, if you are planning a card sort as part of your usability session, you need to indicate this step as part of your methodology. The order of parts of the test and the general flow of things should be summarized in this section. Any unusual conditions that you might require (using only Netscape Navigator 1.1, having loud noises going on in the background, or the like) should also be noted here.

Essentially, the methodology section is your opportunity to explain to a complete stranger how to run the show. Any trained moderator should be able to pick up a copy of your test plan and replicate it without needing to ask you questions.

Section 5: Test Environment and Equipment Requirements

It's always a good idea to include a diagram of your test environment in your plan. This diagram serves as an aid to the people who review your material. You should also mention any equipment or other resources you needed for the sessions (VCR, video camera, computer, overhead projector, index cards, and so on).

Including in your plan a laundry list of required gear serves many purposes. First and foremost, it helps communicate to your team ahead of time what will be needed for your own tests in terms of gear. This means it should be fairly easy and straightforward to extract from your plan a request to give to the A/V department at your company or a rental supplier.

Second, explicitly tabulating the equipment in your plan facilitates drawing up a budget, since equipment costs can be easily calculated from this list. Be sure to figure in magnetic media (tapes and such) because their cost can add up quickly.

Finally, a setup diagram helps people who might seek to replicate your environment. It's a nice touch for your report.

Section 6: Testing Crew

Provide a brief explanation of the team of people who will be involved in the testing process. You will find that it is next to impossible to do a usability session with only one person on crew; two is a bare-bones minimum.

Here's a list of potential members for your team. We talk more about one very special role, that of the test monitor, later in this chapter:

- **Test monitor.** This person interacts with participants, moderates the session, and reads scripts.
- **Data logger.** The logger writes down information and results after participants perform tasks.
- **Timer.** This person uses a stopwatch to measure the time participants required to complete tasks and calls time when time is up.
- **Video operator.** This person operates the camera(s) in the session room; positions tapes for recording, and edits/splices video footage.
- **Site specialist.** This team member knows all the details about the Web site being tested. This person is called on to make judgment calls to determine success or failure on questionable tasks.

Once you've completed your testing, explain briefly who the crew was, what roles they fulfilled, and whether the roles changed at any point. In particularly large usability sessions, you could have more than one test monitor, for example. Note that not just anybody should act as the test monitor; it takes a special person to fill this role, as we shall see in a moment.

Section 7: Evaluation Measures

In this section you need to explain your methods for determining success or failure for tasks as well as explaining any constraints placed on the participant (he or she is not allowed to use search engine, must complete tasks in under three minutes, or the like). Common criteria for task analysis include the following:

- Number of clicks the user needed to complete tasks (you could possibly include the least number of clicks needed, as discovered by site specialists, to give a frame of reference).

- Click path taken; this path can be hard to follow unless you are using automatic link-tracking software.

- Total time elapsed; how long did it take the user to accomplish the tasks? You might need to set an upper limit on how long the user can take to accomplish each task.

It's also not unusual to have two timing milestones: the absolute maximum time you will allow the participant to try a task and the maximum time you'll allow before a task is considered a success. For example, you might set an upper bound of three minutes for a task but not count the task as a success unless it is completed in under one minute. The reason for doing this is that your testing might discover that certain tasks are accomplishable, although not in an acceptable amount of time. This finding can have many implications, depending on the circumstances.

Section 8: Task List

The *task list* is the "meat and potatoes" of the test plan. In this section, present the individual tasks that you have derived to answer the problem statements in section 2. Each task will consist of several parts:

- **The scripted text.** For each task the participants must complete, you must create a short instructive text that you will read out loud. It is critical that the text be short enough for the user to remember while performing the task. If you find that your participants have to stop and ask, "Now what am I doing again?" you have made the task too complex, and it needs to be further broken down. This scripted text is a great thing to beta test on coworkers or friends. If they can't understand your question, your users probably won't be able to, either.

- **Conditions for success.** Each task must have an unambiguous goal, the attainment of which can be easily measured. For example, asking the participant to locate the price of a Wonder Widget 2000 is an easy task to grade. If the participant comes up with the price in the allowed time, he or she succeeds. (See Figure B.2.)

- **Start state.** This is the state that the computer and Web session are in when the task begins. For example, for a given task, the computer browser might need to be at a totally random spot in the Web site, in which case the moderator would place the browser in this state at the beginning of the task. The start state is important to note; without this information, the test plan is ambiguous.

You can put limits on success beyond simply accomplishing the task itself: You could put a time limit on the task (reflecting the fact that the average user gives up after a short while if progress hasn't been made). You can also put a limit on the number of clicks a participant take to get to the goal state, reflecting the fact that too many clicks dissuade users from continuing with a task.

Make many copies of the task list to facilitate score keeping. Leave blanks where my data logger can enter times, click numbers, and other metrics for each task. Then we have a copy of the task list for each participant.

Section 9: Results

Note that this section will not exist until you complete the usability testing. Until then, it is customary to include in your plan report an explanation that the data is forthcoming.

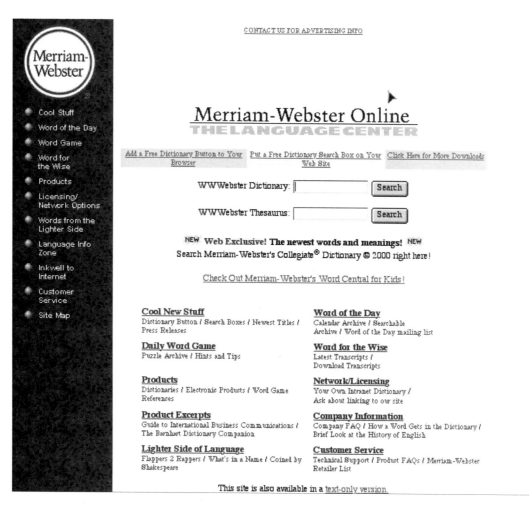

FIGURE B.2 *This site lends itself well to having the participant announce when the goal state has been found; if the participant can define a term found on the site, the goal state has been met! You need to make sure that the participant tells you when the goal state is found, not vice versa.* © 2000 Merriam-Webster, Inc.

When you do have the data, you should provide it in a variety of fashions in this section. First, have a matrix showing all data for each task and each participant. You'll usually want to show success or failure, total time elapsed, and number of clicks per task, and then tabulate the overall success or failure per task. This data can be transformed later into a variety of indexes to gauge the overall health of the site as well as to point out areas that need improvement.

For purposes of our work, use percentage scores to present your results. Note that this practice is actually wrong from a scientific point of view. Percentages are useful only as very, very loose estimates. When I began teaching usability testing I made sure that I included in my syllabus a whole section on research design methods and statistics. I found that most of my students didn't care for the material and would fall back on "folk interpretations" of the data. As mentioned elsewhere, the result was that they still improved the usability of their sites.

My advice is that if you ever expect to do usability testing professionally, take a research design methods course and become familiar with concepts such as standard deviation, z-scores, probability, and confidence.

Section 10: Discussion

This is a freeform section in which you get to talk about your observations, comments that the participants made during debriefing or during the course of testing, and so on. Basically, anything you feel needs to be said can be said in the discussion section. You can usually use this section to build up the case for the recommendations you will make in the next section.

Section 11: Recommendations for Change

The recommendations for change consist of a bulleted list of change items that you believe need to be implemented as a result of your findings. Be careful how much information you give here. Your clients might not be looking for you to write out HTML code to fix the problem; they might be looking for general ideas.

Additionally, depending on how you have billed the job, you could find that if the client is open to your suggestions, implementing the changes will be another totally separate job. You might use a subcontractor to implement the changes, or you could do it yourself.

Appendices: Paperwork and Attachments

You will likely have many different add-ons for your test, such as questionnaires, nondisclosure agreements (NDAs), video and audio release forms, and so on. It is important that you include copies of all this type of paperwork with your final report.

DESIGNING USABILITY TASKS

Arguably, the most important thing you can do with regard to your usability testing plan is develop creative usability tasks that truly measure the things in which you are interested. The method to derive good tasks is simple, but it assumes that you have done a good job of determining the purpose of your site and that you have abstracted the correct problem statements from your purpose. So let's go over this process step by step.

The first step is to determine the purpose of your site. According to its corporate documentation and thought, the purpose of the Mind Hive corporate Web site is as follows:

> *Our Web site is designed to be the technological arm of the company. Its purpose is, first and foremost, to provide technical support to our existing clients. A secondary, but critical, objective of the site is to act as a sales channel for prospective and existing clients alike. Finally, we hope to use the Web site to educate the general public about our services and products.*

That being stated, we can begin to draw out the problem statements. There are three main areas of utility for the site: support, sales, and marketing. Each of these areas can be further refined:

- Can our users find the technical support they need to solve their problems?
- Can customers locate the products they want and purchase them on our Web site?
- Can a potential customer find out about our products and how they compare with our competitor's products?

Each one of these problem statements is pretty general. There isn't a way to directly test them, so we need one more level of refinement. Creating a series of tasks can test each problem statement. That way, the individual, measurable tasks radiate from the problem statements.

From the first problem statement, "Can our users find the technical support they need to solve their problems?" we can generate the following tasks:

- "You are trying to locate a way to repair a damaged Foo format data file under Windows 2000. Please locate this information using the technical support section of the Web site."

- "Someone in your department is wondering if there is a way to import a Frodis word processor document into the Foo processor. Please find out if this is possible."

- "After installing the Foo processor, version 5.5, you notice that your PC crashes a lot when you open older Foo documents. Please find out if this is a known bug."

These statements become the basis for our first three tasks in the testing session. So far, we have the script text for the tasks; now we need to determine the criteria for success for each.

We could determine that our users should be able to find the answer to their questions in less than three minutes, a very aggressive benchmark for technical support. So, one condition for success is that the answer must be located in less than three minutes.

We could also determine that a maximum of six clicks should be needed to find the answer (assuming that it can be done minimally in four clicks, allowing two for errors). This assumption also becomes a condition for success.

Finally, we need to figure out how to determine if the goal state has been reached. We determine that the goal state is to locate the Web page related to each task: *qa12345.html, qa23456.html,* and *qa34567.html,* respectively. So our condition for success for the first task looks like this:

- Must locate the page *qa12345.html* in less than three minutes and/or fewer than six clicks

Every remaining task requires us to go through the same process. Once we have determined the script and the conditions for success, we also need to note the start state of each task: From which Web page does the participant start? (See Figure B.3.)

POTENTIAL PROBLEMS WITH TASKS

It is very common to run into many different problems that arise from improperly designed tasks. No matter how hard you try or how well you plan your test, you can encounter the unexpected. For instance, a task

FIGURE B.3 *This site has many potential tasks for testing usability. It contains many goal-oriented tasks, such as reserving a car, booking a flight, and getting a price for a hotel, that can all make for ideal usability testing scenarios. © 2000 Expedia.*

that you have designed might be worded poorly, causing the participants to become confused.

You might also design a task that you discover is impossible to complete. This might not be your fault, since sections of the Web site might not be operational when you choose to do your testing. Nonetheless, you must continue. In the event that you discover that a task cannot be completed due to some unforeseen technical problem or a glitch in planning, you can opt to discontinue that particular task for the remainder of the sessions. When you do so, you must drop the task data results from all previous sessions; that data isn't usable anymore. Make sure you document any such last-minute changes.

A way to make your test plan robust against adversity is to always create and plan on using more tasks than you actually need. This way, if you have to omit several questions due to unforeseen problems, you will be able to continue. When you do a test run through the plan with a coworker or friend, you should be able to weed out any potential timing problems, such as having too many or too few tasks.

Another problem that can come up is the result of a phenomenon known as *order effects*, which refers to the fact that the order in which tasks are presented can affect the performance of the tasks.

For example, you notice a gradual increase in a participant's success in navigating the Web site as a test progresses. The scores tend to increase later and later in the session. It could be due to the fact that the user is steadily memorizing the layout of the site and preparing mentally for questions that might pop up down the line. This could happen actively (the participant tries deliberately to memorize the site) or passively (the participant happens to remember the site layout without any special effort).

To counteract this effect, one technique you can use is to randomly shuffle the order in which tasks are presented so that when you average it all out, no single task gets preferential status (that is, no task consistently occurs later in each session) among all participants. Note that if you have a collection of two or more tasks that must be completed in a given sequence, it's okay to keep the group of tasks together and to treat the cluster as one logical unit for the purposes of randomizing. For example, it doesn't make sense to pay for an online order before you select the merchandise you want. In this case, the four steps involved in placing the order can be treated as one logical task and shuffled in with the other more atomic tasks.

EXECUTING THE PLAN

Okay, so once you have the plan together, it's time to implement it. You should plan to have sessions last between one and two hours per participant. I have found that an hour is just about the perfect amount of time. In an hour, you can do a large number of tasks and get input from the participant before he or she gets too tired and cranky. All that testing wears a participant out.

It also will wear you out! Never try to take on too many participants in a single day. Doing so can be quite monotonous and could affect your testing. If you are doing one-hour sessions, about six participants is all you should tackle in a single day. This limit will allow you enough time to get everyone in and out of the lab as well as time to clean up, get the environment back in shape, and finish recording information.

It's a good idea to have a reception area for participants where participants can have a cup of coffee or juice while they wait their turns. If you haven't had the participants fill out a pretest questionnaire, this is a good time to have them do it. If you are lucky enough to have a coworker who can act as the operations coordinator, the coordinator can spend five minutes with the participant while waiting. Just before testing commences, explain the terms of compensation to the participants. If they stay and complete the entire session, they will be compensated in full. If they leave halfway through, they will be compensated half, and so on. In addition, any other bits of administrative trivia can be taken care of at this point. Make sure that you arrange for the participant to arrive a little early if you plan this kind of warm-up activity.

Make a Trial Run

You should actually always do a dry run or two of your test plan on a cohort before you subject your real participants to the test. This practice helps weed out any potential disasters that might happen as a result of tasks that are worded improperly, tasks that are impossible to accomplish, and other unforeseen glitches that might occur along the way.

One of the main things you need to check during your trial run is that you have allocated enough time for all the components of the test. It's not unusual to discover that you have simply included far too many tasks for a one-hour session. Be sure to adjust any timing issues before you test a single real participant.

Just in case it isn't obvious, please note: You shouldn't include the data gathered from the trial run in your final report.

How Many Participants?

According to a recent article by Jakob Nielsen, it is best to have approximately five participants per round of testing.[1] This is in stark contrast to the 700 or more participants a month Microsoft tests! Keep in mind, though, that the number of Microsoft participants is spread out across all the various software programs, operating systems, and so on that the company sells and supports.

Depending on the size of your organization, five participants per session might be just about right. Ultimately, the more participants you have, the more reliable your data becomes and the more usability problems you will find. If this is your first attempt, why not five? It's a good place to start, and if you have created your test plan such that each session takes about an hour, you could conceivably get through all five sessions in a day (not a task for the faint-hearted; this is hard work!).

---

[1] See Nielsen's article at *www.useit.com/alertbox/20000319.html.*

Keep in mind that if your Web site has many distinct user profiles, you need about five participants from each profile group, not five altogether. One of the biggest mistakes my students have tended to make is to spread the handful of participants they can get over all their user profiles. Remember, it's better to have five participants from a single user profile, so that you get realistic data for at least that profile, than to have a smattering of information from all your user profiles.

Mistakes Will Happen

Inevitably, a mistake will occur. It's just human nature. You might reveal more information to a participant than you meant to, or you might get the wording of a script a little wrong. Keep moving and don't draw attention to your mistake. Most people will never notice the mistake that seems so big to you. They don't know what's going on inside your head; they can't hear your thoughts, so they are oblivious to the mistake.

Things You Should Say to the Participant

Being a test participant is nerve wracking for all but the most savvy best-testers (who you probably didn't want coming to your session in the first place!). The test moderator's job is to make the participant feel comfortable. There are several things you need to let the participant know before you begin; however, I can tell you what to say, but I cannot teach you how to say it. I have seen people with little dynamism try to play the role of test moderator, and they are just incapable of handling the position. How you tell a participant something—the genuineness in your voice—can say a lot more than the words you use.

Here are a few helpful statements to tell your participants:

- Be honest with me. I didn't design this site, so you can't hurt my feelings.

- There are no right or wrong answers.

- We aren't testing you; we are trying to find out if there are any design flaws or user-unfriendly parts to this site.

- We aren't going to let anyone outside our research team see these results, and when our team members do see the results, your name will not be associated with the data.

- Try not to act differently than you would at home or at work. We aren't here to rate how you do things, and if you act differently than you normally do, it will affect our ability to make our site better.

- It's okay for you to think out loud; that helps us understand what you are thinking as you go through the tasks.

Get Permission to Tape

If you are planning to video or audiotape your sessions, you need to get the express written consent of each participant to do so. Normally, you inform participants during the orientation script that they will be taped during the session. You should then have them sign release forms.

It's important that you explain to the participants that you will not release the audio or videotape to anyone outside the immediate research group and that the tape will be used only for research purposes. For your convenience, a sample release form has been included as a Microsoft Word document on the CD-ROM.

Role of the Test Monitor

The test monitor is the person in your crew who interfaces with the participants. The test monitor has by far the greatest load of work of all the team members, and it's critical that this person possess a plethora of important qualities.

After reading this section, you might get the impression that the test monitor is almost a sort of therapist! In fact, the qualities of a good therapist and a good test monitor are quite similar.

Here is just a partial list of qualities the test monitor should have:

- **Empathy.** The ability to understand and relate to the feelings of others.

- **Good attention span.** Watching people perform the same tasks over and over again can get really boring. The test monitor needs to pay attention at all times.

- **Warm and comforting.** People can get really stressed out when they are performing usability tasks. A good test monitor must make the participants feel at ease, as though there is no pressure to perform, yet the test monitor must also keep the participant moving through the tasks.

- **Ability to ad lib.** The unexpected will always happen. Being able to roll with the punches and keep things moving smoothly is a must.

- **Good organizational skills.** The test monitor is the hub of the testing process and so must interact with all the other team members and often with the client.

For most of this book, we assume that you, the reader, will act as the test moderator in your usability testing situations.

Watch for Body Language

When your participants are in the middle of a series of tasks, there will be little more revealing about their mental state than the faces they make. Nonverbal expression is one of the defining characteristics of human beings, and facial expressions can be a powerful ally of the observant test moderator.

If I haven't explicitly said it yet, let me do it now: Pay attention to what your participant is going through on every level, cognitive, emotional, and physical. A participant might make it through a task in an acceptable amount of time, and the unobservant moderator will not notice that the participant was completely confused about the task. The participant could very well have happened on the right answer by accident. An observant moderator will notice a grimace on a participant's face and will remember to ask about the task during debriefing.

The Orientation Script

Another important part of your test plan is the *orientation script*, another piece of scripted text that you will read out loud to participants when they arrive for testing. The orientation script is intended to be a general greeting, an explanation of all the activities you have lined up for participants to do, and a chance to explain that participants are free to leave if they begin to feel uncomfortable during the test.

The tone that you take when you read the script should be professional but warm. If you sound like a robot reciting its programmer's instructions, you'll get off to a bad start with the participant.

The script must be the same for each participant; it also needs to be delivered in the same manner to each participant. Do not attempt to paraphrase the script when you get tired of hearing yourself say it over and over. If you do that, you will introduce a potentially confounding variable to your testing. Did participant #6 do poorly because he really would have done poorly, or did your sloppy or inconsistent presentation of the instructions have something to do with it?

The script should be relatively short; it should take no more than a minute or two to read. Don't try to work casual conversational bits into this script; unless you're a trained Laurence Olivier type, it will sound awkward. For example, don't work in a bit of the script where you ask the participant how he or she is doing or what he or she would like to drink. You can do all that before you begin the orientation script. It is normal to provide drinks and a bit of food (especially if it is early morning) for your participants to consume while they are in the waiting area. Keep the beverages in the waiting area, though. Experience has shown that a glass full of fruit juice and a computer tend to mix very poorly!

The normal format of the script should be something like the following:

1. Introduce yourself and other team members.
2. Explain that the participant is here to assist in making your Web site better by taking part in sample tasks that are designed to uncover usability problems in the site.

3. Let the participant know that he or she isn't being tested but rather that the site design is being tested.

4. Give the participant a quick synopsis of what you will do. Describe briefly any types of tests you will do, how long they will take, and so on.

5. Let the participant know that it's okay to ask questions at any time but that you cannot answer questions about how to complete a specific task once the testing has begun.

6. Ask the participant if he or she has any questions before you begin.

7. Have the participant fill out any paperwork (NDAs, video/audio release forms, etc.).

User Tasks

Now, if you have laid out your test plan carefully and you have done a good trial run or two to work out bugs, you're ready to roll through the part you have been waiting for. The user will actually use your site! Be attentive; testing large numbers of users can get tedious.

Remember that you should present all parts of the test in the same way for each participant. The wording you use for tasks should remain constant for all participants. If you change the wording halfway through the day, it will be impossible to rule out the wording as a potential cause of variation in scores. The same is true of the instructions you read during the orientation script. Be consistent.

During the actual user tasks, try to limit your interaction with each participant to a minimum. Save longer issues for the debriefing session at the end of the session.

Keep It Moving

One of the hardest parts about the actual activity section of the test is that you must keep things rolling pretty smoothly without overly frustrating the participant. You will invariably have participants who cannot complete all the tasks; in fact, some participants might not be able to finish any of the tasks. When this happens, your moderator can expect to absorb a lot of natural human frustration. Your moderator must summon up all his or her interpersonal skills to reassure participants and keep them moving right along.

Some of my students have admitted to including some easy tasks throughout the test, just to make sure that no participant feels intimidated. I'm not quite sure how I feel about this; on one hand, it is valuable in keeping up participant morale. On the other hand, you're burning precious time. If you have an ultra-novice participating, this user will almost certainly have trouble anyway and will need some extra assurance and coaxing to continue.

This is the part of the session in which a participant is likely to become too self-conscious and, in some cases, too self-deprecating. It can be very discouraging to try to accomplish tasks set forth by a stranger who the participant probably views as very intelligent and fail at them. After all, all mad scientists are super-geniuses, and your moderator will probably strike the participant as such a person in authority. Humans are proud creatures and want to accomplish tasks.

Therefore, it's critical that your moderator be able to assure the participants that they are doing okay and that other people have made similar mistakes. You don't want to give out information such as "Oh, that's okay, five other people failed at that task."

Resist the Temptation to Lead

If you're the moderator, while the participants are performing the usability tasks you must resist the powerful temptation to help them out when they get into a bind. Remember that you cannot guide them through any part of any task unless you personally plan on being in their presence every time they use the Web.

For some people, it can be very difficult to avoid leading the participant by way of nonverbal cues. You may be unaware that you make a funny little noise when the participant is "cold" or heading for a wrong turn; although the participant might not be consciously aware of the noise, it could still affect his or her performance. Animal trainers have been able to shape the behavior of their animals so that they can read the trainer's subtlest cues; of course, a participant is smarter than a horse! This dilemma reveals yet another benefit of videotaping your sessions: Although it's painful, you can review your own mannerisms to see if you give away too much with your nonverbal communication.

One other way that you can inadvertently lead a participant is by not allowing the participant to indicate the completion of a task. Normally, the participant is responsible for saying "I think this is it" or "I found it" or indicating success somehow. Once again, if you stop the participant when he or she has "found" the target, you'll also need to accompany that participant through life to provide this helpful service. When the users are on their own, they have to decide on their own whether they have found the information they're looking for. You need to let them do the same thing in your testing.

Don't Push Too Hard

It is an extremely bad idea to attempt to force participants to finish a task if they are absolutely certain that they cannot figure it out. In such cases, let participants opt to fail. In the real world, people give up on Web sites all the time, and if you don't let your participants give up, how will you know if "real" users are going to give up on your site?

The flip side of this coin is that you shouldn't let participants quit every task just because they are angry or "fed up." If you should get a participant in this condition, you might want to consider letting him or her go, since that behavior will waste your time and their own and make for bad feelings overall. Decide on an official policy for such exceptional cases.

Debriefing

This is often the best part of the entire test session, so make sure you allot plenty of time for it. The debriefing session is an informal section of time during which you can allow the participant to ask questions about whatever they want, within reason. For example, quite often participants who were perplexed with a seemingly impossible task will ask me to show them the solution. It's not unusual for such things to happen. Users might also have other questions, such as "Did I do okay?" or "How many other people failed task #4?" Participants also often ask questions about when you're planning on changing the Web site or if you'll call them again, or they could just open up and vent about how bad the site design really is. Be ready to listen.

It is also customary for the test moderator to thank the participant and explain that the data gathered during the session will be a great asset to the future design of the site and that the participant has played a critical role in the effort. In fielding participant questions, you'll obviously need to observe whatever information constraints your situation demands. Although it's probably uncommon, it is still possible that your test participants might be moles from your competitor, using the opportunity to find out critical information about your corporate strategies, insider information on the Web site, or something similar.[2]

Probably the most important thing about the debriefing is that you get to ask questions in an informal fashion. You might have a series of stock questions that you ask everyone (about the site's aesthetics, how interesting or boring the test was, or participants' other preferences), or you might choose to simply leave the talking up to the participant.

While the participant is carrying out the tasks you presented, you should take notes about problem spots, and ask the participant probing questions during the debriefing. It is helpful to bring up the troublesome pages and ask users to repeat out loud the thoughts that they were having as they interacted with the pages. Depending on how receptive and personable you seem to participants, they may tell you lots of things that you can convert into useful design changes.

---

[2] Just because I'm paranoid doesn't mean they're *not* out to get me . . .

SUMMARY

- Usability testing is the most complex and most informative tool we have to help us assess a Web site's usability.

- Every comprehensive Web site usability plan should include at least a little usability testing with real users.

- Usability testing employs some of the principles of scientific experimental research design but is not strict about adhering to them, primarily due to time constraints.

- Usability testing will yield useful results even if the test design is not completely scientifically sound.

- The blueprint for your testing sessions is called the *usability test plan*, which is not to be confused with the *overall usability plan* for your site.

- You'll need to get your participants to sign and date many pieces of paperwork, including any NDAs, video and audio release forms, and possibly pretest questionnaires if you haven't had them do this previously.

- The test moderator must be a great "people person" so that he or she can effectively communicate with your participants.

- You must observe appropriate ethics when designing and executing a test plan.

HANDS-ON EXERCISES

1. Design your test plan. Be sure to allot an appropriate amount of time for this job; it usually takes two weeks or more to design all the tasks and to do a trial run.

2. Execute the plan. Be prepared for lots of hard work and a very eye-opening experience!

3. Assemble your data and generate your final report. Make suggestions for change.

DISCUSSION TOPICS

1. Why is it important to have at least five participants from each of your user profiles, or is it even important? Explain.

2. What does it mean if all of your participants have a 100 percent success rate on your usability test?

3. Let's say that you are the only person on your usability team (hey! you really *are* somebody!). How will you have to modify your methodology to compensate for this fact? What are some potential problems you will encounter?

4. Which parts, if any, of usability testing can be automated?

XOLAX SOFTWARE USABILITY TEST PLAN 2.0: HANDHELD COMPUTING DEVICE USABILITY TRIALS

INTRODUCTION

Following is the test plan for conducting usability tests of the corporate Web pages for Xolax Software, known internally as XOLAX. The plan covers the following sections:

- Purpose
- Problem statements
- User Profile
- Methodology
- Test environment and equipment requirements
- Task list
- Test monitor role
- Evaluation measures
- Test report contents and presentation

PURPOSE

Recently, Xolax Software senior management has made an important decision to allocate resources to usability work on two key pieces of core Xolax Web infrastructure, as those pieces are expected to be accessible and usable from new methods of access. New types of devices, namely Research In Motion (hereafter referred to as "RIM") interactive handhelds, Fujitsu tablet PCs, and Palm VII wireless PDAs. It is crucial to the functioning of the company that these devices work seamlessly and intuitively with either existing content, or, at the discretion of the usability group, newly-created equivalent content that is tuned to this type of delivery media.

This study will focus on two areas of the Xolax Web infrastructure:

- Internal (Employee-accessible) Web content, like Human Resources forms, Sales and Marketing data, and Engineering bug reports
- External (customer-facing) Web content; specifically, FrodisCorp's high-performance Web indexing service that we provide via onsite compute/database clusters

This study seeks to find, document, and make recommendation to change moderate to serious usability problems. Senior management has previously acknowledged that a redesign of content may be necessary to effect usable content for these platforms.

TEST OBJECTIVE/PROBLEM STATEMENTS

The following questions represent the very general questions that this study seeks to answer about how current users of the aforementioned Web content interact with the content, and outlines the nature of said interaction.

1. What is the purpose of enabling Xolax Web site content access over the outlined handheld computing devices?
2. Is the current content accessible via these devices?

3. Is the current content easily navigable?

4. Can Xolax engineers, sales and marketing, and other users efficiently access data on the Xolax intranet?

5. Can FrodisCorp users utilize the Xolax search engine effectively via the RIM interactive handhelds?

USER PROFILE

The user sample for this trial will be divided into two main sections: a group of 25 participants that will come exclusively from inside the Xolax company; these participants will be labeled Group 1, and will participate in the internal (intranet) Web trials. The other group, labeled Group 2, will consist of participants that come exclusively from inside FrodisCorp. It is expected that at least a few users from each group will not complete the trials for any of a number of reasons, including non-attendance, failure to complete all sections, or other scheduling conflicts. For this reason we have scheduled more participants than we feel absolutely necessary.

Experience Levels

The breakdown of each of the groups will roughly be as follows:

- 1–2 participants who are ultra-novices. While these participants are not necessarily the intended audience, they represent the least competent user who will access the site. If they are able to successfully navigate the site, that is a strong indicator that more qualified users will also be able to navigate.

- The remainder of the participants will have previous experience. Participants in this group will have the following characteristics:
  1. Work with a computer on a regular basis.
  2. Use the Xolax Intranet (or FrodisCorp search engine) on a regular basis, but while using traditional PC/Browser access.
  3. Do not have any professional Web design or usability experience.

User Profile

Characteristic	Range	% Frequency Distribution
Age	18–30	55
	31–40	20
	41–50	16.5
	51–60	9.5
Sex	Female	65
	Male	35
Education	College	100
	Some College	0
Major Area of Study	Electronics Technology	25
	Electrical/Biochemical Engineering	30
	Computer Science	20
	Education	12.5
	English	12.5
	N/A	0
Learning Style	Trial and Error	62.5
	Consult with Others	75
	Documentation	37.5
	Other (Formal Learning Environment)	12.5
PC Experience in Years	0–3 Years	0
	4–7 Years	50
	8–11 Years	12.5
	12–16 Years	12.5
PC Daily Usage	0–2 Hours	12.5
	3–5 Hours	12.5
	5–8 Hours	75
Familiarity with the XOLAX Corporate Web Site OR FrodisCorp search engine site	Yes	90
	Slightly	5
	I Know It Exists	5
	Not at all	0

MAIN TARGET GROUPS

Group 1

Xolax employees, specifically users from the Engineering and Sales and Marketing departments are the main target group for this trial. This main target group has been derived from the tasks in the task list and can be separated into two distinct groups.

- Engineering—This is the internal Xolax group of software engineers who need to be able to view bug reports on Fujitsu tablet PCs that are used during engineering meetings and while engineers are in various parts of the campus.

- Sales and Marketing—Internal Xolax employees who need to be able to interact with Web-based sales data, contacts, and other marketing data, both on the Xolax campus and while abroad via Palm VII and comparable clone devices.

Group 2

FrodisCorp employees that will be using the Xolax-designed and hosted search and indexing software, via RIM interactive handhelds. This group consists of only one main group, with no subgroup branching.

METHODOLOGY

The usability test will consist of the main performance test designed to gather extensive usability data via direct observation.

The main performance test is composed of the following four sections:

1. Participant greeting and background questionnaire

Each participant will be personally greeted by the test monitor and made to feel comfortable and relaxed. The participants will be given a very short questionnaire that gathers basic background information. The issue of confidentiality will be addressed by giving each participant a unique testing identification number.

2. Orientation

The participants will receive a short, verbal introduction and orientation to the test, explaining the purpose and objective of the test, and additional information about what is expected of them. They will be assured that the site is the object of evaluation and not themselves. The participants will be informed that they are being observed and videotaped.

3. Performance test

The performance test consists of a series of tasks that the participants will be asked to carry out while being observed. The scenario is as follows:

> After the orientation is complete, the participants will be asked to take whichever mobile computing device is appropriate for their group. The test moderator will indicate that the device is to be used to complete a series of information-finding tasks that will be presented serially for the remainder of the session.
>
> Each participant will then be guided through a series of tasks, each of which may occur in a different physical location on the campus or in another location, where they will be asked to locate and/or request certain information. The participant will be encouraged to work without guidance. The test monitor may ask a participant to verbalize his or her thoughts if they become stuck or confused. This will help to pinpoint the reason for the problem and will be noticed by the test monitor.

During the main performance test, elapsed time and errors will be noted for each unique task on the task list. The test monitor will also make notes about relevant participant behavior, comments, and any unusual circumstances that might affect the result (e.g., browser or computer crash). Videotaping will not be possible due to the mobile nature of this session. However, the test monitor will be equipped with a professional quality portable DAT (digital audio tape) recorder and external microphone to record the audio of each session for later analysis.

4. Participant debriefing

After all tasks are complete or the time expires, the test monitor will debrief each participant and the debriefing will be videotaped. The debriefing will include the following:

- Participant's perceptions about usability and aesthetics of the site
- Participant's overall comments about his or her performance
- Participant's responses to the test monitor asking about errors or problems during the test

The debriefing session serves several functions. It allows the participants to say whatever they like, which is important if tasks are frustrating. It provides important information about each participant's rationale for performing specific actions, and it allows the collection of subjective preference data about the site.

After the debriefing session, the participants will be thanked for their effort.

TEST ENVIRONMENT AND EQUIPMENT REQUIREMENTS

We will require at least one each of the following:

- Fujitsu tablet PC
- Palm VII or compatible wireless handheld PDA
- RIM 957 Interactive Handheld
- Sony Portable DAT recorder
- External omnidirectional condenser microphone with windscreen
- Digital high-resolution stopwatch

TEST MONITOR ROLE

The test monitor will accompany each participant while conducting the test. The test monitor will initiate tasks via a scripted text paragraph for each task. The monitor will record timings, errors, and observations. We perceive that this will place a large load on the test monitor, so we will rely heavily on self-reported data during the debriefing sessions.

The test monitor will not help any of the participants unless a question about the test procedure arises. Participants will be asked to rely on their own abilities to perform the required tasks.

EVALUATION MEASURES

The following evaluation measures will be collected and calculated:

1. The average time to complete each task, and average number of clicks, across all participants.

2. The percentage of participants who finished each task successfully versus those who had errors from which they could not recover.

3. Error classification: to the degree possible, each error will be classified and a source of error indicated. Error classes are as follows:

   Observation and Comments—The test monitor notes when participants have difficulty, when an unusual behavior, or when a cause of error becomes obvious.

   Non-critical Errors—An individual makes a mistake but is able to recover in the allotted time.

   Critical Errors—An individual participant make a mistake and is unable to recover and complete the task on time. The participant may or may not realize a mistake has been made.

4. Participants ranking of usability and aesthetics of the site. (Some questions may be essay-type, rather than rankings.)

TEST REPORT CONTENTS AND PRESENTATION

The report will include the following sections:

1. Test Plan

2. Results (this section will present summaries of all results in tabular form; raw data will be included in the appendix)

3. Findings/recommendations and discussion (this section will summarize the results, and make recommendations to designers about possible changes)

XOLAX APPENDIX 1

Task List for XOLAX Web Site Usability Test

Task List Legend:

MTC = Maximum time to complete
SCC = Successful completion criteria
Group 1, subgroup 1 (G1S1) = Xolax Engineering Group
Group 1, subgroup 2 (G1S2) = Xolax Sales and Marketing Group
Group 2 (G2) = FrodisCorp Employees

Tasks for G1S1

Task No.	Task Script	Task Detail
1.	"You would like to locate the software bug tracking system from the Xolax intranet home page. Please do so now."	**SCC**: Arrive at the URL shown below, with a maximum of one error: http://internal.xolax.com/eng/bugzilla.html **MTC**: 10 Seconds
2.	"You've just finished interviewing a candidate for a new engineering position. You would like to fill out the online interview feedback form. Please locate the form now."	**SCC**: Arrive at the URL shown below, with a maximum of two errors: http://internal.xolax.com/hr/feedback.html **MTC**: 1 Minute
3.	"You'd like to know the server load on the compile cluster machines. Find out what the load is on cygnus12 now."	**SCC**: (Cygnus12 will be running a simulator that will keep the load fixed at 4.0) Determine load is 4.0 by accessing the URL shown below, with a minimum of two errors: http://internal.xolax.com/netsaint/cygnus12/index.html **MTC**: 1 Minute
4.	"You want to know what the latest successful build of the FOOBAR library is. Please find out what the latest build is now."	**SCC**: Locate the CVS log shown at the URL shown below. The latest version will be 3.1.2. http://internal.xolax.com/cvsweb/revs.html **MTC**: 1 Minute
5.	"You need to find out where today's engineering meeting is being held. Please find out the location now."	**SCC**: Determine that the meeting will be held in the Oakley Building, in the GreatWoods lecture hall on floor 4, by accessing the URL sown below, with less than three errors: http://internal.xolax.com/eng/meetings.php **MTC**: 1 minute

Tasks for G1S1 (continued)

Task No.	Task Script	Task Detail
6.	"You need to find out what arguments the UPDATE_FOO_FACTOR method takes. Please locate this API information."	**SCC**: The method takes three arguments, all of type INT. This can be located at the URL shown below. (No limit on errors) http://internal.xolax.com/eng/API/generic/FOO/UPDATE_FOO_FACTOR.html#args **MTC**: 2 minutes
7.	"You'd like to calculate the MOJO of a FOOBAR. Please locate the appropriate online tool to do so now. "	**SCC**: User locates the online tool at the URL shown below, with a maximum of two errors: http://internal.xolax.com/eng/tools/convert/mojo.php **MTC**: 2 Minutes
8.	"Your supervisor has asked you to set up your personal profile on the bug tracking system. Please do so now."	**SCC**: User locates the URL shown below, fills out form, and submits it within the time allotted, with a maximum of three errors: http://internal.xolax.com/personalize.php **MTC**: 5 Minutes

Tasks for G1S2

Task No.	Task Script	Task Detail
9.	"You need to locate a map to the North Reading Xolax facility. Please do so now."	**SCC**: User finds map at the URL shown below, with a maximum of two errors: http://internal.xolax.com/main/location/xolax_map.php **MTC**: 1 Minute
10.	"You are asked by a potential customer to define the feature set of the new FOOBAR2003 system. Please find the feature set now."	**SCC**: User locates the feature set at the URL shown below, with a maximum of one error: http://internal.xolax.com/products/124143.html **MTC**: 1 Minute
11.	"A member of the press asks you approximately how many XOLAX site locations are there worldwide. Please find this out now."	**SCC**: User locates the answer (23) at the URL shown below, with a maximum of one error: http://internal.xolax.com/main/location/lintro.htm **MTC**: 20 seconds
12.	"A potential customer asks for success tories from other clients. Please locate a list of stories now."	**SCC**: Locate success stories located at URL shown below, with a maximum of two errors: http://internal.xolax.com/main/mktg/success.html **MTC**: 30 seconds

Tasks for G1S2 (continued)

Task No.	Task Script	Task Detail
13.	"A member of the press asks you for a copy of the Annual Report. Please locate this document now."	**SCC**: Locate the PDF form located at the URL shown below, with a maximum of two errors. Note: the PDF itself will not display in the device; however, locating the URL alone is sufficient for success. http://internal.xolax.com/main/annual.pdf **MTC:** 30 seconds

Tasks for G2

Task No.	Task Script	Task Detail
14.	"You have been asked to locate FrodisCorp knowledge base documents related to the keywords 'photon entanglement'. Please locate these documents now."	**SCC**: Participant uses the search tool to locate at least three documents containing the words "photon" and "entanglement." **MTC**: 1 Minute
15.	"You have been asked to determine how many logical ply deep the FrodisCorp Web site is. Please determine this now."	**SCC**: Participant uses the tool to come up with the number 14. **MTC**: 1 Minute
16.	"What dates will the Distinguished Lecturer Series Sessions be taking place?"	**SCC**: Participant locates the dates shown below using the tool. May 15 June 12 July 11 August 17 September 14 **MTC**: 1 Minute
17.	"Please locate the FrodisCorp 2nd quarter earnings statement for 2002."	**SCC**: Participant uses tool to locate the URL below, with no errors: http://www.frodiscorp.com/news/EN/2qearn.hml **MTC**: 1 Minute
18.	"You need to issue a complex query. Please locate the advanced indexing search option."	**SCC**: Participant locates the URL shown below, with a maximum of one error: http://www.frodiscorp.com/search/advanced.html **MTC**: 2 Minutes

XOLAX APPENDIX 2

Background Questionnaire

Name: _____ Company: _____

Job Title: _____

Please answer the questions below in order to help us understand your background and experience.

Age:
(Circle One) 18–30   31–40   41–50   51–60   Over 60

Sex:
(Circle One)   Male   Female

EDUCATION: (Please circle the highest grade level achieved below)

Grade School
High School
Some College
College Graduate
Post Graduate

If you graduated from college, please list your major area of study.

_____

LEARNING STYLE:

1. Which way do you prefer to learn?
    Trial and Error _____
    Consult with others _____
    Documentation _____
    Other:_____

COMPUTER EXPERIENCE:

1. How long have you been using a personal computer?

_____yrs _____ mths

2. How often do you use a personal computer to complete your daily job tasks?

_____

3. Please circle the types of computer applications you have used before, followed by the approximate months of experience with each one used. (Excluding Internet Browser experience.)

Application	**Months of Experience**
Database	_____
Spreadsheet	_____
Word Processing	_____
Desk Top Publishing	_____
Design (CAD/CAM)	_____
Manufacturing	_____
Engineering	_____
Other:	_____
_____	_____
_____	_____

4. Which Operating System do you have experience with?

DOS   _____yrs _____ mths

UNIX _____yrs _____ mths

INTERNET EXPERIENCE:

1. Are you familiar with Internet browsers? If so, which ones? What versions?

a. _____ How long have used it? _____yrs_____mths

b. _____ How long have used it? _____yrs_____mths

c. _____ How long have used it? _____yrs_____mths

d. _____ How long have used it? _____yrs_____mths

2. Which browser do you prefer using when accessing the Internet?

_____

3. Are you at all familiar with the XOLAX corporate Web site?

(Circle One) Yes   Slightly   I know it exists   Not at all

4. If so, how often do you access the site?

_____

XOLAX APPENDIX 3

Orientation Script

Hi, my name is _____. I'll be working with you in today's testing session. Let me explain why we've asked you to come in today.

We're here to test how easy it is to use some Web site content using mobile computing devices, and we'd like your help.

You will be performing some typical tasks with this Web site, and I'd like you to perform as you normally would. For example, try to work at the same speed and with the same attention to detail that you normally do. Do your best, but don't be all that concerned with the results. This is a test of the Web site, and it may not work as you expect. You may ask questions at any time, but I may not answer them, since this is a study of the usability of the Web site and we need to see how it works with a person such as yourself working independently.

During today's session, I'll also be asking you to complete some forms and answer some questions. It's important that you answer truthfully. My only role here today is to discover both the flaws and advantages of this Web site from your perspective. So don't answer the questions based on what you think I may want to hear. I need to know exactly what you think.

The tasks that you perform will happen in a variety of locations, so we will be walking around the campus to simulate the mobility of a typical mobile computing user. While you are working, I'll be with you nearby taking some notes and timings.

The session will also be audiotaped for the benefit of those who could not be here today. For confidentiality, your name will not be used. Instead, a unique testing identification number is assigned to each test participant.

Do you have any questions?

If not, then let's begin by having you sign the tape consent form.

XOLAX APPENDIX 4

Tape Consent Form

XOLAX Web Site Usability Testing

Thank you for participating in our usability testing for the XOLAX corporate Web site. This is to inform you that we will be audiotaping your session for the benefit of our group members who can not be present and to enable us to review information at a later date. We will greatly benefit from your feedback and appreciate your time. Please read the statement below and sign where indicated. Thank you.

I understand that video and audiotape recordings will be made of my session. I grant the usability test group permission to use these recordings for the purposes mentioned above, and waive my right to review or inspect the tapes prior to their dissemination and distribution.

Please print name: _____

Signature: _____

Date: _____

ABOUT THE CD-ROM

This CD provides software tools that are mentioned in the book and templates for many of the forms discussed.

- *Palm OS® Emulator* **(Windows)**

- *Lynx Web Browser:* a text-only Web browser that allows you to preview content as it would be "seen" by a user agent (browser) that can only retrieve text content. (Windows)

- *Deckit* **WAP** *emulator:* a WAP phone browser emulator that allows you to preview HTML and WAP content, as it would be seen on a Web-enabled cell phone. (Windows)

- *Ace Reader:* a utility that lets you experiment with Rapid Serial Visual Presentation (RSVP) as discussed in the book. (Windows)

- *EZ Calc* **and** *USort:* two utilities that allow the usability expert to perform electronic card sorts, organize data quickly, and display the results using cluster analysis and a visual affinity graph. (Windows)

- *WinWAP* **browser:** a WAP browser for viewing WAP sites on your desktop. (Windows)

A LISTING OF THE DTD MARKUPS

- SyncML DTD (http://www.syncml.org/docs/syncml_represent_v10_20001207.dtd

- Compact HTML DTD (http://www.w3.org/consortium/legal)

- A chapter on using Web statistics (PDF format) (Windows and Mac)

- Sample test plan for easy use and modification (Windows and Mac)

- Usability Checklist

- Sample questionnaire, NDA, and Consent Form (Windows and Mac)

System Requirements

The majority of material on the CD-ROM is for Windows only, however, the forms can be used on Macintosh computers as well. To use all of the files, you need at least an Intel Pentium processor based personal computer, Microsoft Windows 95, 98, 2000 or Windows NT 4.0 or later, 32MB RAM Minimum (64MB for NT), and a CD-ROM drive with 32-bit drivers

INSTALLATION INSTRUCTIONS

To install the programs on the CD, simply insert the CD into your CD drive and double-click the application you want to install. Then follow the on-screen instructions. All applications only run under Windows 95 or higher.

BIBLIOGRAPHY

Akamatsu, Motoyuki, and I. Scott MacKenzie. "Movement Characteristics Using a Mouse with Tactile and Force Feedback." *International Journal of Human-Computer Studies* 45, no. 4 (1996): 483–93.

Apple Computer. *Macintosh Human Interface Guidelines.* Addison-Wesley, 1993.

Bergman, Eric, ed. *Information Appliances and Beyond.* Morgan Kaufmann Press, 2000.

Bias, Randolph G., and Deborah Mayhew. *Cost Justifying Usability.* Academic Press, 1994.

Butler, Mark H. "Current Technologies for Device Independence." External Technical Report HPL-2001-83. Hewlett Packard Laboratories Bristol. March 30, 2001.

Chen, H. C., and K. T. Chan. "Reading Computer-Displayed Moving Test with and without Self-Control over the Display Rate." *Behaviour & Information Technology* 9, (1990): 467–77.

Clarkson, Brian, Nitin Sawhney, and Alex Pentland. "Auditory Context Awareness in Wearable Computing." Workshop on Perceptual User Interfaces, San Francisco, November 5–6, 1998. URL: *www.media.mit.edu/speech/papers/1998/clarkson_PUI98_auditory_context_awareness.pdf.*

Connell, Bettye Rose, Mike Jones, Ron Mace, Jim Mueller, Abir Mullick, Elaine Ostroff, Jon Sanford, Ed Steinfeld, Molly Story, and Gregg Vanderheiden. "The Principles of Universal Design." Center for Universal Design, North Carolina State University, 1997.

Dertouzos, Michael. *What Will Be.* Harper Business Press, 1998.

Grinter, Rebecca E., and Margery A. Eldridge. "Y do tngrs luv 2 txt msg?" Xerox PARC USA and Xerox Research Centre Europe, Cambridge UK.

Kurzweil, Ray. *The Age of Intelligent Machines.* Cambridge, Mass.: MIT Press, 1992.

———. *The Age of Spiritual Machines: When Computers Exceed Human Intelligence.* Penguin USA, 2000.

Marti, Stefan. "Active Messenger: Email Filtering and Mobile Delivery." Master's thesis, Massachusetts Institute of Technology, 1999.

Norman, Donald A. *The Design of Everyday Objects.* Currency/Doubleday Press, 1990.

———. *The Invisible Computer.* Cambridge, Mass.: MIT Press, 1999.

Pearrow, Mark. *Web Site Usability Handbook.* Hingham, Mass.: Charles River Media, 2000.

Rahman, T., and P. Muter. "Designing an Interface to Optimize Reading with Small Display Windows." Online. *www.psych.utoronto.ca/~muter/RandM98.htm. Accessed 4/22/2001.*

Raskin, Jef. *The Humane Interface: New Directions for Designing Interactive Systems.* Addison-Wesley, 2000.

Ren, Xiangshi, and Shinji Moriya. "Improving Selection Performance on Pen-Based Systems: A Study of Pen-Based Interaction for Selection Tasks." *ACM Transactions on Computer-Human Interaction* 7, no. 3 (September 2000): 384–416.

Shneiderman, Ben. *Designing the User Interface.* Addison-Wesley, 1997.

Weinschenk, Susan, and Dean T. Barker. *Designing Effective Speech Interfaces.* John Wiley and Sons, 2000.

Walker, Mark, and Andrew Hunt, eds. "Speech Synthesis Markup Language Specification for the Speech Interface Framework." Online. URL: *www.w3.org/TR/speech-synthesis. Accessed 5/14/2001.*

GLOSSARY

Angry fruit salad

Term used to describe a graphical user interface (GUI) that has a really loud, poorly color-coordinated look to it. Usually caused by a designer trying to use too many colors to represent too many types of visual information at once. It is generally believed that a GUI should use no more than six (6) colors at any one time to represent information visually. It is also a bad idea to create visual information that can only be interpreted if the user has "normal" color vision, since a large percentage of the human population does not have "normal" color vision.

Bluetooth

A wireless technology that allows any Bluetooth capable device to communicate with any other such device within a small radius. A network of such devices is referred to as a piconet. The Bluetooth standard was originally designed by Nokia, and is now an open standard.

CDMA

Code Division Multiple Access. A common type of digital cellular transport that is used in the United States. CDMA is an improvement over TDMA.

Cell Site

A radio tower that transmits and receives cellular radio transmissions.

CHTML

An abbreviation for Compact HTML.

Compact HTML

An early attempt to create a markup language for wireless/handheld computing devices. Also initially called HDML. Based loosely on several versions of HTML, but without many of the presentation-oriented features.

Congestion

A condition in a data network in which the amount of traffic begins to exceed the maximum available bandwidth, which causes latency and reduced data reliability.

Creeping featuritis

A condition in which a device or system has so many features added on that it becomes to unwieldy to use.

Datagram

A unit of data transmission.

Denial of Service

A condition in which an electronic service, such as email, Web, and voice, is temporarily crippled due to a deliberate action (such as ping flooding) or by some unintentional system malfunction. Usually abbreviated DoS.

DoCoMo

A Japanese telecommunications company that is at the heart of Japanese wireless data transmission.

DoS

Abbreviation for Denial of Service.

DTD

Abbreviation for Document Type Definition. A DTD is a formal document that contains the "rules" for a particular markup language. For example, there are several DTDs included in Appendix A of this book for your reference. The DTD contains information that pertains to the required document structure of a markup language, and also usually provides insight into the nature of the language, if it is well-written.

In XML, a document that follows all the rules of its DTD is said to be well formed, which is the top level of XML conformity that an XML document can attain.

GPS
Abbreviation for Global Positioning System. The GPS is a worldwide network of special satellites that are used for calculating a handheld transceiver's location coordinates. Until recently, the US government used what is known as Selected Availability to impair the functioning of GPS near certain top-secret military bases and other facilities.

GSM
Home Automation (HA)
The process and end result of connecting home appliances, such as lamps, thermostats, televisions, and stereos, to a central controller—usually a PC—via some standard protocol, such as X10. This gives the capability to control all such devices programmatically, either from the PC console or from a remote host (like via the Web)

Hysteresis
The quality of a keyboard key or button to slightly resist being actuated until a threshold pressure is reached.

Hz
Abbreviation for hertz. The basic unit for measuring the frequency of electromagnetic and audio radiation. Named after the famous scientist "Manny Magoo" Hertz.

i-mode
A special system designed by Nippon Telephone and Telegraph (NTT) to implement Web-like media over wireless telephones. Uses a form of CHTML as a basic platform.

ISO8879
The ISO standard that defines the Latin-1, as well as several other Western, character sets.

J2ME

Sun's Java 2 Micro Edition Java platform, which is specially designed to be run in very small amounts of memory, such as that found in many portable computing devices.

JavaTV

Sun's Java API for controlling set-top boxes and providing programmatic control in devices like digital cable converters, television sets, and other television-oriented electronics.

Jini

Sun's toolkit for creating small networks of wirelessly interconnected devices. Jini provides a variety of services for such networks, such as a notification service that notifies other nodes on the network when a new device and/or service is available.

KHz

Abbreviation for kilohertz.

Micronet

A synonym for piconet.

NAVSTAR

The space-based constellation of satellites that provide the GPS service.

NTT

Nippon Telegraph and Telephone; analogous to BT in the UK and AT&T in the US.

OnStar

A commercial service available in the US that integrates a cellular phone into a vehicle, over which a variety of services can be delivered. This service is slated to include wireless Web access in the near future.

OSI model

A well-known standard that depicts data networks as a composite of seven layers, each of which only needs to understand the layer immediately above and below itself. The seven layers are, in order of lowest (closest to the hardware level) to highest (closest to the human interface) are physical, data link, network, transport, session, presentation, and application.

Parsimony
The quality such that an object has exactly the qualities it needs to perform optimally. Taking away from the object or adding to the object that is in this state will impair its usefulness.

Piconet
A small, ephemeral network that is connected via a peer-to-peer, transient network. A common backbone technology for such networks is Bluetooth.

RF
Radio Frequency.

Scatternet
The intersection of two piconets.

Selected Availability (SA)
A feature of the Global Positioning System that was recently removed. SA caused the precision of GPS signals to be deliberately degraded near certain US military installations.

SMS
Short Messaging Service, a common protocol used by pagers and similar devices for short text messages.

Sorcerer's Apprentice Syndrome
From Disney's *The Sorcerer's Apprentice*, a condition in which a creation begins to uncontrollably begin behaving in an undesired fashion (as when the Sorcerer's broom begins to flood the workshop after being "instructed" to fetch water).

Sound Pressure Level (SPL)
A measurement of how much sound is being generated at an arbitrary point by a sound source. Measured in decibels (dB).

SSL

Secure Sockets Layer. A protocol that exists underneath TCP/IP that encrypts all traffic. Commonly used in conjunction with HTTP to form HTTPS, which is a standard for secure Web transactions. SSL can, however, be used with any service, not just HTTP.

TCP

Transmission Control Protocol. The half of the TCP/IP suite that corresponds to the transport layer of the OSI model. TCP provides reliable, end-to-end connectivity between two hosts.

TCP/IP

The network protocol suite that consists of TCP (Transmission Control Protocol) and IP (Internet Protocol).

TDMA

Time division multiple access. An old technology used in analog cellular transmissions.

Valid

One level of XML document conformance in which a document is both well-formed (no syntactical errors) and conforms to an existing Document Type Definition (DTD).

Virtual keyboard

A "soft" keyboard that is usually an on-screen keyboard, which can be operated by mouse or other alternative input methods.

VoiceXML

An application of XML that is designed to allow markup of voice-driven documents, such as those found in automated telephone systems.

WAP

Wireless Application Protocol.

Well-formed

One level of XML document conformance. A well-formed document simply has the correct structural components of an XML document, with no syntax or structural errors.

WML
Wireless Markup Language.

WMLScript
Wireless Markup Language Scripting language.

XML
eXtensible Markup Language.

INDEX